Confessions of a Closet Mystic:
How I Learned to Connect to Divine Love
(and you can too)

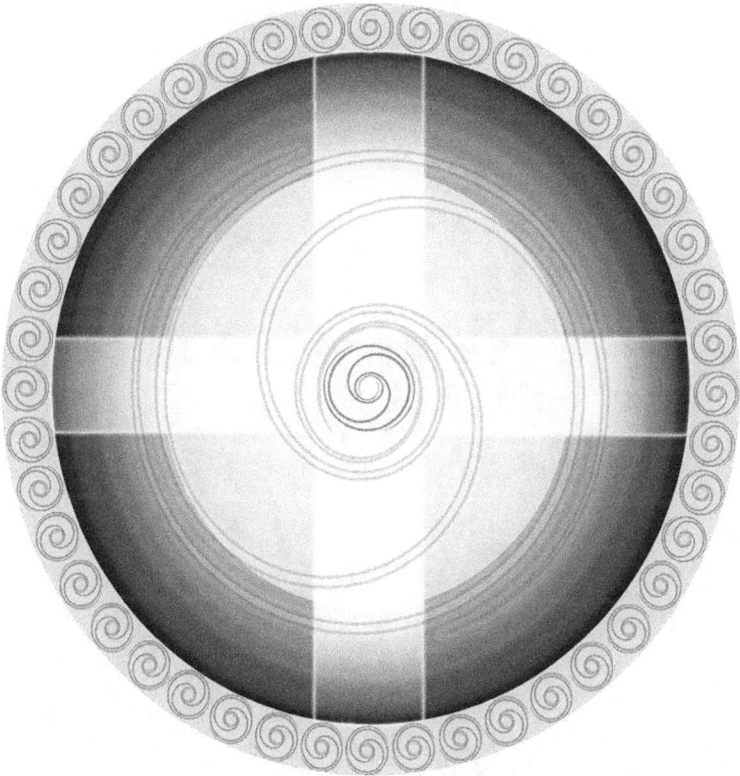

Julia Turner Hultgren, MSW

ISBN: 0615615767
ISBN-13: 9780615615769

Table of Contents

CREATING STRUCTURE

CULTIVATING AWE

CREATING STRUCTURE + CULTIVATING AWE = PASSION

Introduction

All pathways lead to the center

In late March of 1998, I was meditating with a Wayne Dyer cassette, his *Meditations for Manifesting*. I had been doing this meditation pretty much every day for about a month. It's a technique for inviting positive things into our lives. Wayne directs the listener to chant with him the sound, "AHHH," which he says on the recording, is the sound of the Creator world wide. About two weeks into the meditation, I realized if it was really for contacting God, I should ask for good things for ALL people, not just me. As directed in the tape, I focused on sending energy and light out from my forehead into the world, blanketing all that I could imagine, as far away as possible. I had already had experience with sending light this way while praying for others. It feels really good to do it. It feels pure and clear, like drinking a cool, fresh glass of water, because the light comes from the core of my being.

After about two weeks of shifting the direction of my prayers and sending the "AHHH" energy out, I started to "hear" voices above the left side of my head. What you should know about me is that I access trance states easily. So while I was "hearing" these voices, chanting, and sending light and energy out, I felt like I was in my own little wave/light machine. Sometimes my head rocked and my body swayed with the pulsing energy of it, as I sat on an old green couch in a musty-smelling basement. The voices identified themselves as "God" and "Jesus." It felt like I think heaven must feel. They were unimaginably kind in a boundless way. It felt like true love going into the very deepest part of myself.

After that, Jesus started coming to talk to me by himself. He started telling me a story that I found too hard to believe, so I put the tape player back in the drawer for several years, like Peter Pan's shadow. I knew IT was there. I just didn't know what IT was. I told only my husband about it. I told my meditation teacher I thought errant spirits were playing a joke on me. She said, "Ask them to stop." And they did. After all, I am not a devoutly religious person. Why in the world would JESUS be talking to ME?

I thought surely if it was real, someone else would be able to see or sense the connection. But no psychic ever mentioned it, "Hey Julia, there's this spirit that looks like Jesus who wants to get through to you." "Hey Julia, did you notice there was this spirit following you?"

In 2002 or so, I went to a Caroline Myss workshop in Denver. At one point, I had written her a letter and said something like, "I think I must be crazy but…." During the workshop, she looked out into the crowd and said, "If you are receiving spiritual guidance, you should take it." I felt sure she was talking directly to me. I have taken a lot of Caroline's advice over the years and have felt really, tremendously rewarded for having done so. We adopted a baby from China. When I had the initial idea, I remembered her voice from a previous workshop saying, "If you HAVE to be a rescuer, find someone who really needs rescuing." Not once did I ever regret we made that decision.

You know all the advice that you have given people over the years, and how you feel so rewarded when someone, anyone at all, takes it? When I think about how I could be different, about why they talk to me, that's who I am. I am that "anyone at all." I'm the antithesis of Mikey on the Life box. Remember him? "Let's get Mikey to try it. He hates everything." There were lots of times in my life earlier when I wished I wasn't so impressionable and easy to manipulate for other people's goals. Sometimes I felt like the Eveready bunny where people would wind me up and point me in a direction and off I'd go, doing their bidding. But on the other hand, because I am able to hear advice or read a concept in a book and apply it, my life has been incredibly enriched. And even though sometimes the risks feel like taking a swan dive into the unknown, where I can't see ten feet in front of my face, it also feels free.

I live in a realm beyond lucky where I have an amazing life partner. I am always holding a real person's hand while I am diving into the unknown. He doesn't hear the voices or see the people, but there he is, diving right beside me.

So with all these great resources and experiences, I asked the question and gave HIM, the spirit masquerading as Jesus, permission to talk to me again. I thought, "Why not? Even if you ARE an errant spirit, what do you have to say?"

Well, as it turns out, quite a lot.

It is a complicated story, for a very simple message. I hope you will bear with me in its telling. When I presented it to my writing coach, Molly Wingate, she said to me, "Julia, if you are going to tell this story, you have to be credible. Your reader has to be able to trust you."

I had so hoped to be anonymous!!! I am an upper-middle-class housewife and mother-of-four-turned-social-worker, who never in her wildest dreams would have sought this kind of role. Who would choose this? Even as I write this, I think about what a comforting feeling it is to hide under a bed.

What follows is the story about how I grew into a person who could receive spiritual guidance for the purpose of telling this story. It covers more than twenty five years of my existence, as I learned to become a mystical person who repeatedly surrenders my life to spirit. It also is the story Jesus wants me to tell you about how HE grew into a person, over thirteen lifetimes prior to the lifetime where he became the Christ, who could become the spiritual guidance he was receiving. The reason I can tell this story, he says, is because we shared thirteen lives together prior to him becoming the Messiah. We then shared a fourteenth life, the one they call the culminating life, where I was the "other" Mary at his tomb.

This story was received through many months of channeling information from Jesus and a cast of other notable spirits. They include his mother, Mary, the apostle Peter and John the Baptist along with occasional angel choirs. I am fortunate that I have so many friends in the physical realm who believe me, believe IN me and have been willing to dedicate their time to this project, sitting with me while I channeled, and helping to develop the material we were receiving.

There are three parts to Jesus' personal development, as he has shared through me. First is where he learned to *receive* spirit and universal, divine wisdom over thirteen lifetimes prior to becoming the Christ. During those thirteen lifetimes of *receiving,* he and I, as his companion, learned to **cleanse**, **center**, **create structure** and **cultivate awe.** These are the necessary steps, they tell me, in developing a relationship with the divine. The other two parts of his personal development in becoming the Christ were *seeking* and *sharing* universal wisdom and divine love during his lifetime as Jesus. While some of the *seeking* and *sharing* events and processes are mentioned in the channeled portions of the book, and are used in my workshops, they are not the major thrust of this endeavor.

This is a book about how to *receive* spiritual guidance, experience divine love and learn to become a vessel for universal energy. It is organized this way: First, I tell about my experience where I learned to **cleanse** in this lifetime. The chapter following gives channeled examples from previous lifetimes I experienced with Jesus where **cleansing** is utilized and discussed. Second, I tell about my experience in this lifetime as I learned to **center**. Following that are channeled experiences from previous lifetimes with Jesus where centering is utilized and discussed. Next is a chapter of channeled material from the earlier lifetimes with Jesus where he and I learned about **devotion,** because when cleansing and centering are used frequently in a daily practice, a pathway is worn through all the daily confusions of life. The connection between self and spirit is easier to access. It becomes instinctual to make an overt connection to spirit. The next chapter is about how I learned to **create structure** in this lifetime. The chapter following it is channeled material from previous lifetimes I experienced with Jesus where **creating structure** is utilized and discussed. Next then, is the chapter about how I experienced and **cultivated awe** in my life. What follows is channeled material from previous lifetimes with Jesus where **cultivating awe** is utilized and discussed. Finally is the chapter on **passion**, because when **awe** is **cultivated** within a **structure**, from a **devotional** practice of **cleansing** and **centering**, **passion** is possible.

For clarification purposes and general interest, the last three chapters contain information about the mission of our project and information we have received about who Jesus was and what was happening with and around him at the time of the crucifixion.

What the spirits have told me is: This is a formula for raising the levels of energy on the planet. This is a way for you, the reader, to personally experience and access universal wisdom and divine love. This is THE WAY Jesus was talking about, but it is THE WAY told with a different set of parables. This time the parables are in the guise of past lives I purportedly shared with Jesus. I understand the idea that Jesus and I shared past lives requires a huge leap of faith. It implies an enormous level of buy-in that I don't always possess. Sometimes I have to put my objections aside, take my ego out of it and simply become the messenger.

The compelling aspects of the message are thus far two-fold for me and my readers. On an individual level, we are finding personal connection to the vastness of the universe. It is not simply an enormous, neutral echoing chamber. Instead the universe possesses an all encompassing feeling of love and kindness. This experience of love and kindness completely reframes the context of our existence. It's the feeling of absolutely knowing that we are precious and cherished children of the universe. Knowing this is all that matters. It becomes perfectly clear that each being on the planet is contained within the context of this energy. We are all part of this perfection. When we act out of that perfection, we become co-creators of the context in which we live.

On a community or global level, the reason for pursuing this connection becomes exponentially more profound. We have all the tools we need for envisioning and manifesting an evolved society in which we recognize each individual's connection to that perfection. The more of us engaged in this visioning process, the greater the energy for evolution becomes. Those of us who witnessed the bloody barbarism of the 1968 Democratic Convention in Chicago, where our society turned on its own youth, the promise of its future, are fully cognizant of the necessity for this evolution. I'm sure there are many other examples we could list. But that is the one that reminds me of the dysfunctional nature of our society.

If identifying the perfection in yourselves and others doesn't turn out to be your experience while engaging with this "how to" manual, then at the very least it is one incredible whopper of a story. I can already feel the wind rushing against my ears as I dive into the unknown.

The "Q" in all the channeled sessions is identified in an appendix immediately following the chapters. What we found early on was that readers were becoming distracted by the person asking the question, which seemed to distract from the information presented. Each person who sat with me was fully invested in helping uncover the most significant information as it related to their experience. What's great is they all come from different perspectives and backgrounds, so the flavor of their questions really helps to flesh out the material from different points of view. We repeatedly found topics about which I, Julia, often held a different point of view or opinion than the questioner, the spirits, as well as the personality of the past life I found myself in at the time. To simplify that process, questioners became "Q." However, that didn't seem fair either, in case the reader especially identifies with the point of view of one particular "Q." Hence I decided an appendix of the channeled sessions as well as the identity of each "Q" was appropriate.

What also is important to mention is that most of the information I channeled was totally new to me at the time. When I really think about it, it blows me away. How did I get it all? I have no way to know how to answer that question. I have never trained as a psychic, nor do I consider myself to be one. Even though I am bright, I honestly don't think my personal imagination or memory is especially superior.

When we began to pursue this information, I didn't really have an awareness of the mechanism of how I received it. I simply went into trance, saw pictures and received words. Simultaneous with the "seeing" and "hearing" came a deep "knowing." I'm very clear it's a knowing I don't possess unless I lift my awareness to different levels. Further into the project, I began to understand that how I best accessed information was by first becoming rooted in another life. Once I was rooted in the life—the more I channeled the easier it was to become "rooted" earlier in each session—I could also see from above the life. I could "be" the character and I could also "see" him or her. I was both in it and observing it. Having the vantage point of seeing from above the life then connected me to having an understanding of what came before and after what I was observing. Now when I am channeling and rooted, within certain parameters, I can often cherry pick from different periods to pull information together, sometimes thousands of years apart. I currently only have the ability to "see," "hear," and "know" answers to questions which concern the line of wisdom relevant to the way Jesus learned to receive and use universal wisdom and divine love. I can also "read" the best path for individuals to interface with that wisdom. What I don't "know" and can't access is information about how other world religions developed, or Atlantis or the Pleidians.

The following are excerpts from channeling sessions where we learned what, exactly, was the point of the information I was receiving, and how it should be organized.

Spain, 48 A.D.
Excerpted from Number 4, February 6, 2011

Q: What's the knowledge you have a sense of needing to bring forward?

Me: The knowledge I am holding is multifaceted. There's this thread of lives that Jesus and I had together. When we started out, we didn't have the capacity to conceptualize the big picture. It was over a matter of lifetimes where we could--as I say this, I am seeing a rose opening in my mind's eye—condition ourselves to the point where our minds would open to possibility. And those were the lives we had together, bouncing ideas off of one another, until we were to this point.

Q: Yes, can you ask where did it originate?

Me: The knowledge is universal truth. It's sort of like how they are finding in each human cell is DNA to create the whole body. It's similar to that. It's knowledge that's just there. It's knowledge that's in the air. It's just a matter of being able to fit our dimensionality, or our mind strength around it. It is knowledge that anyone can have. It doesn't really take going to the four corners of the earth to pick it up. It is universal wisdom.

Q: Why did he choose this?

Me: The more knowledge he gained, the clearer he became that life was pure and simple. No matter what level you were operating on, no matter the level of sophistication or intelligence, it boiled down to one small kernel of truth. We could just love one another and open ourselves to the other and we would heal. And we could heal to the point where we could have a communion with God and the Universe. He was showing people the way to have deep fulfillment. The God that came before, the one of the ancient Jews was very judgmental and hard on people. Jesus had the ability to understand that it didn't have to be that way. It could be about grace, gentleness and loving. He felt he had an important message to share with all the people. Not everyone is ready to receive this information. We had those 13 prior lives where we had been preparing our minds and our spirits to open to this information.

Q: Is it kind of like today, where people don't want the knowledge, they don't want to change, they fear people knowing more than they do, or having a different set of knowledge?

Me: It's not so much not wanting to. That was his point about compassion. It's more that they can't wrap their minds around it. He was one to say, "Let's make it so that it is a simple loving message."

Q: Why have you surfaced at this time?

Me: There is so much searching now that there is an opening and longing for the information. I'm seeing a standing ovation. There are enough people who are at this point of inquiry in their spiritual seeking. It's time to supply some answers to their seeking. It's also time to create a written historical basis, too, for future generations to study.

Q: Can you ask about where it originated, where you learned it? When it was known in the past?

Me: Since it is knowledge that's available to everybody, the wisdom I am holding is, how do you get yourself into a position to access it?

Q: Are there some specific points you can make in terms of the knowledge?

Me: Ultimately, I am supposed to give a structure for the pursuit of it. I'm seeing this web. For the people who are committed, it's important to follow a framework. If you're not going to study it through Catholic mystics, Kabalists, Sufis or trained spiritual masters, then it's good to have a structure for it. The reason I am telling this now is to organize the pursuit of universal wisdom.

Q: These pieces of knowledge will become clearer?

Me: The knowledge I have is to help people learn to go with the flow of the universe, in their highest and best use, in this lifetime.

Q: We talked about your role as being a disseminator of information.

Me: I have been conditioned in my life to be a receptacle or conduit for this information.

Q: What is your interaction with the knowledge and what conditions are best for it to blossom? What are the ways for it to be best universally received?

Me: Jesus is saying to me, "A book, we're going to write a book." He's saying what needs to come first is how it occurred for him and me. That is the story of the lifetimes that we had together. In the telling of the story it becomes apparent what's necessary to be a good receiver. He is saying it is as important as the knowledge itself because people don't know how to first receive it. There are all of these seekers and they want desperately to be able to get the information, but first they have to prepare themselves. I keep seeing a rose opening. You have to have the opening, and you have to have space between the petals. This knowledge can't come into a cork. To get this knowledge, you can't come into it saying "I know, I know, I know." You have to come into it saying, "I'm open and I'm willing to learn." He's saying it's not only the lifetime where he was the Messiah that's important—and clearly, people weren't appropriately conditioned to receive that information then—that's when he thought he could do it for them. You position yourself so you can be a recipient of the information.

Q: Why do you think people resist these universal truths? It could help them; it could make their lives better.

Me: Well, it isn't in a familiar form. People think they know. They are so sure that they know. The form isn't something they have seen before, or felt before, so until you have lived a lot of lifetimes and have a very open mind, you are generally not prepared to accept it. If you are a newer soul, it's very unfamiliar to you. It's more like a porous piece of coal versus a diamond that is multifaceted. A diamond refracts all the light, because it has all the different facets and you can see through it.

A newly cast soul is like a piece of coal. It's the manner of being tumbled around and compressed in different lifetimes that you are able to use the information. Those of us who can perceive or pursue this can bring the others along. We provide the environment for the opening to occur.

Q: We started to talk about how to proceed on this project. This is a book you will be writing?

Me: Apparently. I guess our lifetimes together equal opening ourselves to the processes. He says he didn't perform miracles. He found the perfection in people to reflect. He found the core truth inside of people that allowed them to recreate themselves. It isn't about being perfect, it's about getting your own self out of the way enough that you can bring universal energy inside of yourself, and then send it outwards so that you can be possessed of—not possessed by—universal energy. He talks about the powerful refractions of

11

the light coming into you, that you are then able to send out. You become a receptacle for concentrating universal energy to then disperse. That's what great healers are able to do.

He's saying that sometimes people happen on to that energy on their own where they get themselves out of the way, to allow the energy to come through. He says there is also a formula for it and that's what the other practices are about.

Q: You don't need someone leading you through. Is this something people can do on their own?

Me: Yes, some people can. Jesus says the more you do a ritual, the better you are at it, the more your energy lines up with it. People would be far better at making change if they would line themselves up with the different flows and not get stuck in judgment. He says Christianity   was never meant for the purpose of judging others.

Rome 50 B.C.
Excerpted from Number 19, June 11, 2011

Me: Anything that builds connections is worthy in the same way. Because it always has the opportunity to build energy exponentially. It's where the sum of the parts is greater than the whole. It's not just a little greater than the whole. A huge amount.

Q: It builds upon itself. Does anything come first?

Me: Cleansing, and you can use any of the elements to do that. Jesus, Mother Mary and Peter are saying there are many different ways to cleanse and most people who do this work are conscious of the cleansing aspects

Grounding is really important.

Q: So we want to cleanse and then ground?

Me: Yes, cleanse and then ground. The cleansing helps to create a space to receive. Once you ground, you can open yourself up to receive. It is better not to open yourself up to receive until you are grounded. Then you create the structure. Cleanse, ground, structure and receive, which means to open. I am to start with one of the stories where we learned cleansing.

They are saying it's a good way to format the book, to start with one of the stories about cleansing. Then it's good to do one of the stories about grounding; then it's good to do...

Q: Enclosure...And reiterate that through the lives? The book will recount the cycle of cleanse, ground, structure, receive.

Chain Gang, Part II 510 B.C.
Excerpted from Number 23, August 4, 2011

Me: I had been asking the question about awe and where it will fit in. They are saying when you are connected with the awe in yourself, it comes from being cleansed, being centered, having structure and the awareness that every moment is a miracle. When you are in that space of allowing and possibility, everything seems awesome, everything seems inspiring.

I did have this question: What does it mean to connect to the hearts of men and women?

When they talk about connecting to the hearts of men and women, it's always with the idea that we need to be coming from awe and inspiration within ourselves. When we do that, we will make a connection. Our goal is getting to the point where, when we are delivering this material, when we are acting out of it, it is coming from the honest place of inspiration and feeling like life is a miracle. Energy is best served finding the awe and inspiration and acting out of that. Awe is waking up each day and saying, "It's a magnificent day. I feel so inspired, I feel so lucky, I am so happy to be who I am in this moment." It's one of those things where if you feel it you don't have to say it because it radiates off of your skin. You have found the portals in the air where you are moving with the flow. You feel exquisite every single moment. It is taking ownership of it yourself. It is being a co-creator of that identity. It isn't something that is bestowed on you. It's claiming your birthright to feel inspired and awe.

Q: I was having a light bulb moment. It makes total sense.

Me: I'm getting that, too. Yes, absolutely, we get too wrapped up in what is going on with other people. Then we forget to claim our own space.

Q: Exactly.

Me: It isn't about being bestowed anything. It is always a choice that we are making in every moment, to choose to feel awe and choose to feel inspired. It is the point we always want to reach regardless of the circumstance. Absolutely, they are saying to me, when you are standing in the grocery store and feeling frustrated, yes, you can then take it to the next step and say, "In this moment, I am supposed to be here, and isn't it a wonderful place to be?" That's the next step. "I am so happy to be exactly where I am."

It is a space I have claimed for myself. I am grateful to have the opportunity to do it, yet it is the part where I become a co-creator, and I accept responsibility for being exactly where I am in that moment.

So that's what they are saying: It is the point of being a stakeholder. It is a co-creation. It is taking ownership. It is beyond the gratitude part. It is beyond the humility part. And it is OK, because it is the part where you are coming from pure awe and inspiration.

1

I Want My Story to be Told

First, I cleansed so that I could learn to listen...

"I want my story to be told," Jesus says to me while he sits with me on the concrete bench in the garden. We are surrounded by big-leafed, waxy green shrubs. The light is a little dim, like dusk. Jesus looks like himself, with his shoulder length wavy chestnut hair and neatly trimmed beard. He has on a white robe, sandals and a long red vest.

I'm at Omega Institute in Rhinebeck, New York, deeply in trance, while reclining on a back jack, the most comfortable apparatus for meditation I've experienced. Omega in Rhinebeck is that glorious spot where some sort of transcendence is bound to occur because the setting is so ideal. A former Jewish boys' summer camp, it has a lakeside setting and many small buildings and dormitories, with some larger buildings for group meetings and meals. Multiple groups meet here at the same time. There is always someone interesting to talk to. As cell phone reception is almost impossible, telepathy is a desired skill for being in touch with anyone else. My husband was here with me last summer and knows this, so I am settled into a calm, semi-somnolent state for the week.

We're on day three of processes with Brian Weiss, M.D., the renowned psychiatrist who has popularized reincarnation over the past three decades. We are in training for facilitating past life regressions with clients. During the week, we experience many group processes and then see some people pulled up on stage for individual regressions. I am finally slowing down to the rhythm of Brian's verbal cues. The first day of processes,

> I am on a Viking ship in torchlit darkness, feeling the bracing sea air on my face, smelling the rank body odor of my sailing comrades, experiencing the swell of excitement that comes before plundering the northern coast of Ireland. Then Brian's lilting voice comes through, encouraging the room of 120 therapists, social workers and yoga instructors into the process, going down a beautiful staircase, completely severing me from my pre-marauding delight. I wonder at the regret I feel.

By some weird fluke I've already been on stage. I was actually the first in the training to experience a one-on-one regression with Brian. He's demonstrating a dramatic way to assist a client into trance.

> Looking into his eyes, from a chair in center stage, my crossed arms are leaning on his right arm and hand which he is holding horizontally in front of me. As he puts his left hand on my forehead, I slump into a heap as he pulls his right arm out from under my arms. There are audible gasps from the audience. I emerge as a Nazi messenger pilot in a bright red plane with black swastikas encased in white circles on the wings. I experience an "Uh-oh" moment, when first seeing those swastikas in a room where I think there are many Jewish people. Luckily, the pilot I was never engaged in combat. Whew!

Later that night in the dining hall, I experience my 15 minutes of fame as people ask me what it was like to regress in front of the group. Altered states are easy for me. If he'd asked for volunteers, I would not have raised my hand. I always like to give people who haven't had as much experience or opportunity as I have had their turn to be center stage. As it happens, I was asking Brian a question about the eye roll test we were practicing that hypnotherapists can use to determine the how hypnotizable their clients are. It is kind of cool, watching people who do it well. Their eyes roll up into their heads and they close their eyelids over the whites, eyelashes fluttering like butterflies on the way down. I was having a hard time with the exercise. I said to him as he walked through the group, "I can't do the eye trick, but I know I am good at trances." So he said, "OK, we'll do an exercise on stage in a minute, and you can come on up and demonstrate."

A woman in the shamans training group with whom I had dinner one night has already walked away in a huff due to my challenging her commitment to her craft when learning she gave her 12-year-old son Ritalin for ADD.

Our beautiful young friend from Prince Edward Island, with alabaster skin and china blue eyes, has already had traumatic recall of the hours and minutes surrounding Jesus' crucifixion, during one of the group regression exercises. She stays agitated even when she is out of trance. Her hysteria is amazing and sincere at the same time.

And I have already told my new, good friends about my personal experiences with Jesus coming to talk to me. This is Wednesday in late October, 2008.

In this group process still being lead by Brian, I am asking Jesus how, exactly, he wants me to tell his story, as we sit on this bench in my garden together. "Do it using automatic writing," he says, "like you did in a previous life." I tell him, "People talk about you all the time." "Yes, but they have the story wrong," he says. He holds my hands and looks steadily into my eyes as he says this to me. He probably realizes my first inclination is to run away, even though I know he can always find me.

*****

It had all started in the fall of 1996, twelve years earlier. I had experienced a mysterious illness where my heart raced and I couldn't catch my breath. It felt like my bronchi were frozen stiff. At 38, as fit as I have ever been, playing tennis five times a week, I hugged the banister as I edged up the narrow stairs covered in plush, taupe carpet, in our delightful Cape Cod home. For the first time in my life, I was afraid to go to sleep; thinking I might not wake up. I gripped the heavy cotton top sheet as I lay in bed with wide open eyes. I wore a heart monitor for a day or two. Our internist found a functional heart murmur, but nothing else. And, after a couple of weeks, my breath came back.

My husband, Claes, and the children and I had recently been to San Diego to visit with my mother and grandmother. My interactions with my mother were disquieting as they often were, but enough to cause these intense psychosomatic symptoms?

One day soon after, as I drove to the grocery store though the winding oak-lined streets of Lake Forest, the Chicago suburb where we lived with our three children, a thought popped into my head. Out of the blue, a voice I later learned to trust had an idea for me. I would learn to meditate! It was an idea that suddenly made abundant sense and found resonance deep within me. My dad meditated when he was alive, and my grandmother still did. Two of my friends meditated in a group with a woman in town. I got her name and called her up.

Jackie was in transition when I first met her. She and her girls were staying in the coach house of the large grey Queen Anne home as you rounded the corner from Washington to Illinois. It was set way back in the wooded portion of the yard, almost to the bike path that ran alongside the train tracks behind it. Going upstairs to the living room, I found it was filled with worn comfy chairs and wicker with random cushions. There were windows on three sides of the coach house. The late September breeze created a ballet of tree branches on the other side of the glass. There were three other women there the first afternoon, besides me and Jackie. Jackie had recently been to a workshop where she learned a new process and bought soul cards.

> She guided us into the process which took us down a forested stream, with a leaf floating on the water. During the process I also saw a scene where a child and I were watching a parade of Roman soldiers. I was wearing a rough brown robe and my hands were old, gnarly and misshapen. Next, a guard with bright orange feathers in his helmet leaned down to snatch the child away from me. A feeling of foreboding rose in the pit of my stomach before the scene shifted back to designing my special place.

In all the years in between then and now, my special place hasn't changed. It's in the mountains in a grove of Aspen trees, next to a stream. In an instant, I am able to be there, creek side, with the sun on my face, the golden leaves of the trees catching the light. The breeze is always cool and refreshing, like springtime or early morning. A mountain peak is a bit away and I know I can walk there in a short while.

After the meditation, we all shared our experiences and the consensus was that perhaps I'd had a past life recollection. It's funny because from the perspective of today, I have no doubt that's exactly what it was. But then, on my first day, I guess I was waiting to get permission from the experts.

I was lucky to be in a group with seasoned meditators. Sometimes the viewfinder that is our connection to past lives and other altered states needs a bit of assistance knowing the way there. The energy of the seasoned meditator provides that. I always recommend to my clients that they start meditating in groups if they wish to more quickly develop their ease in achieving altered states.

Besides that, Jackie Jackman was born and raised in Northumberland, England. Her voice is so gentle and engaging, with an accent that is surely more closely related to the faerie realm, and waves from Northumberland seafarers lapping against the shore, than anything found here in America. Following her voice in guided meditation felt like an easy connection to far away worlds.

Also, after the meditation, Jackie brought out her soul cards and we each drew one out of the deck. Mine was a face with a big open mouth. Jackie looked at it straight on and then side ways, and then looked at me carefully as if pre-gauging my response. Then she said, "I hope this doesn't offend you, but this looks like a vagina to me. I'm wondering what's up with your mother."

Mom had recently moved to San Diego to live with Grandmother. Daddy died of lung cancer in 1990, and after that my previously bombastic and confident mother seemed rudderless and needy. Before she moved, she kept dreaming up these large schemes to save children worldwide that she designed and conceptualized, but wanted me to put together for her. Every time I saw her it seemed like she was handing me sheaves of paper with lists of people to call on her behalf to get things moving, me, with my three small children. She, with nothing pressing in her life. When I avoided doing these things, she called to argue with me on the phone, which always left me in bed the next day, exhausted, with a swollen face from crying. It would be lying to say her move to San Diego wasn't a huge relief to me. So yes, I knew it was possible that the yawning mouth on the soul card did indeed represent my mother.

After that first afternoon of meditation, I was accepted into the group, and the wonder filled realm of altered states opened to me. Jackie moved to a small house a few blocks from ours, and Monday night was meditation night. One of my first nights there,

I bi-located to a place where a man named Bill Smith was struggling on Lake Michigan with his sail boat. The waves had capsized him off his boat, and somehow I reached out to him and helped him get back on. He said, "Oh, thanks!" Then the scene shifted, and next I was a blond knight, strapping on battle hardware, getting ready for a practice round of swords with a comrade. Later I went back to Bill Smith to make sure he was OK. He was sitting on the side of his boat in a navy wind breaker, eating what looked like peanut butter crackers. He was taking his boat back to the harbor, seemingly in good shape.

After that night, my meditation experiences were not so dramatic. I spent my time in the group dutifully following Jackie's prompts or going to the white space filled with nothingness, until at the end of the time, she called us back to our spaces in her basement. We opened our eyes to the luscious rose candle burning in the center of the room. At some point after I started meditating, I learned that sometimes newbies get a Cook's tour of what's possible, which is why I could regress and bi-locate early on. It whet my appetite for lifelong commitment to the practice. Certainly I was hooked!

In the spring of 1997, Jackie made an announcement that her friend, Terrance Lovewave, was coming from Santa Fe to read astrology charts the next month. Always up for an astrology reading, I took the number and made an appointment.

I am a Capricorn, and as all Capricorns know, Saturn is always with us. It constantly reminds us of responsibility, whether it strictly belongs to us or not. Every successful Capricorn I know has learned to shoulder that responsibility right along, without breaking stride. This astrology reading was no different, in many ways, from any other I've had. Saturn was still in my chart, exacting demands in my life, this time in the guise of my mother. What was different was Terrance Lovewave. Sitting in one of his friends' kitchen in a nearby suburb, he said to me, "You have to listen to Caroline Myss. Everyone is! Here's the number, order her tapes from Sounds True. Another Capricorn client I had with mother issues started listening to the tapes. Her mother came to her in a vision while she was running a marathon. After she finished the marathon she learned her mother had passed on."

We were in the process of moving to a larger house just west of downtown Lake Forest. I listened to Caroline Myss' *Energy Anatomy* from start to finish while sponge painting our older daughter's new bedroom sage green and pink to match the Laura Ashley bedding she had chosen. I was so entranced with her message that I went over in the afternoons to paint while the older two children were in school, and our wonderful child care helper and friend, Kimmie, came to watch our little two-year-old at the old house. Being engrossed in Caroline Myss and her stories opened up a whole new world for me. I especially enjoyed it when she said things like, "If your spirit guides tell you to move to North Carolina, how will you meet your perfect destiny there if you don't go?" I wasn't ill, so to speak, but I liked the idea of screening thoughts like a sieve. There were many larger pebbles in my internal self that benefited from being identified and pulled out. Who was I really and how did I hold energy?

The most important concept I received while listening to those tapes was that thoughts matter. Before the tapes, I believed that thoughts were my own private arena. I didn't realize they were important enough to influence others. My favorite story Caroline tells is about the woman involved in a car accident who leaves her body temporarily. As her spirit rose she heard the people in the cars lined up behind the accident. Most people were irritated at the delay, but ten or so cars back, a woman prayed, "Oh dear God, if it is an accident, please let everyone be well and safe." The out-of-body woman noticed the license number of the car and returned to her body because it wasn't her time. When she was able, she located the other woman by her car license number and thanked her for her prayers!

It was such a huge awakening to me to learn how much impact thoughts and prayers have. I started monitoring my thoughts, every morning waking up with the intention to listen to what I was saying inside of myself. And, most importantly, with regard to my mother, every time I thought of her I sent her light. If I found myself arguing with some thing she'd said or done, I interrupted myself and saw light beaming from my forehead, all the way across the country from Illinois to California and surrounding her.—Because, regardless of the state of our relationship, I wished her comfort and care in healing thoughts.

In retrospect, I realize this was a foundation piece of my learning to cleanse. Being able to shift thoughts to more positive ground is incredibly important. If we can shift out of the chatter in our heads, it allows a space for universal energies to come through, giving us access to a relationship with the Divine. If we are stuck in our heads, nothing else can come in.

Additionally, when I was in my early 20s, some 30 years ago, I learned my body functioned better if I avoided sugar, grains and foods with a high glycemic index, although I know we weren't calling it that yet. As an adult, I have always been a diet and exercise hound. I like the lighter-than-air feeling I get from being lean and trim. There's also a huge energy payoff for eating natural foods. I am usually game to go on a diet with someone.–"Sure, let's do it!"—or to head off for a hike, go to the Y or Jazzercise. The long, dreary Chicago winters were particularly hard on my moods. I noticed they fared much better the winters that I headed out for a two-or three-mile walk most days in the early morning hours. It's hard to manage this work of connecting to the universe if you aren't feeling good.

Also around this time, in meditation class someone had asked about their spirit guides. Like, how do we know who they are? Jackie replied, just ask and they will show up for you.

I have this perversity about trends. If everyone is doing it, I think there must be something wrong with it and look for a different path. For instance, I read in *Time* magazine years ago that people were signing their kids up for the "correct" nursery school when they were born. I thought, "Oh, man, that's the lamest thing I ever heard." So when everyone else was jockeying to get their kids into Joytime down the street, I signed our son up for nursery school at the Presbyterian Church with amazing Tiffany windows saved from the Great Chicago fire of 1871. "Now that," I thought, "is an awesome place to be."

So when everyone was talking about discovering their spirit guides, I knew mine would be Native American because I had such an aversion to the idea. "For heaven's sake," I harrumphed to any one who would listen, "does every spirit guide have to be Native

American?" By then I knew that the spirit world delights in nothing more than playing little games with us. One day, stepping out onto the freshly hosed clay tennis courts of the Lake Forest Club for a match, in my knife-pleated orchid skirt, my first spirit guide introduced himself, as he hovered directly above my head. His name is Red Feather. Later, during meditations and various parts of the day, especially a day of cooking in preparation for a party, the rest of the gang introduced themselves. There is another Native American named Blue Cloud. She is the only female. Then there are Gabriel, Raphael and Ishmael, the angels. I remember Raphael because he was my son's second favorite Ninja turtle, the red one, and Ishmael looks sort of like Harpo Marx, with large tufts of white hair. When ever I am the butt of a celestial joke, like endlessly lost car keys, I always think it is he who set me up, silently laughing hysterically off to the side of the room. And of course, Gabriel, who is the messenger.

Even though I was raised in the Unitarian Church, by intellectual parents who were never able to wrap their minds around the stories in the churches, I grew to love the Presbyterian Church on Sheridan Road. Claes and I were married in the chapel of the church by a lovely young minister named Harry, who, after combating Hodgkin's disease as a youth, was dealing with leukemia as an adult. Younger than us, he was still able to ask us the hard questions about our commitment to each other and what we thought that meant over the course of our lives, as he counseled us before the wedding. With our son in nursery school at the church, and Claes organizing the church's men's softball team, it was a place we could begin to belong in a community filled with Armour, Swift and Walgreen family members. I joined many committees over our years there and Claes and I taught eight or nine years of Sunday school, kindergarten through third grade. When we reached third grade, we began all over again with kindergarten curricula when the next child left the nursery at the church, where Kimmie was regent. And that, to this day, is what comprises my Biblical knowledge. But it must have been effective because what I noticed, after about the fourth year of teaching Sunday school, was that I believed ALL the stories. Somehow, to my mother's complete horror, I had become a believer.

If anyone takes the time to peruse the Sunday school curriculum of the Presbyterian Church, what you will find is the best and the brightest of the New Testament, with a couple of Old Testament stories thrown in for good measure. We loved to prepare for the class with Jesus in the boat with his Apostles, hooking up magnets to fishing lines on dhal rods. I always imagine that fishing day nearly two millennia ago must have borne a strong resemblance to Ernie on Sesame Street standing at the side of his vessel in his red and blue striped shirt, yelling, "Here fishy, fishy, fishy!" while fish jumped into the boat.

Because no one ever told me how to hold those stories, there was little concept of the more heavily handed Old Testament. I took a childlike delight in the miracles, and would often find myself reciting the phrase, "Knock and the door will open," in the back of my mind, underneath all the other thoughts of the day. I believed, in the purest sense with all of my heart: with God, all things are possible. The fact that I had Native American spirit guides never served to contradict that feeling.

On the Fourth of July, 1997, after attending the always-charming Lake Bluff parade, I was driving home alone in my forest green Taurus station wagon along Sheridan Road. Claes and the children were still at the little fair at the end of the parade route, with its bouncy blow-up toys and cotton candy. The oak leaves on the trees far above me were fully leafed like a canopy above the street. I mentally prepared for the potato salad and fruit tarts I was throwing together for the group picnic we would be sharing with our neighbors and friends for the festivities later in the day. A cardinal flew so close to the windshield of the car that I nearly hit it. I jerked my body away as we are prone to do in case of impact. I was exactly passing the Presbyterian Church chapel where Claes and I were married.

Tying on an apron in my pretty white kitchen with blue and white striped wallpaper after arriving home, I picked up the wall phone to check messages for the coordination of the day's events.

27

On it was a message from Grandmother: "Julie, call me, it's about your mother." With shaking hands, I quickly dialed the phone. I learned my mother had lung cancer. It was advanced. She was thought to be close to the end.

The next six weeks were like a whirlwind, much faster than our usually action packed life. We had a trip planned to see Claes' sister and my brother in San Francisco, our older daughter was on her way to YMCA Camp in Wisconsin at the end of the month, and we were moving! We quickly made arrangements for our older two children to fly to San Diego from the San Francisco trip to see their grandmother. I planned to go as soon as we became settled in the new house.

The first week of August, while unpacking the new house, friends invited us to a dinner party at their home. I had a horrible cough but went anyway. Our hostess had put Oriental lilies in the centerpiece of her oval dining table, so, along with the cough came the brain splitting headache I get from lilies. A friend of theirs was a social worker who did hypnosis and thought he could help me with the cough. In the middle of the dinner party, I dutifully followed him into the family room. The ceiling light poured into the chasm in my head, as he tried to hypnotize me. It might be the only time in my life where I have failed to go into trance at whim. I felt so tense and awkward, in this bizarre turn of events in the middle of a dinner party, with glaring yellow light around me. There was no chance of an altered state. As it panned out, the social worker turned up a week or so later coughing as well. The conclusion drawn by him and our host, a clinical psychologist, was that it was a psychic illness that I had picked up from my mother, which he then received from me. I had not heard of such a thing, but it certainly would explain the mysterious frozen bronchi I had experienced the previous autumn after visiting my mother in San Diego. It was like a vicarious health premonition.

In the next few days, Grandmother called and said it was time for me to go to San Diego. There wasn't going to be as much time as we had hoped. I quickly bought a ticket and got on a plane that day. Heavily sedated and gasping for air when she wasn't taking oxygen, Mom opened her eyes and said, "Scary" when I sat down beside her. Grandmother explained that she was worried about how she appeared to me. In a peculiar way, when she turned her head sideways, the light from the window shining behind her head, she looked like a baby bird with its head tilted up to receive food from its mother. Instead she gasped for breath. Odd, because that is what she always said the babies in our family look like when they are freshly born, baby birds. Bird to bird and dust to dust. By the next day my siblings were all there. My younger sister had arrived with her girlfriend to help care for Mom a week or so earlier. A trio of Mom's closest friends from Illinois had come as well. She died in the afternoon of August 12, with all of us in a circle holding her hands, wishing her *bon chance.*

Even in retrospect, that summer seems like a distortion in time to me. In the fall my younger sister called to say, "I miss Mom the way I wanted her to be." Yes, I knew exactly what she was talking about. I wasn't getting much sympathy for my mother's passing from family or friends because it was no secret that our relationship was difficult. But it didn't stop the deep wells of longing I had for it to have been different. In the first meditation class of the fall, though, as I went into trance:

> We were making something out of clay. While I shaped an object on the pottery wheel, my mother's small freckled hand slipped into mine. I knew she felt the loss as I did. Tears seeped out of the corners of my eyes.

Caroline Myss had a weekend presentation in Oak Brook later that autumn, and I went with a couple of friends. One friend and I were perfectly awful during Ron Roth's benediction on Saturday morning when he mentioned the "attitude of gratitude." I about died laughing—the kind of laughing where snot was coming out of my nose and tears were rolling down my face, snorting and choking to keep from laughing out loud. For some reason, I was feeling incredibly transformed and superior that day. But the joke was on me after the break. I left the bathroom with a tail of toilet paper tucked in to my pants, trailing behind me forty or more feet into the meeting room on the red carpet!

Caroline spoke about archetypes that weekend, which fascinated me. After I went home that Sunday afternoon I saw all sorts of religious symbolism that I had never noticed in my house before. Every where I looked was a cross or an "X," on the backs of chairs, in our art work and sofa cushions. But the most striking symbolism we had in our house was my husband's early American pottery collection that he had begun the year before he met me. Nearly 100 crocks, or "vessels," as my sister called them, comprised the collection. Wow! Vessels! I wondered what that meant. I also started feeling like the *Twilight Zone* when I realized our son was born on one of the reputed days of Jesus' birth, our older daughter on a Sunday during Good Friday/Easter season and Claes exactly five weeks later, Pentecost. Our toddler daughter was born during a full moon, a high Jewish holiday and the Autumnal Equinox all in one! The only one missing was me. And then I got it. Oh yeah, 1/12, or 1of 12! It was a little bit apostle-ish and a little bit Wicca at the same time. At that point I was humored by, and felt safe in, the ambiguity.

In our new house, just west of town, we backed up to an open area and a stream, which held many natural delights. Once, the stream flooded a bit in the late autumn months. A family of bright white egrets stopped by for a couple of days to visit with our big willow tree, as it draped its long tendrils into the silver-shadowed water. They splashed in the newly created pool. Then they headed on their way to a more southerly destination.

Somehow we ended up with one of those bird clocks that we finally put up in our kitchen—the clocks that have a different bird call with each hour. The only bird call we knew to set the clock by was the mourning dove. Both Claes and I had separate but equally meaningful experiences, waking to their cooing in safe, comfy beds when we were children. It was at this time that I learned the call of the cardinal, the beautiful red bird I now associated with Grandmother. And one day, when it wasn't the cardinal's hour to chirp on the clock—instead it was more like 1:20 in the afternoon—I heard the magnificent serenade of a cardinal, seemingly from above my head in the kitchen. I ran outside in the front lawn to look up at the house. There he was in his brilliant crimson coat, on the old white-shingled roof, singing his song for the millennia, like an escaped soloist from the choir in Handel's *Messiah*. The wonderful thing about that cardinal's song is that every time he sang, he sang with complete abandon. It was always the best song he ever sang. And every time he sang, I could feel the energy of that song rising from the depth of my spirit and filling my whole body with joy.

It seemed like there was something potent coming, but when it finally did come, holy cow, was I not ready for it! I was constantly dreaming "training" dreams about ceilings bulging with water, or practicing on the trampoline with my tennis drill friends, whose names in real life sounded like "trinity" and "vessel" (I don't know about other people's universe, but mine slays itself with its cleverness and sense of humor!), or about living at the base of a vast mountain I was charged with climbing.

I have never been an *Oprah* watcher, but many of my friends are. They tell me all about what was recently on her show. I am not very attached to the television and prefer to read instead. But once during that time, I had a very detailed dream about being Oprah's gardener on an estate she had very near Market Square in Lake Forest. The estate was on a southwest corner, completely out of my imagination. The yard had a high metal fence, with rows and rows of lush evergreens descending in height as they came away from the fence. The greenery was very deeply vibrant, comforting and somehow womb-like. I felt safe and significant there in my role as Oprah's gardener.

The flavor of the dream seemed like "loving kindness." It felt somehow related to a dream I'd had many years earlier, after my small son and I joined Claes in his life in Lake Forest. When Claes and I married in 1988, my life shifted in a huge way. I went from being a barely-making-ends-meet single mother whose ex-husband randomly paid child support, to living in one of the most affluent communities in the country. Soon after we married, we moved

31

into a charming Cape Cod house in a *Pleasantville* neighborhood. There were towering oaks with an occasional shagbark hickory or sugar maple thrown in on quarter-acre lots, where the streets dead ended into a picturesque community park. The houses had their own individual designs and construction, and each was more captivating than the next in Hansel and Gretel appeal.

As I began my career as a stay-at-home mom in this storybook neighborhood, I asked Claes how he saw my role. He said since his office was in the home, he felt like he had a limited ability to develop a social life, so he would appreciate it if I would put one together for us.

This I thought I could do. I'd always had mountains of friends and been in the thick of many social milieus. I had also been in the hospitality industry for part of my career and could throw a party together in a heartbeat. Little did I know that Lake Forest was a hot bed of Martha Stewart clones ("Martha who?" I asked the friend who told me this, single motherhood not affording me the opportunity to keep up with who's who of the celebrity circuit) and expense account entertainment. Any party given was met with cynical assessment of its value for opportunism. The first summer we were married, we invited the neighbors over for a cookout and one of the young dads asked Claes what he was selling. After having several such parties that met with meager success, Claes and I began to doubt our ability to attract friends. We would huddle in bed at night and ask each other, "Do I have bad breath?" I felt like somehow my first failed marriage had branded me as insufficient for Lake Forest society. I slunk around with deep guilt for my inadequacy.

Then one night I had a dream that changed my life. I was running along the softly undulating curves of Sheridan Road with the minister of our church, just as it passes Lake Forest College. The trees were fully leafed and it seemed damp out, as though a soft rain had recently fallen. I had one child strapped to my right leg as I ran. I turned to the minister and said, "I worry about my arrogance." Then the scene changed and we were inside the chapel where Claes and I were married, only instead of matching the church, it was about three stories high with paned glass walls and ceiling. In the middle of the chapel was an enormous black cauldron, about 20 feet high, from which fragrant steam emanated. As we stood next to the cauldron, the minister asked me, "You're a cook aren't you? What would food be like without any spice?"

I woke up from that dream feeling like somewhere out there was approval for me being exactly as I was. I honestly woke up from that dream echoing Sally Field accepting her Oscar at the 1985 Academy Awards: "I can't deny the fact that you like me, right now, you like me!" And, as with the dream where I was Oprah's gardener, there seemed to be a space reserved especially for me, that perhaps one day I would grow into.

Going to meditation class was like developing this wonderful, secret, magical life. Many years later, at one point in my training in various forms of hypnosis, I learned that the center for laughter is very near the center for meditation, prayer and hypnotic states in the brain. When I was training with ASCH, the American Society for Clinical Hypnotists, more times than not, I found myself heartily belly laughing while being brought out of trance by my dentist, podiatrist and psychiatrist classmates. We all know that person who laughs so loud, it's hard to believe. Well, that person is me, or my younger sister. My daughters, after years of not wanting to sit with me in the movies, are growing up to learn to their horror, that some of them also have THAT laugh! Given that, it is not at all surprising that many of my trance experiences are filled with humor. One of my favorite guided meditations at Jackie's was when she led us into a state where we grew our higher spiritual selves from inside of ourselves to outside of ourselves. Mine grew and grew until it turned into the Stay Puft Marshmallow Man from *Ghostbusters!*

Another time during meditation class:

Shifting out of the white space at the end of the process, I am in a night scene. I am jostled in a crowd of people and we are escorting the procession carrying Jesus' cross down from the hill where he was crucified. There is torch light. I smell oil burning and I hear the sound of people quietly sobbing, and low singing. I do not know who I am, but I am seeing the scene from inside the rim of the hood I am cloaked with. The skin on the bodies around me glow with gritty, drying sweat. I know I have deep sadness below the dull resolution to complete the many tasks ahead of me.

The second most important thing I learned from Caroline Myss is to follow coincidence.

Both the friends with whom I went with to see Caroline that fall meditated with Wayne Dyer's *Meditations for Manifesting* tape with significant results, so I thought I should try it. This began my dedication to "The Rule of Twos," as I call it. Sometimes I hear something that sounds intriguing and I put it on a mental 'to do' list. A book to read, a recipe to try, or, in this case, it was a Wayne Dyer recording. When TWO sources spout the same recommendation, I know it is the universe delivering a message to me. It is telling me to DROP EVERYTHING and fully immerse myself in that particular recommendation. "The Rule of Twos" has served me well over the years. I just do it, with no questions asked. This time was like all the rest. I was completely rewarded when I initiated the behavior recommended by following the Rule, which was to meditate with Wayne Dyer. Of course, any recording of his is wonderful, based on the depth of his voice alone, but after we recovered from Christmas that year, I thought I should get serious about a daily prayer and meditation practice. Every morning, before awakening the children for school, I carried my handled teak tray filled with candles downstairs, lighting them just prior to chanting, "AHHH," which was a call to the Divine to engage with me in my life. Sitting on the old green and gold tweed padded sofa in our bowling alley-sized basement, I concentrated on opening the chakras between my root and crown, pouring energy out into the universe. After a couple of weeks or so of this, I grew bored with visualizing easier cash flow and a thinner body and shifted to focusing instead on world peace and a safer world for children.

What follows reminds me in so many ways of Bill Cosby's routine on Noah. As children, we laughed hysterically as Noah asked God, in the voice of Bill Cosby, "What's a cubit?" Of course not knowing what a cubit was ourselves, it made perfect sense that Noah would be confused. It didn't occur to me until much later to ask, how did Noah know it was really God talking to him? How does anyone know for sure?

And then one day it happened during the meditation.

> Voices in my head that identified themselves as "Jesus" and "God" began a conversation with me. First, what they said was, "We are sorry it has been so hard for you." Then, "We wanted you to stretch." And last, "You have done a good job."

The compassion pouring out to me was incredible, like a balm to my spirit, where everything that had once felt raw and tender was smoothed over and made whole. Honestly, the only way I know how to describe the pulsing energy of a prayerful meditative state is that is like the rushes we had as kids getting high on marijuana. The waves of energy fill the body and flow through it in such a similar fashion. However, these rushes are totally encompassed by loving kindness. When there is spiritual energy involved, as when a message is coming through, the waves are that much more intense and crystalline.

After that occurrence in my basement in Lake Forest, I have had an internal knowing, an unshakable certainty, that the universe equals benevolent, loving energy. The rest of the stuff that we get wrapped up in our lives is just drama, story and mental gyrations to help us through the learning. What I've come to understand as a mental health practitioner with the primary intention of sharing this adoring support and solace from the universe, is having that connection is the experience people need to have to begin the healing process. It is the message I feel compelled to share with every client who walks into my office. Because until that connection is experienced personally, it is hard to conceive of the deep love and kindness that pours through it, or to know that it is intended equally for everyone.

The next time I meditated with Wayne Dyer, Jesus came alone. This time he said to me,

> "You were James Madison in a previous lifetime and Claes [my husband] was William Tecumseh Sherman."

OK, so now I'm coming out of the meditation thinking, "Who IS this talking? And, what do you think you are trying to pull over on me!" I did not tell anyone about it for a long time. Who can you tell this sort of thing? It was like a *Candid Camera* moment, when I was looking around for the joke to be on me, but the only place to go with it was inside my own head. Was I nuts? Because it felt entirely more extreme than just being crazy!

I thought, "I'll do it one more time and maybe I can get some serious answers." I know my hand was shaking, and my body thrummed with intensity the next day as I lit the candles on the tray, settling back into that old green sofa resting on old green carpet in my musty-smelling basement. This time as I became settled and focused in to the "AHHH" meditation,

> Jesus came to me and he said, "Mary, thank you for teaching me bodies are beautiful." And he held some shrubbery aside for me to walk through as though he was going to show me a scene.

I shuttered the picture in my mind, opened my eyes, turned off the tape and, blew out the candles. I marched up the stairs with the tray in my hands. I put it in the bottom dresser drawer in my bedroom and slammed it shut!

This was late March, 1998.

2

Cleansing

Getting SELF out of the way, in order to receive...

When I was growing up I lived in suburbs of Chicago. Grandmother and Granddaddy spent part of their time in San Diego and part an hour north of Kansas City. When they were in California, occasionally they sent us a crate of juicing oranges. Setting the crate on top of the oval, olive green laminate-topped kitchen table was only the beginning of the best kind of anticipation. As soon as one of us wedged a screw driver under its lid, the greenish-orange sweetly acrid fragrance of fresh juicing oranges wound itself out of the crate. We cradled the oranges to the sink to rinse them, and cradled them again in paper towel to the empty refrigerator drawer, made ready for their presence.

Sunday mornings we often had a big brunch with softly scrambled eggs, patty sausage, the grainiest toast, fresh fruit and coffee cake. But the undisputed star of our Sunday brunch was freshly squeezed orange juice from our California oranges. Its flavor was so sweetly delicate as it danced down our throats. Even the pulp seemed to instantly dissolve on our palates. Unlike other household chores, the child chosen to squeeze the oranges for juice Sunday morning felt they had been conferred a special honor.

One Sunday morning I must have been the first child to awaken and begin helping with breakfast, because I found myself dreamily squeezing the oranges for brunch. Clad in cotton shorts and a T shirt, my sleepy self was coaxed into full awakening as I pressed down on the handle of the juicer. At the exact point where the pressure on the squeezing paddle released the first rush of juice from the orange, the sweetest essence enveloped the space around me. It was as if the whole life of the orange, from seed, to tree, to the heady fragrance of the blossom, was encased in that moment. It's one of those moments in my life where time seemed to stand still. I felt like my identity was absorbed into the experience of that second. I was the orange and the orange was me.

"Cob web juice," I said. "It's like cob web juice."

"How do you mean that, Poolie?" Dad asked.

"It's like all the cob webs that have collected in our brains and throat overnight are suddenly cleared away with our freshly squeezed juice."

My dad, ever one for glorifying the cleverness of his children, called freshly squeezed orange juice "cob web juice," from that moment on.

As with cob web juice, there is a moment of complete stillness, awakening and openness that goes hand in hand with **cleansing**. We are suddenly immersed in a slowing down of consciousness that voids the previous context of our awareness. It's a yawning, a stretched out segment of time that we meld with. Identifying such moments, as with cob web juice, is what helps to orient us in the void. It creates a soul memory so that we remember how to return to the stillness. In my experience of squeezing juice oranges, my awareness stopped in the space of gorgeous sensory information. I opened from sleepy pre-adolescent into, "I am so totally in this moment of oranges" mode. Immersing myself in natural sensory information is usually a good way for me to engender a cleansing experience. The first time I squeezed juice oranges, I had no idea what magic was in store for me. However, after having that experience once, I knew I could return to it. I knew I could choose it.

In writing this passage, Claes and I had a conversation about what it was like for him the first time HE squeezed juicing oranges at Grandmother's. We both remember that potent instant when we first experienced the juice being released from the orange with absolute clarity.

Cleansing doesn't create shift, but it allows it to happen. Sometimes we turn into empty vessels with no new information filling us, after clearing the clutter in our minds away. Clearing our minds of conversation and argument creates an opening where redirection can occur. Meditation is a great assistant in slowing down our processing enough that we can choose the exact moment in which to create the opening. It's like knowing when to push in the clutch of a manual transmission vehicle. You know the moment where there is no gear engaged? It's an abeyance, an opening, a space of nothing. What is that moment filled with? Possibility, right? It's the time when everything around us is on hold. We are simply in the space of that moment. It's a clearing, a lack of connection. It feels like an infinite number of choices are surrounding us. If we understand the mechanism of this opening, we can consciously engage with it when we are seeking a shift in our lives. Or, we can just hang out there because it feels good. The more we practice it, the better we get at it.

With a manual transmission vehicle, the choices of what gear we can shift into are somewhat limited to the speed at which the vehicle is moving. The same is true for us and the energy level on which we are resonating. Sometimes if we want to shift into another level of consciousness, we have to raise or lower our energy to do that.

The following are the lifetimes Jesus and I shared where **cleansing** was highlighted. In the first life, **Innsbruck**, the cleansed space is occupied by the spark of life within a little girl, which her family cherishes and protects. It is from that sacred cleansed space that the family creates a new existence after severe trauma. In **John the Baptist,** some choices about how we determine the direction

39

of the shift after cleansing are illuminated. From the purview of the "other" Mary, those shift choices fall under the heading of "shape shifting." Last, from a discussion contained within **Jesus at a Roman Party**, "shape shifting" is defined.

Innsbruck, 730 B.C.
Excerpted from Number 15, May 2, 2011

Me: I am going into a valley. It is near Innsbruck, Austria before it was a village. There is a beautiful, wide river, surrounded by mountains, before there were buildings there. The year is 730 BC. I have wooden shoes on and I have little, thin legs. I am a little blond girl wearing a white dress. I am walking along the river. The wooden shoes are too big for my feet. They belong to someone else. But it is springtime and there are lovely wildflowers. I have made a crown from them. I am seven or eight years old.

Q: Are there people around?

Me: I am with my mother. She is a buxom woman with cinnamon-colored hair. She has on roughly woven fabrics in natural and dark colors. The necklines of both of our dresses are gathered, where you pull a string through. We have taken some old crusts of bread to feed the ducks along the river. The fish come and eat the bread. My mother works in a tavern and this is her day off, or she has time to be with me outside. I help out in the tavern, too.

Q: Is it just you and she who are together in this life?

Me: My father works near horses of people who travel. He is a very simple, slim man who is clever and remembers tales. He sometimes travels with the gentry to take care of the horses and sometimes he is a stable man. I think my grandfather works at the tavern also where my mother works.

40

He is not the owner. We are simple people and we have enough. I have a place to sleep in straw, not too near the fire because it would catch, and warm enough. I have enough to eat. I am loved--really, really loved.

But now I am seeing later in that life, some kind of terror. Dark people come with horses and light our village on fire. They are unkind to my mother. I don't see what happens to her, but I can hear her screaming. My father is maimed. I'm still seeing my grandfather is there and my mother is there. These are dark people. I can't really see them distinctly. I see dark energy around them. They are really unkind. My grandfather barters with them. He and my mother will do anything to keep me untouched. And after that they tire of us and our village, because they have burnt it. There isn't much left after that. There are just a handful of villagers left. They go someplace else to ravage and pillage. We have this broken family now. I think what happens with my father is first they maim him and then he gets gangrene and dies. It is an unpleasant death. The idyllic childhood that was so lovely and safe was covered by an ominous dark energy after that. My poor mother. She was so ruddy and buxom and happy. Now she is thin and wraithlike. My grandfather is hunched. They are scared. They are really scared. Because I have been untouched, I still have a spark of brightness, I can feel it inside. I know that I have to keep it hidden. I am out of sync. It doesn't belong there anymore. It isn't enough to sustain everyone else. I quietly nurture it myself and I learn to make beer like my grandfather. I am a beautiful young woman. Jesus is one of the dark people who came. It was one of the lives where he experienced going along with the crowd. I don't think he was the ringleader.

Q: He was a follower?

Me: Yes, he was a follower. He didn't stand up and say, "This is wrong." I saw him again later in that life. He, of course,

41

was not a very nice or bright person. He didn't recognize me, but I recognized him. I was able to rebuff his attention. He'd lost some teeth. I was satisfied by having the ability to do that, knowing he was no longer anyone who could hurt me or my family. I would go and sell my beer in a bigger town. I can see my casks of beer in a cart. I grew to have some affluence with the beer that I made. With my grandfather, we were able to rebuild our business.

There are a couple of lessons here. One of them is that when what you have in your heart is the desire to nourish others and the desire to have an honest living, it is easier to prosper. The other one is that when you have a spark of goodness—I'm seeing this spark inside…

Q: Little tiny flame…

Me: …cherish it, protect it, develop it, and hold it dear with all your might.

Q: Are you able to see that spark you've cherished and nurtured after you have grown into a beautiful woman? Do you get accolades with your grandfather for the beer?

Me: Yes.

Q: What is the reward?

Me: Gradually my mother and grandfather are able to let go of some of the fear. It isn't a fast transformation, but eventually they are able to relax somewhat. We are always vigilant about protecting ourselves. It's my feeling that a new lord had taken over the castle nearby and the dark men were with that lord. Eventually, as with all things, they pass. And they had no interest in our village any longer because they burnt it and nothing was left. We kept our energy small and protected. We kept it sort of under a bushel while we quietly went about our business of building community again, without attracting attention. We deliberately asked for protection to stay under the radar. We made a conscious effort to keep from being noticed. We didn't make a big noise. We didn't ever really trust again. I don't think I ever married in that life. We always were modest. Quietly, simply we just held on to one another and took care of our own in the village. And we sustained each other, keeping our energy small. We made a concerted effort to shield ourselves using intention, kind of like a psychic flexing, to keep from being noticed, to be allowed to go about our business. And as with all things, the old lord was vanquished, too. The new people who came to live at the castle didn't engage with us so much. We lived in a place more like a posting inn. We lived on the way someplace. We were a little outside the range of the castle. We didn't ever fully live in our bodies after that. We were always a little timid. There was not the same kind of great joy. That was too big of an emotion for us to have again. It was too scary to occupy that space.

Q: Almost as if, if they were too happy or joyous, it wouldn't be cautious enough.

Me: We were so fortunate before those people came and we couldn't reclaim that space again. It seemed too dangerous. So we kept our simple little lights inside ourselves separately.

Q: Under that bushel.

Me: I am seeing that light inside a person, a little flame inside of the solar plexus. It's the third chakra, right, that's around the stomach?

43

Q: Right, the color yellow.

Me: The color yellow, really? I am seeing it related to a golden goblet. There is some sort of vessel holding or creating a space there. There's something about the light in the stomach and the beer that we made that cleansed and nourished. Holding the space for the goblet is there, as that is where the energy of the goblet resides. When we talk about vessels, sometimes they are spoken about in terms of being the womb. I'm not seeing that as the relationship here. I'm seeing the relationship as the golden goblet, the spark of life, the spark of will to go on, and being cleansed all occupying the same space inside of a person. It is right here in the solar plexus/stomach area. It has to do with nourishment.

Q: That area, according to the teachings I've learned, is all about self. Your second chakra is your womb.

Me: Right, and often I've heard that the chalice, the Holy Grail, is related to the womb, and I'm not seeing the idea of the vessel as being the place where children grow. This is saying to me that the chalice in this relationship is related to shifting and nourishment.

Q: Feeding your soul.

Me: Exactly. And there's a spark of life. I have such an aversion, I don't know what it is, to using the word "power" in these processes. I have to really search for the more appropriate word. There's a life-generating essence that comes from that area. It is similar in some ways to the energy of the womb, but it is a personal generation. It's not creating another life, it's creating YOUR life.

Q: Correct. The one above the womb is the chakra that is you. So having that spark of life feels to me that's where it exists, in that area, and that's what you cleanse, or shift, and nourish to take care of self.

Me: Right.

Q: Not others.

Me: I'm seeing the natural residence of the gold goblet right where that spark of flame was. In the past I have read that the chalice of Jesus is associated with the womb of Mary Magdalene. And what they are saying is in this process where I am bringing forward the information of Jesus' lives, the gold goblet is a function of the third chakra area, and it has to do with nourishment. It can be nourishing for others, but it is the idea that first you must nourish yourself. You MUST guard the flame that is the little flicker of light inside of you. That has to be the primary focus of your life. Only after that is sustainable can you give any nourishment to anyone else.

My grandfather and my mother in Innsbruck always maintained their kindness, even after these atrocities occurred. They felt like they had to sell their souls, but they never let it break their spirit. They were able to reorient themselves and live kind lives even afterwards.

Q: Lesson there. They had to nourish their flame.

Me: At first all they could do was nourish mine. It's the idea of living simply that is so paramount when you are under adversity. When you have circumstances that are adverse, it is important to return to the simplest processes you know. To rebuild it has to start all the way down at the most basic level. How do you best center yourself? What is the best thing that you know you can create? Go back to the simplest form of whatever it is that you know, because sometimes it is hard to sustain yourself under adversity.

Q: Gratitude?

Me: I don't think they could even go to the gratitude part. I think they had to shift their energy to keep the flame alive before they could be grateful.

Q: Was that all the work that they could do? Keeping that alive?

Me: Keeping that alive inside of me, their little child, is all they could do initially, as they were beginning to heal. And they had to give it to me cleanly, without rancor. It was a huge endeavor for them to shift their energy in that way.

Q: Were you able to give it back?

Me: Once the men with the bad energy tired of us, we were able to rebuild. My grandfather always had his ability to make beer. At first they took it from him as soon as it was made, but eventually they tired of harassing him.

Q: So you saw the pre-Jesus.

Me: They were able to keep the men away from me. Then I saw him later when I was driving some beer to the market. I had the satisfaction of seeing him in a decrepit form. He'd lost some teeth and he'd lost some of his importance. I was able to ignore him.

Q: He didn't recognize you?

Me: No. But it gave me satisfaction to know that I had that ability to be strong, to have succeeded under the adversity he had been party to. He was dissolute and ineffectual, basically. He had lost his ability to hurt me.

Q: The lesson in this life is taking care of that inner spark.

Me: And if you have an opportunity to work in a field that nourishes others, that's a very gratifying way to live.

Q: Still feels like passion belongs there, but not quite in this life. I want to put passion in. Where you nourish others and nourish self can be a passion, yet in this life it feels like the struggle to keep the light alive...

Me: Right. We never had that kind of passion again. There was passion to begin with. Love and kindness...it helped to have had that experience to come back to, you are exactly right. To measure against and come as close as we could.

In the excerpt from the **Innsbruck** regression, originally the word "cleansing" wasn't used with regard to how the mother, grandfather and child responded to their great trauma. When I was going through the lives to discern which fit best under the recommended criteria of cleansing, centering, creating structure and cultivating awe, this was still the one that felt most like cleansing to me. When I was in the regression, I had the experience of them letting go of their judgment, hatred and fear of the dark energy that had nearly destroyed their lives, and to begin to nourish the flame that was inside of them. They only wished others well, and it was a choice they made. They consciously reoriented themselves to make the best of the lives they had left. Dark energy had no place there.

But because the actual word "cleansing" was not spoken during the recounting of that life, in a subsequent regression, I asked permission to use that word with regard to this past life and it was given.

Amazingly, there were settlements outside of where Innsbruck is now in 730 BC. I am confused about the word "castle" as I am not sure whether that is an accurate description of how people lived at that time, but that is the word that came.

John the Baptist, about 33-34 A.D.
Excerpted from Number 2, October 27, 2010

Me: I see horses.

Q: Horses. Tell me about the horses.

Me: They're running. There are riders on them. It's a big field area. The boys are riding the horses.

Q: And who are the boys to you?

Me: James and Jesua, who are my sons. They are fourteen and sixteen now. They are training the horses. They are really good-looking boys. Strong. They are off in a paddock area.

Q: And who are you?

Me: Mary, their mother.

Q: OK, so there is fencing around to hold the horses in.

Me: It's a good-sized outdoor paddock. I'm looking over the fence at them. I am really proud of them. The boys are so close. They have big, joyful energy.

Q: What happens next?

Me: I'm here to tell them it's time to clean up for supper. There's going to be an announcement at supper. Their father is home. It's an occasion.

Q: And what's the announcement?

Me: He's going to take the boys to Galilee. It's a surprise.

Q: Is Galilee a long way for them to take a trip?

Me: Not so far. It's a gathering. John the Baptist will be there. They will get to see him. They are excited. He is their friend. He's been traveling.

Q: So tell me what the boys look like now that you have them in front of you.

Me: James has dark eyes and curlier hair. He's the older one, and his hair is darkening more than Jesua's. Jesua has big, blue eyes and straighter, lighter blond hair, kind of strawberry blond.

Q: Strawberry blonde, like his father?

Me: I wouldn't say his father's hair is strawberry. I am the blond one. Jesua's hair has a reddish tint, but it is very light. My hair is blond. It is curly like James and light like Jesua. He has my blue eyes.

Q: OK, and if you had to, how old would you say you are? How old would you say Mary is?

Me: In my 30s.

Q: And how old would your husband be? How old is Jesus?

Me: He's a couple of years younger than me. He's in his 30's also. He's come in and he has just met with John the Baptist. The boys have an important lesson, and it's about the power of water.

Q: Can you tell me a little more about that?

Me: Water is one of the elements. It's the element that is associated with emotions. And it's about transmutation and emotional cleansing. It's how to imbue water with energy

and how to make it sacred. John has used the water for purification and clarity.

They have a group that is meeting to talk about water. The
boys are excited because it is the next stage in the development of their knowledge.

Q: When you say it is the next stage, were they being
groomed for anything?

Me: It's a privilege and an honor. The descendants of King
David are meant to stay knowledgeable and current. They
are not receiving the same tutelage that Jesus did. They don't
have to travel as far because it is a more cosmopolitan time.
There are bigger centers of civilization with knowledge.

Q: So it is more about the importance of education in the
David family, not so much being Jesus' sons.

Me: Education is important for descendants of King David.
Jesus takes it very seriously, and he knows that the boys are
ready. I have had the lesson and so has Mother Mary. We are
both excited for the boys. It's a very festive event, that John
has returned, and the boys get to go.

Q: Very good. So what happens next? Are you getting ready
to go on this trip?

Me: I'm not going and neither is Mother Mary. Only the boys
are going. We have already learned what they will learn. It's
the power of water and its ability as a vehicle to help shape
change and shape shift.

I'm confused about whether it's an ascendancy tool, such
as becoming more involved in and open to universal learning, or whether it's a tool that actually helps you shape shift,

and I think it's both? That's what's coming. Different people specialize in different uses of water.

Q: And is this shape-shifting tool, is it learning thru the Gnostic group, the David family or the Essenes? Who is teaching this?

Me: I'm seeing it came from a long journey, where we rode camels over the desert, to a point where China and India meet. I'm seeing a map in my head of the northeast border of India with China.

Q: So you think this ability is from ancestors of people in China and India?

Me: Yes. That is where we went, and John was with us. They taught us this.

Q: Can we ask a detailed question about those natives in India and China? Can you get information about them?

Me: Let's ask.

Q: Were they simply normal beings that learned on the planet or were they advanced as beings and brought this knowledge to the earth?

Me: They are Shaman, and so they are both. They have red dots on their foreheads. You have to train to learn this. It's sacred knowledge.

Q: Did they learn this sacred knowledge just by being human beings? Or is this learning from another universe?

Me: I think it's originally from Atlantis, and it's a lot like crystals. But water has a different quality than crystals. Water has permeability and it melds in an easier way, so while crystals are better for giving and directing energy, water is better for shifting or transmuting energy.

Q: Crystals are better for directing energy, but water is better for transmuting?

Me: Yes, transmuting, melding or, sometimes you need to cleanse before you supplant information. I see in my mind wiping emotional turmoil out of a body, and then a re-infusing it with the water that had been imbued with healing properties. And crystal energy is kind of zing-y. It infuses with energy and it's similar to combustion-able energy. Crystals are more like lasers. And water is used to cleanse and to shift. The Shaman studied and carried the knowledge for hundreds of years before we got there. We had heard about it by chance. And each of these Shamans had a raven they carried on their shoulder.

The shape shifting is an embodiment of the energy and knowledge, so when they have a raven, it becomes the vehicle for the knowledge. So maybe it's not exactly shape shifting? Some of them did that though, they'd run as animals. It's sort of where the vampire, werewolf story comes from. Some of them were able to do that.

It's a similar skill to bi-locating. They bi-locate inside another animal. They use water to facilitate the ritual that goes before that.

Q: They used the water to facilitate the ritual?

Me: Yes, like baptism. It's the idea of cleansing and supplanting with spiritual energy. That's how John used it for the religious ritual. But it was from having learned it from the Shaman.

Q: Can we use those rituals to bi-locate today?

Me: Anybody can bi-locate. For shape shifting, it's a matter of transmuting your energy into the energy of the animal. It helps if it is your totem animal. It helps if you are familiar with their energy. My daughter in this life was bitten by an eel in Mexico. She put her foot in the ocean and the eel came and bit it. She has that totem now, so if she wanted to, she would have an easier time bi-locating as an eel. Not that she would want to, she was so freaked out when it bit her. It's similar to when people are bitten by a dog. The dog wants to claim them in their tribe, like blood brothers. It becomes easier access to that energy. Because it's such a huge invasion, we are not used to it. When people train dogs for violent purposes, they have violated the dog.

Q: Let's ask Mary to go back to our scene, so we can discover a little bit more about your life at that time. So what do you see next? Do we go on to meet with John the Baptist?

Me: The boys go with Jesus. I am not there, but they tell me about it. It's a group of about ten select people. It's at night and it's quiet. John has to be careful who knows he is around.

I think Mary Magdalene wants to come and they tell her a wrong time. They want her to be SOMEWHAT engaged, but she isn't closed-mouthed enough to be fully engaged. She comes later for the tail end of it. This men and women thing is an interesting dichotomy. Because women are better channels, they are more permeable. They are more in touch with the energy of water. They are more emotional. But because they are more permeable, they have a harder time holding knowledge in secret. There's this issue of men and women. Men aren't as good at receiving the information because they are so rigid—these are vast generalities—and women are more instinctual because they bond with babies. The really good ones learn to read the baby's energy. Women have an easier time as channels, and are more permeable, so they are easier to cleanse. They hold on to things less. They can move on more quickly. They don't hold a shape as well because they are like water.

Q: But you say the men hold the knowledge longer.

Me: Well, they are more rigid, so they aren't as good at receiving. That's why Jesus has to do the vision quests. It's harder for him, as well as the boys, to get the knowledge. But because they have less permeable structures, it isn't as easy for them to dissipate the knowledge either. It isn't as easy for them to talk about it. So when we're talking about secrets, it's only women who have been men often times in past lives, who have a better conceptualization of how to become less permeable.

It's really the older souls who have been both men and women, who are the better channels. They are both permeable, so they are receptive, and structured, so that they can hold it. They can receive and hold the information.

Q: I wonder if we could ask some questions.

Me: Sure.

Q: These are big concepts. One question is: who were the women in early Christianity? Who were the movers and shakers who went along with John and any other of the disciples in early Christianity?

Me: It was a group of women affiliated with the Essenes. There was some wealth in that movement. I believe Mary Magdalene was affiliated with that movement. There were still the same reservations about which women to trust and which women could hold the information. Time was short. There was a timeline and it wasn't about discriminating against the women. The assumption was that some of them would know anyway, because they were so intuitive, by being in the environment. That's how some of the Essene women got their knowledge. Time was too short to officially induct them. The only women who truly had the knowledge were me, "other" Mary, and Jesus' mother Mary.

Q: So "me" meaning the "other" Mary, Jesus' wife. So just you and Mother Mary were the only two?

Me: Yes, we were the only women because time was short. The boys had been going with their father for so long and there were the other disciples who followed Jesus who were also practiced. There were levels and levels of knowing. The knowledge they were meant to carry wasn't for generations. It wasn't like the knowledge I was to carry. So they didn't have to be as adept. The Essene women were probably more able to gather information than the male disciples. But they weren't ever officially inducted, as I had been, or like the boys were officially inducted. It was John who carried the wisdom of the water. He was the one who had it as his specialty and was fully engaged with water.

Q: Let's go back to "were never officially inducted." What does that mean? Does that mean the women weren't recognized as holders of the Christian knowledge?

Me: Because they are better mediums, they weren't invited because of the fear it would take them too deep. There wasn't the trust. They weren't meant to hold the knowledge forever. They had their own rituals, and this helped them to intuit. They were not excluded because they weren't smart enough, or wise enough, but because they were too smart and too wise. They weren't meant to be the keepers of this knowledge. That's why only two women were inducted.

Q: Tell us a little bit more about the boys and what happened to them. We know their names are James and Jesua. We know they are at least teenagers. In your life that you are living with Jesus, they are 16 and 14 years old. What happened to the two sons in that life?

Me: Oh, they went to France with me after the crucifixion.

Q: And then what happened in France?

Me: They became minstrels. They told tales and James played the lute and Jesua played a reed. It was a little bit of a disguise after we first arrived in France. Because you didn't know who would appear. We didn't carry a lot of wealth with us to France.

Q: Were you with them when they were minstrels?

Me: No, when I was young I liked to travel, but when I grew older I loved a warm hearth, a soft bed and good food. I was always happy to take in a traveler.

Q: And did you continue to live in France until you died?

Me: Yes, I did.

Q: Do you remember the name of the last city you lived in?

Me: Oh, you know, it was near where Montpelier is today. It's hilarious to me, because it's what the Madison home was called in Virginia. And whenever I look on the map to where the "Marys" landed, and see that's where it is, it always makes me laugh.

Q: There are no coincidences. How old would you say you were when you died?

Me: Oh, 76.

Q: Oh, that's old. Now what did the sons go on to do? They were minstrels?

Me: They were bawdy boys when they were young. They were never ones to turn away a pretty face. But they grew. James had some property. Jesua went with the church. He became a pastoral counselor.

James had property with animals. He liked farming, raising crops and training horses. He became landed gentry. It was before Catholicism. And Jesua became a spiritual leader.

Q: Jesua did?

Me: That's probably where the confusion is about whether Jesus also went to France because his name is so similar to Jesus'. He liked totems. You know, in China they have totem poles. He had seen them, and he liked them. He carved totems. Out of block structures, log pieces. The little ones had heads on them, like the Native American witch doctors. Similar features.

Q: Well as a spiritual leader, was Jesua known as Jesus' son in the Christian community?

Me: No. There was some need to maintain a low profile. And it was also the Eastern influence where the boys and Jesus learned how to put the ego aside. They had already learned the lesson of what happens when you become a spectacle.

Jesus always struggled with the ego piece when he was alive. You know, he knew he was great. He attracted crowds. But he didn't want to become the embodiment of arrogance. He experienced frustrations because he was the holder of the knowledge. Yes he had the wisdom and yes he had the energy, and when they are put together, they want to be arrogance, but they are not supposed to be.

Q: So they lived their whole lives incognito, really not being known to anyone except the immediate disciples?

Me: Yes.

Q: They all protected the boys? So the entire Christian movement that was growing, no one ever knew except for the immediate disciples?

Me: While Jesua developed a following in France, it was less Roman, more Gnostic, more Essene and more Earth Goddess. The Romans really distanced themselves from the earth-worshipping piece. And it has continued to plague them, as you know. They don't have the power that they could. They barely assimilate the transmutability power of the water. They totally neglected the pieces of the earth. Shamans always use earth in their ritual. Catholics don't really use it until death. And then it is just in burying the dead. A lot of the power is lost when you are only willing to give it to the dead.

Q: We are really looking at the energy of water as being a huge force in the knowledge that has been lost.

Me: Well, they lost the powers of all the elements. When the boys were going that night, it was about the water, but they also had the lesson of the earth. They also had the lesson of the wind and the air, and they also had the lesson of the fire. It isn't unlike Shamanism. It isn't unlike Wiccan knowledge.

Q: And you say most of this came from Atlantis.

Me: Well, the water Shamans had gotten that knowledge from Atlantis. I think the earth may have been a different lesson from a different group. The reason Jesus became so powerful is because he had braided the four elements. He became fully inducted into the wisdom of the water, the wisdom of the earth the wisdom of the air and the fire. And he knew how to use all of them. We had been trained in that.

Q: Could you do that?

Me: Yes, even now I know that I can do that if I want to. Sometimes you find a religious healer who happens onto a capsule of that energy and is able for some time to be a healer. Or there are these capsules of energy that happen when you have groups of people where healings occur, like with Caroline Myss and Brian Weiss. The point is for everyone to learn to do it themselves. And when you go to a healer, you are using them as a conduit for the healing. We get very complacent about learning the knowledge. We can all heal ourselves, like the Christian Scientists said, but we chose not to.

Q: With the 2012 vibration shift, will we be able to use the four elements?

Me: Sure, if we are open to it. When I was at Brian Weiss' training, I ran into people who were at Shaman school. And I had an argument at dinner with a woman who had put her ADD son on Ritalin. And I asked her, "Aren't you being a little lazy here? Are you really following the path?" We get used to these crutches. Your body is a temple, but it is hard to be so pure. You have to keep your mind in the place where it is free. It's a discipline. There are a lot of people who have to take themselves away from society entirely to be able to do this work.

Q: So if you looked into the future of the next couple of years, do you see our generation as a whole getting closer to these old practices of the four elements?

Me: Yes, because there is a collective movement that is happening all over. The first step is to make your self a vessel. You can't be rigidly judgmental and be permeable enough for the knowledge to enter you.

We have a lot of trouble with rigidity and permeability. How many women do you know who are an emotional mess? They are far too permeable. They have not enough boundaries. And then how many men do you know who are far too rigid? They are not permeable enough. It's a huge dichotomy. It's the two-headed dog.

Q: But it seems like it would be so wonderful for our society to get back to this knowledge that you and Jesus used, in the future.

Me: Yes, it's a matter of choice. It's the Yin and the Yang. Does the Dalai Lama have any women close to him in the high camp? I don't think so, not yet. I think they are just starting to tap women. There's the necessary feature where women have to accept the masculine in them selves, and men have to accept the feminine in them selves. There's a process that has to be undertaken. You see it more and more. The older souls are taking it on when there is the gentle man and the powerful woman. It's the embodiment of the dichotomy.

After this second regression, I was driving home from Denver, where it had occurred. I had this picture of John the Baptist, beheaded, as I was driving that I just couldn't shake. I didn't remember it from teaching Sunday school, but it could have been too gruesome to include in the text for kindergarten through third-graders. My friend Kat, later to become a facilitator, whom I met at Brian Weiss' training, was brought up going to Catholic school. I called her and asked, "Was John the Baptist beheaded? This really seems like something I shouldn't get wrong!"

She said, "Hold on I'm driving, I'll call you back." In the meantime she called her husband who Googled John the Baptist. Not only did I learn, yes, John was beheaded, but also that he was betrayed by a woman, Salome. I had been feeling a bit sexist about the information I had just shared, that they hadn't trusted women enough to train them fully in the rituals of water. Instead I had a feeling of "correctness" about the information I received, like a missing puzzle piece when I learned their instincts had been correct. But not soon enough to save their good friend, John the Baptist.

I also read in Fodor's Guide that Montpelier, France is a relatively new town. That area wasn't named that at the time just after Jesus was crucified, so I am perplexed about how that relationship transpired at this point.

In the regression that occurred July 26, 2011, we asked the question, "How do we define shape shifting? Is it simply the ability to send our energy to another location, like a ventriloquist sends their voice? It seems like there are different levels of sending energy, and perhaps praying for another is the first step? Next, allowing universal energy to come through us to send out seems like a more advanced step? Then there are the personal manifestations of shape shifting, such as bi-locating or embodying an animal, which seem to be even more advanced forms of shape shifting? And finally, for the purposes of the processes we are pulling together, it seems like the idea is to consciously draw and combine group energy to send out, to envelop, embrace and heal?"

Here is the response we received:

Jesus at Roman Party, about 18 A.D.
Excerpted from Number 22, July 26, 2011

Me: Let's talk about shape shifting. How do we define it?

Shape shifting is simply the ability to redirect energy. A kind thought even comes before prayer, because prayer usually implores the intervention of a deity. "Oh, dear God, please help so and so..." An even more rudimentary form of shape shifting, where you stop and re-direct your energy is a kind or generous thought. "I hope they are OK." "I just wish for them to be healed and well, safe and protected." "Boy, take a look at that gorgeous woman."

The first step of shape shifting is a conscious thought. It is a focused intention. The processes we are investigating are for healing. They are for physical healing, for spiritual healing and for networking. These processes are so people can learn to connect to universal wisdom, healing and love, for the purpose of manifesting and shifting the orientation of the planet. It is not for the purposes of material manifestation. What people need to know about it is, the more they engage with this work, the more their lives will flow really well and the things they need will come to them.

Q: Right.

I'm getting the word "allowing" and the word "grace" a lot. Those are two key things I think people need to understand.

Me: Absolutely, allowing and grace. Grace is multi-faceted. One part of grace is receiving energy you need for healing, such as "living in grace." Additionally, when you are living in this grace, it also is the circumstance where things manifest for you. It's an energy you receive and it is also a manifestation.

Q: It's like when you are aligned with the universe, they will provide.

Me: Right.

Q: With the flow of it, it just comes.

Me: Right. There are two parts to grace. One is the flow and the other is the manifestation. As for allowing, I see allowing as being the pure vessel that the energy comes through. Allowing is the ability to hold judgments in abeyance for a moment. Your vessel is clear so that only the good energy is allowed through--my hands are ZZZTing, I feel like I don't even need a magic wand--you don't have to give judgment away or cut it off. Just allow it to be over there so that you can have a clear vessel for receiving. "I am feeling this energy coming through me. I am a clear vessel for the purpose of holding and transporting the energy of wisdom, kindness and love." This brings up another point. The energy is not neutral. It is definitely imbued with kindness, love, healing and wisdom. It is a big embodiment of loving kindness. Another piece of recognizing this energy is it comes as sweetness. It's a very appealing, darling, joyous sweetness. Some of the spirit groups are kind of heavy handed and they are into rigidity and structure. The message for our group is like my mom and grandmother used to say, "Honey draws more flies."

Q: Right.

Me: It is sweetness that is the draw for this. I did the est training. We've all done these rigid structural things, blah, blah, blah that are hard on us. That's not the purpose of this work. Good to know, I am down with that.

Shape shifting:

It is a kind or generous thought or action.

Again there is a definite need for structure because you can be an enabler if the energy isn't focused and grounded in respect. If you are doing a kindness for someone so that they can't be strong on their own, then it isn't kind. It's creating weakness. That's where the strength and respect has to come from.

Shape shifting is the ability to move your energy away from judgment and forgive. To forgive means to let go while being grounded in respect for your own as well as others' personal growth.

The next step of shape shifting is personal manifestation. If you want to you can bi-locate. There are many bells and whistles that go along with it. It is special, yes, and it is a cool thing to be inside another animal's head for a while. But that is not the purpose of this exercise. For our purposes, the definition of shape shifting is to concentrate our energies in the clear vessel inside ourselves with strong allowing. Then we redirect it in ways it can heal. Though I guess for me, personally, I just hope I have a really good sense of when it is appropriate to use it and when it isn't. I still feel like I have to take an enormous amount of time to evaluate boundaries. They are saying to me they understand my confusion and it will come, we will get it. What they are saying about how to make sure that we don't undermine someone else's ability to grow themselves is to always focus on their magnificence. I'm not really sure what that means. I am seeing tennis. To keep hitting them the ball so that they have to give you their best shot. Don't give them an easy shot. Keep feeding it to them so they stretch and grow.

Shape shifting is the ability to redirect energy.

They call it shape shifting because it is important that it holds a shape.

Q: So that they recognize it.

Me: The reason for this exercise is to see where we can take it so that we can help others heal. When we have a circumstance in our life where we have an energy sponge and it feels like endless drain on our energies and intention, we have to learn how to hold ourselves separately from that situation. We need to learn how to hold our energy in a structure and still connect to the hearts of men and women.

After this regression, while we were both still in the trance energy field, we sat down to map the shape shifting model:

<u>Shape shifting</u>
Shifting away from judgment or any emotional attachment=
Cleansing
This creates the space for:
Allowing
Allowing then becomes the opening, through which universal energy 'ows,
Shape shifting occurs when that universal energy is directed outward:
A kind thought
Prayer
Forgiveness
Bi-locating
Sharing an animal's body
Healing energy

3

You Were an Innkeeper's Daughter

...and then I learned to slow down my life to center in each moment...

"You were an innkeeper's daughter," Jesus is saying to me. "You lived near Pella and I stayed at your father's inn. I was in Macedonia as part of a Grand Tour, studying Alexander the Great and Aristotle." He is showing me scenes where he helps my father thatch the roof of the inn, carries water from the well for me to cook with, and splits firewood for the great fireplace in the hearth room. "You were 18 and I was 16," he says. I'm getting the sense of being a pretty young woman, with long, wavy almost white blond hair. It is the shy beginning of our relationship, where I am impressed with this handsome, educated foreigner. Even though I am older, he is far more confident. "We had two boys together, who are currently your husband and your son."

It is March 16, 2003. I am at the Vista View Congregational Church in Colorado Springs, praying for peace, three days prior to our country's pre-emptive engagement in Iraq. I arrive by myself at the tidy, contemporary church, with the spectacular view of Pikes Peak. We are new enough to the 'Springs that I am still emotionally transported every time I stop and fully accept the grandeur of the peak. It takes more than a moment for the depth of feeling to fully register. When it does, it feels like floating. As I arrive, the dusky shadows of the snow cap are banked by the rose glow of the setting sun behind it.

There are only five or so of us waiting in the vestibule for the sanctuary to be readied for our devotion to a cause that by now seems futile. I am contentious in my belief that there are no weapons of mass destruction. It is and has always been about oil. Something about living in altitude has honed my convictions. I have a sureness about "knowing" things that feel like they come into my head from the high air in waves. Claes would have come with me, but he is back in Illinois, running his business there for a few days this week.

The hour of prayer is broken into four segments, with Psalms and hymns at the beginning of each, and then prayerful silence. Jesus comes to speak with me intermittently, just as I deepen into the personal devotion portions of the service. It reminds me of how Maude stalked Harold at funerals in *Harold and Maude,* one of my all time favorite movies. I know the potential for "Psst, over here," always exists, now, when ever I enter an altered state.

"You were the "other" Mary at my tomb," he continues in explanation. My relief is significant in not having been Mary Magdalene in a previous life, but I cannot honestly exclaim, "Oh, good, that explains everything!" At this juncture, in this deep trance, I have not yet begun experiencing anxiety at the inherent responsibility in this new identity revelation.

After that first series of encounters, exactly five years earlier, I told Jackie that errant spirits were bothering me. She said, "Ask them to stop." I did that, basically saying, "I don't know who you are, or what your agenda is, but you are clearly yanking my chain and I want none of it. I am not amused by this practical joke!"

The five years in between visits from Jesus have been action-packed. That is how we live life. We put an addition on to our house in Lake Forest, requiring semiregular attendance at the almost comical city architectural board of review meetings. The officiousness of the appointed official can be a marvelous vignette of practices to avoid. And then, we lived through the mess of remodeling and the always-illuminating discovery of costly hidden deterrents to streamlined construction, under the earth and in the attic that stressed our budget near to shattering.

I made alternating trips to San Diego with my brother and uncle to look after Grandmother, who prepared to die after the swift departure of my mother. Usually accompanying me was my then-youngest child who was not yet in school. We were so often in southern California that she developed a crush on the albino python at the San Diego zoo. Wedged between depressing appointments with the realtor and the banker at Grandmother's behest, were fleeting trips in the fog to check in with the massive serpent. His bulk seemingly never budged from its corner appointment in the open air snake house.

In late February of 2000 Grandmother called me, saying, "Who is coming at Spring Break?" When I replied our older daughter and me, she said, "You had better all come." Later that week, in the fresh snow of our family room deck, I saw a lump of something red through the wall of glass. Pushing the door open through the drifted snow, and stepping outside in the chilled morning, the lump turned out to be my precious cardinal. He had a broken neck from flying into the glass. "Oh, Grandmother," I whispered as the sob caught in my throat.

A couple of weeks later she called again and asked, "When are you coming?" I said, "We'll be there in two weeks, Grandmother." She answered, "I think I can make it that long."

I arrived at her little house near San Diego with our oldest daughter. She had grown so wraithlike, with skin like the Thanksgiving turkey plastered on her tiny, bony frame. She was hooked up to oxygen, interviewing a hospice nurse, while wrapped in her fluffy pink robe. After the hospice nurse left, she told me all about the turns in her health, the heart that did not pump efficiently, the diuretics that made her dizzy. And, finally, finished with recounting her medical tales, she straightened with alertness and said, "Enough about me! Tell me what is happening in your life."

For another hour before bed we talked about the children and Claes, she nodding with sage advice and understanding.

The next morning, I found her leaned up against a wall, breathing heavily and disoriented. That day she wandered in and out of lucidity. At one point she smiled coyly and talked about a divine dress, a handsome dancer, and a spectacular ball. Claes and the other children arrived, and we wondered what else we should do? I had fierce, specific instructions NOT to call the hospital or emergency care from Grandmother herself. Clearly she was meant to be in charge of this very important aspect of her life. So we sat with her and helped her hobble around her familiar space, feeling woefully inadequate in this end-of-life transitional care.

On Sunday, April 2, I checked in with her in the morning when I awakened. Her eyes opened and she smiled. The next time I checked in, she was gone.

The summer after Mom died, we began the process of adopting a baby girl from China. I knew Grandmother was preparing to leave us and I knew the grief of her passing would be more than I could bear. The week after we returned from Grandmother's memorial service, we received the call from the adoption agency. We had a new little daughter!

During this time, we saw the better part of our savings evaporate largely due to bad investment advice followed by bad personal choices as we encountered our first financial bubble. We knew it was time to move on. Our trip to China filled us with confidence for more successful adventures.

Why not move to Colorado Springs? We had family in the state and we were already feeling the need to live our convictions. We wanted to be outdoors and connected to nature. We love it here. The sunshine is such a balm for the spirit. We are outside nearly every day. We live in the seasons of the peak. We are excited for the first dusting of snow in early autumn, the massive ice encrusted cap in the winter, and its bare baldness in the hot summer months. We live in the seasons of the winds, in solid homes that brace the nearly hurricane strength squalls coming over the mountains to the top of the ridge where we live, lifting and demolishing trampolines with some frequency. We live in the seasons of the mule deer, catching rare glimpses of bucks with entwined antlers and limping limbs just before Thanksgiving, and the first precious sighting of newly birthed fawns at Summer Solstice. But most of all, we live in the seasons of Ute Valley Park, near our home.

A seemingly random event propelled me to Ute Valley Park in early 2005. We had hiked there on occasion before then, but that day I was looking for solace and escape. Claes was away again and a needy friend was incessant in her pursuit of my attention. Contemplating the options that took me out of cell range, I settled on Ute. At Ute I could enjoy the midwinter sunshine, breathe deeply and take the dogs. I always think the reason people have dogs is that it is so easy to please them. And once they are pleased, they are the most jovial companions imaginable. Whenever I think of our dogs, our big Lab, Cammy, who has since passed on, and Harley, our fluffy Rottie mix, I think of them smiling over their shoulders at us, with lolling tongues, at Ute Valley Park. It's a simple but potent formula for sharing pleasure called "walking the dog."

That day began my nearly daily constitutional at Ute.

According to a pamphlet I bought at Garden of the Gods book store, Ute Valley Park is 338 acres of a pre-historic stream valley carved into uplifted white quartz sandstone beds from more than 60 million years ago. They call this uplift "Rocky II" in the series of ancient to new mountain ranges found in this area. For those not familiar with the Rocky Mountains, Ute is in the foothills paralleling to the east the newest of the three mountain ranges that counts among its members Pikes Peak. Prior to the uplift, Ute evolved from a marine to beach environment, hence the weather and winds from the ensuing eons have shaped the sandy ridges into a comfortably worn enclosure. It abuts a similarly sized tract of land owned, and kept largely in its natural state, by Hewlett Packard. Surrounded by high cliffs and ridges, Ute offers full vistas to the east, with perfect pine protected sanctuaries for contemplating the sunrise. In the cold winter months, we head up the first ridge trail in the sunshine to keep warm. During the summer, we reverse our route to end at the natural spring, for canine refreshment. I especially like the days where nothing immediately pressing calls for our attention, and we can do a diagonal figure eight intersecting the center of the valley, where the sand is deep and the length of the gully accompanies us. This hike is something like four miles, and consumes at least a full hour.

I can honestly say that of all the natural wonders I've experienced since we moved to Colorado, the bulk of them have occurred at Ute. Harley loves the coyotes that visit the park in late summer and often will run with them. Once we heard her, "barking, barking, barking," from far away. When we called to her, trudging up the hill into a clearing surrounded by pines to see where she had gone, she finally arrived with her newest discovery. With her were two teen coyote pups. All three were fresh faced and electrically charged with their chance encounter. After introducing her friends to us, and after we told her how happy we were to meet them, Harley finally was persuaded to leave her young, new friends. We think sometimes she regrets she doesn't live at Ute with them.

And once, in between Christmas and New Year's, I had a moment to escape the closed-in spaces and dry stale air. If I left just before dawn, I could fit in a quick hike up the ridge with the dogs. The trail was eerily lit by the glow of the morning moon, casting blue shadows through the trees in the cool, misty air. As the dogs and I made our way over the foot bridge and up the rock incline, first we felt and heard before seeing, air moved by vast wings over our shoulders toward the valley. Stopping to intently listen, we heard the adult hooting of owls over excited chirrups of their progeny. Then the air moved again. As they all launched off the cliffs and over the valley, larger wings slowly and confidently pushing the air, to the quicker pumping of young owl wings, and the even more rapid panicked flutter of their prey. And then a quiet "thunk" of capture, and the garbled trill of young conquest. And again, slow large moving wings, and calm hooting. Palpable pride of the adult owl in the success of its young encased us in a treasured instant.

We can't wait for the return of the mallard family the first week of April and the determined whir of hummingbird wings in May. The whole glorious summer is filled with first sightings of wild flowers, and the vanilla-scented discovery of holding a sun lit pine tree close. I love best the moist mornings of dew on my old tennis shoes. In this dry climate, damp air is a rare treat. I think of Ute as my labyrinth and walking meditation. It is the wise earth I trust to hold my moods and moments.

I practice many of my "consciousness" exercises here. One of the times I went to see Sonia Choquette at a workshop in Denver, she advised distancing self from troubling circumstances—she said something like, "Don't allow the adversity in your life to define you"–so I often imagine challenges in a hobo's knapsack on a string, which I gleefully cut as I walk. It never bothers me to abandon them at Ute. The ancient-ness of Ute fairly exudes from the ground, so easy is it to imagine full tribes of Native Americans living there. With teepees lining the valley, during long, harsh winters, they would have been protected from north winter winds. Or sometimes I begin the journey with an intention. I stomp my desire to hold a concept, or relationship, with a different mindset into the ground with a purposeful stride. Or even other times, I practice aligning my energy with the fabric of the park. This is an endeavor that seemed to just "come to me" during a group meditation I was leading. It usually results in the greatest lift in spirit, or shift in perception. First I find a focal point. Sometimes it is a tree fifty feet ahead, but just as often it is the horizon. Then I open my heart and abdomen energy, like unzipping a sweat shirt to the navel. Next I beam that energy out, out, out, all the way to the focal point I have chosen. And then, after a moment or so of absorption, the focal point sends the energy back to me. This rebounding of energy continues until I pass the focal point, as with a tree, or can't absorb any more energy, as with the horizon.

By 2003 I have already been to see Caroline Myss in Denver in one of her large group lectures. During the presentation she says something to the effect of, "If you receive spiritual guidance, it is a good idea to accept it." I feel that comment is made expressly to me. I've had this nagging feeling about the spiritual encounters I have rejected. "What if HE is who HE says HE is?" On one hand, I have experienced miraculous events in prayer chain at the Presbyterian Church, where people given no chance for healing came away completely unscathed from life-threatening incidents. On the other hand, I feel like I define the word *human,* in "human being." I have large flaws, a big temper and sweeping opinions. If there's a street fight, I feel compelled to be there. In the body of an upper middle class matron, I have the heart of a renegade. I will argue a concept, a right, or an ideal to the death, long after everyone else has capitulated from sheer exhaustion. It isn't very ladylike. If I were choosing a spirit for Jesus to be enamored with and bear children, I wouldn't be my first choice.

After going to see Caroline, I cautiously invite Jesus back into my life, just in case he has something important to say to me.

With Claes traveling so often, I find I have a very vivid and engaging dream life. I can hardly wait to start writing in my dream journal as soon as the children have left for school, and before the youngest has awakened. I make a little note about dream content as I awaken at 5:30 a.m. and am always amazed by how they unfailingly unfold as soon as I resume the exercise when the pencil hits the paper. I dream often about the children and Claes. I dream poignantly about Grandmother's houses in Kansas and California. Those dreams always fill me with longing for her scent of hand-milled rose soaps and the color wisteria I have long associated with her. Those are the days I engage our youngest in perfect culinary endeavors in Grandmother's memory, silently invoking our bond. Our favorite is egg salad with purple onion, topped with avocado and caviar. And I dream with growing frequency about my eyes: my eyes covered in layers and layers of colored gauze, removing my eyeballs from their sockets and storing them in beakers of refreshing fluids for a brief respite, my eyes with multiple sets of contact lenses that I keep peeling off, only to find another layer.

When I was a little girl, until I was about 13, the feature that elicited the most attention was my white blond hair. After the age of about 19, and I began to lose some of the adolescent pudginess in my face, more and more people began to comment about my eyes. More than one person has asked if I have a thyroid disorder. (In 1981 Kim Carnes made the song, *Bette Davis Eyes* popular: "All the boys think she's a spy, she's got Bette Davis eyes." Later that year, its parody, *Marty Feldman Eyes,* became the refrain blasting through my head whenever anyone spoke of my eyes. "All the boys think she's a guy, she's got Marty Feldman eyes.") Multiple people have told me my eyes make them uncomfortable in their intensity and the way that they stare. Probably an equal number of people have told me I have the most beautiful eyes they have ever seen. They are big, myopic, light blue eyes with gold flecks, so they often appear to be a shade of aqua. I personally don't think of them unless someone mentions them. Instead I always feel I look exactly like the person I am with.

In 2003, I am going to a past life regression therapist. My close friend in Lake Forest is doing it and says I *must* go. I remember a life as James Madison, staying up late into the candlelit night with an ink-stained hand, writing with a quill pen. I remember dinner parties at Mount Vernon where George Washington thinks it is funny to remove his false teeth while he is eating. Roaring with laughter, we shake our heads at his gaucheness. More important than his false teeth, my heart swells to near bursting when I am with him, so deeply do I love George.

I also seem to have all the requisite coincidences that past life aficionados deem important for "verification" of a previous life. First, I was born 1/12. James Madison was the first of 12 children. Second, my birth initials were "JM." Third, my middle name is Hamilton. Fourth, I am from an old Southern family on one side of my family and early Quakers on the other—both originating in this country in the 17th century, with Virginia roots. Fifth, I grew up on Liberty Bell Lane, sixth in Libertyville, IL, seventh, graduating Libertyville High School in 1976. Eighth, I was editor of my high school newspaper for which I received the journalism award and ninth, I also received the history award. My high school boyfriend's birthday was the Fourth of July. One of my best friends, a very tall and slim young man, was named Tom. He was president of student council. In college, I felt like I lived in that time period. I thought I might have been French and run salons in Paris during the French Revolution, so much of a Francophile I have always been. I sobbed for the vision of John Locke when I read his *Second Treatise of Government.* But if Jesus hadn't said so, I never would have considered having been James Madison in a previous life. And I still wonder, in 2003, what possible difference it makes in the overall scheme of things. Why does he think it is important for me to know that?

Once, returning from a regression session, I lie down on the leather sofa in the family room and close my eyes. Often the regressions sap my energy and I am disoriented in the physical realm. This time a whole life flashes before me. I am a witch being burned at the stake. As I burn, my spirit raises her fist to the sky, saying with high drama, "As God is my witness, I will live again!" In a small space of time, I have a deep level of memory. Grandmother and I were actual witches together in that life. She has predeceased me and I am caught, tried, and deemed guilty. People I know in my current life have betrayed me in that life. I begin to have a glimmer of understanding of just how complex relationships can be.

No wonder Grandmother gave me The *Witch of Blackbird Pond,* almost as soon as I could read!

And that year, Jesus begins making night time appearances when I awaken to mull over a problem. He gives me advice. While sleeping with Claes on the futon outside of our bedroom on the deck, in the middle of the summer, I am suddenly awake. Sometimes when I awaken like this, I reach alongside the bed to grab my glasses to see the sky. It is endlessly midnight blue with the brightest stars. The air feels crisp and cool on my face, while I am burrowed deep underneath the down comforter in my worn Lanz nightgown. It is during this little piece of heaven that Jesus comes to me and says, "Your mind is too busy. We can't get through to you. You need to take art classes."

The vibrant colors of the pastel medium are big enough to encompass my moods. My teacher tells me they are pure pigment. I don't have to bend my emotions into pretzel shapes to fit them into the vast, deep colors as I spread them on the cushy suede paper. My teacher at the community college wants me to damper their vividness down—color mostly, but in fits of paranoia, I think she suspects the bigness of my moods–in blending the backgrounds with the display fruit she brings for us to paint. I feel like Clifford, the big red dog, trying to play hide and seek, quashing my energy into table fruit. Every process she recommends starts to look muddy maroon and yellow. Hmm. These are not the colors of my spirit I want so badly to express. She and a local artist in the class are horrified by my purple iris with the red background that I secretly paint at home and shyly, slyly show to the class.

My drawing class, on the other hand, is mostly in black and white until we get to the colored pencil assignments. I feel trapped by the commitment each lesson takes. Every afternoon while our youngest watches "Dora" on television, I'm sitting at the kitchen table with the serape blanket assignment taped to my board. My coral striped flannel robe is blackened with permanent graphite damage at the rolled-up sleeve. Once I get started it isn't so bad. My mind goes AWOL relatively soon after I locate the roll and stripe of the blanket where I left off. Who knew there were so many shades of grey?

Even as I struggle with the suffocating, endless feeling of each project, I sense my mind accessing more degrees of energy in daily life. My impatience stretches like newsprint transferred onto silly putty, distorting and contorting with pooled emphasis in the wrong places. I begin to realize there is really no place I need to be with any sort of urgency. Now when I find myself stuck, somewhere, I sink into the small things around me: the way the sunlight caresses trees' leaves in a benign flicker of light when I am caught in traffic, which movie stars have the most cellulite on the magazine covers in the line in the grocery, and what my nine-year-old dreamed last night. The din of activity I have grown used to shutting out as part of a purposeful life begins to clamor in a different, less discordant way. There is a newly developed quiet space in my brain and in my spirit. It now has permanency, as the most fundamental state of being upon which all other moods and circumstances are layered.

Back in past life regression therapy that fall, I have more defining moments. Those that forever alter my self-awareness occur when I am visiting with authoritative spirit energy between lives, called "The Council" by my therapist. In one such visit, when I ask them what my purpose in this life is, they tell me I am always a messenger spirit, regardless of lifetimes. I don't really know what that means, but it feels like a good fit with my interests as I always am delving deeply into a new topic to share with others. They tell me I am slated for two more lives after this one and that my last lessons in those lives are about love. In one memorable session, I go to the top floor in a tower which reminds me of the brig of the *Enterprise* in Star Trek. It is eight-sided and has windows on every side. In front of each window is a desk. I am relieved to see the desk where the astrology chart for each life is cast. It is where the lessons we have chosen for our new incarnation are particularly aligned with the planet energy that will support that learning. I feel safe and familiar with planet energies, knowing that with conscious application and effort, they are as easy to access as rich tones on a well-strung guitar.

I also capture raw emotions left by my mother's death six years earlier in one of my past life regression visits that fall. After that session, any slowed time at all creates a fountain of tears on my face. I almost don't make it to the last drawing class at the community college with my final assignment in early December. My face, purple and puffy from unstoppable tears, is too embarrassing to show in public.

After missing most of the water color and oils classes I'd enrolled in at the Fine Arts Center in the spring of 2004, one day I took a quick jaunt at Ute after dropping our youngest at Montessori. I longed to be finished with art classes. I'd had about as much of sitting with outpouring emotions as I could bear. As I walked that day with a yearning heart and a "please let me be finished, please let me be finished," mantra, I heard the voice in my head clearly and distinctly say, "Get a Master of Social Work."

Hallelujah! WOOO HOOO! I was finished with art classes!

In the funny way the world works, when I call Colorado State to see about their MSW programs, they think they will start a Colorado Springs cohort in January 2006. I need to get some class work completed, having to update my nearly 30-year-old physiology class and never having had Psych 101 and 102. I have just enough time to complete them and get our youngest launched in school before the MSW program starts.

–About the voice. It was the same voice that told me to learn to meditate many years earlier. It is odd to me that as analytical and curious as I usually am, I still don't know the source of THAT voice, and I am complacent about not knowing. It comes to me in the middle of my brain, almost like reading letters of words it is saying, but not quite. When Jesus comes to talk to me, I see or sense him. His location is more in the realm of the eyelids when they are closed, or often behind the left eye. With the voice, when it tells me to do something, I always think, "Oh, YEAH, good idea!" It's sort of like a, "Hmm, wish I'd thought of that." Its advice always has the quality of a perfectly situated missing puzzle piece.

Because part of my family is from the Old South, I grew up with Br'er Rabbit stories, among other tales, that speak to the ingenuity of African American slaves dealing with oppressive masters. What I most love about those stories are the visceral feelings they evoke of danger and survival, and how Br'er Rabbit was always secretly chiding himself into "correct" behavior that also allowed for his dignity. Br'er Rabbit and the Tar Baby is an especially compelling image for me, as when he kept slugging the Tar Baby, he became even more deeply covered in tar. I know that anytime I connect with anger, it will stick with me always, sucking me back in, even when I have a need to finally be finished with it. I imagine slaves, needing to outwit their heavy-handed masters must have imbued those stories with the harrowing sense of thrill they carry.

Br'er Rabbit's briar patch is another image that delighted and tickled me. "Oh please, Br'er Fox and Br'er Bear, please don't throw me in that briar patch"—which is exactly what Br'er Fox and Br'er Bear did, amusing Br'er Rabbit to no end. The briar patch was Br'er Rabbit's safe and sacred space. Any time you can cajole the universe into catapulting you into your safe and sacred space, surrounded by charmed energy that belongs expressly to you, it is an occasion for great celebration! And that's precisely how I felt about going back to school. What an absolute privilege and joy it was for me to earn a master's degree in social work.

I have always loved school. Not only are there wonderful things to learn there, and amazing books and stories to read, but other people are there with you, learning and reading and sharing the world of ideas. To me, life doesn't get much better than that.

And, as with most decisions I make, the first thing I consider is: will the people be interesting when I get there?

I totally luck out in all possible regards at CSU. Social workers are vastly interesting. And the thing about all of them that I know, without exception, is no matter what they end up doing, they are doing it with the biggest possible hearts.

The first book we read for school is the physicist Fritjof Capra's book, *The Web of Life*. It is the perfect introduction to systems' theory and the interrelatedness of all things. I even read the hard parts, for physicists only, because I think the secrets of the universe are captured in every word, and every line between every word. What Capra basically says is: random challenges from nature have made us stronger and more resourceful as a species. These challenges are non-linear and require innovative solutions from our communities and organizations. When we achieve community buy-in, our solutions are far more encompassing than what we can achieve as individuals. He recommends that we create protected learning environments where the status quo is constantly challenged so that we have a steady stream of new solutions. For the people whose eyes are rolling back in their heads in disbelief about reincarnation and spirit communication, you have my complete sympathy. Everything I think we need to know about universal wisdom is all right there in Capra's work, so you can put this book down now and go get his. Or my favorite, when I find myself unpersuaded by premises in books, I heave them across the room in frustration with some unprintable exclamation. It's immeasurably satisfying.

Because I am so dedicated to studying the work of serious scholars, sometimes I worry about how wiggy people will think I am with this channeling business. Ultimately I know in my deepest of hearts, more important than my feelings of idiocy, is for other people to know the universe is benevolent. That first day in March of 1998, when the entities describing themselves to me as "God" and "Jesus" came through, the indescribable kindness and love was bigger than anything I'd experienced before. It reminds me of *1 Corinthians 13:7* often said at weddings: "Love is patient and kind; love does not envy or boast; it is not arrogant or rude. It does not insist on its own way; it is not irritable or resentful; it does not rejoice at wrong doing but rejoices with the truth. Love bears all things, believes all things, hopes all things; endures all things. Love never ends." I have not yet met the person who comes close to exuding or embodying that sentiment, and when people quote it to me, it has the potential to come across as sanctimonious dribble. Such as when my ex-husband was having an affair and I was eight months pregnant and outraged, those were the words he used to tell me how I should be responding. However, being the recipient of that energy is not sanctimonious dribble. It is awe-inspiring, joyful and completely believable.

The good thing about the vastness of that energy is that connecting with it is a doable proposition. It isn't energy that has to go through a clergy person first, although I think that cute preacher in Texas, Joel Osteen, does such a good job communicating it. It is energy everyone can directly experience.

Plus, what I am finding is thus far people have been very kind when I share my experiences with them. Not everyone wants to hang out with me about it, which is perfectly acceptable to me. But neither do they burn crosses on my front lawn.

I guess too, I struggle with me, the package of the presenter. I am this upper-middle-class WASP-y woman with no single, strong cultural identity. I'd feel a whole lot better about these visions if they were coming from someone with street credibility, or one of my Native American friends. But Jesus recently said to me that I worry too much about that stuff. He said half the time people don't even recognize him, so I basically should just give up the part of myself that worries about connecting the dots between me the person, the vastness of universal wisdom, and what other people think.

My first internship in social work school is at the Jicarilla Apache reservation in Dulce, New Mexico. I learn Motivational Interviewing as a way to interface with clients, and find it an excellent technique for speaking respectfully with my own teenagers as well. Even more exciting, though, is the work the Jicarilla women are doing in exploring ways to heal the old wounds of the tribe. These are the travesties suffered at the hands of greedy and know-it-all whites and religious figures. Using traditional tribal methods, they are planning the process of the Healing Journey for implementation in January the following year. They very generously share it with me in the summer of 2007.

The drive to Dulce is four and a half or five hours each way. I make it back and forth, May through September, for three days at the reservation each week. When I begin going to the reservation, there is still snow at La Veta pass, like blobs of whipped cream soaking into the Oreo cookie crumbs of winter long silt and dirt collected at the roadside. Going south from Alamosa on straight roads through the small towns with Hispanic grocery stores for the first time, I am unaware of the wonder-filled moments waiting for me as I turn west on highway 17. There is a little town with willows along the river, until suddenly after rounding a couple of curves and going down some small hills, I can tell the air is crisper outside the car windows. It is filled with the sound of rushing water as the river grows in strength over my left shoulder. The evergreens are still dusted with white on their top branches. The weight of spring snow becomes denser and curls them over as the canyon wall rises behind the river. The reclining sun knifes through the mountain pass ahead of me in shades of orange and coral. My chest feels sliced open with the beauty of it, and I can barely breathe as the road inclines up the mountain to La Manga pass. As I make this drive a month later after the snows melt, a female moose scales the high roadside fence to my right without breaking her stride, and bolts in front of the car as I reach the pass. I pull the car to the side of the road, my heart beating a stiff staccato as I watch her loping easily into the meadow on the other side. When I look her up in my Ted Andrews book, *Animal-Speak*, recommended by Jackie many years ago, I learn she is the embodiment of "primal feminine energies" for late fall and early winter. I see her magnificence as a blessing for the coming Healing Journey of the tribe.

My next internship is slated to begin in January. I find a job working in Denver in children's public health policy through the NASW lobbyist. As much as I like research, mid-year, six months until I will graduate, I realize my mistake yet again, remembering that I cannot sit all day long as I am doing in this internship. I begin a conversation with the voices in my head about what was it exactly they had in mind for me when they told me to get an MSW. It went like this: "OK, I'm almost finished. You told me to do this, and I have. What do you want me to do now?"

Rummaging around for options, I find a Brian Weiss training for professionals at Omega in October (Oh, yeah, I'm almost a professional now!), but it is full. I am about 120th on the waiting list.

In the meantime, my close high school friend, Tom, shows up with tickets for the 2008 Democratic National Convention in Denver. The days are filled with excitement, attending political lunches and evening entertainment, as news anchors breeze by us in the hallway of the Pepsi Center.

Toward the end of September, I get a call from Omega. There have been cancellations. I have 20 minutes to decide before they give my space away. I give them my credit card number before hanging up. I immediately call Claes, saying, "Honey, I know this will be a surprise, but a couple of months ago I put myself on the waiting list for Brian Weiss' training. It was such a long shot. I didn't even think it was worth mentioning."

I have to say, through all of this, Claes never bats an eye. His upbringing is far more traditional than mine, and still he just rolls with it, coaxing me forward regardless of the outrageousness of the circumstance. This time he says to me, "Julia, I have always felt so lucky to love what I do. I can only wish the same for you in your professional life."

Reading Brian Weiss' books and listening to his recordings is an incomplete outline of the real person. He has such lovely, generous energy. A courtly gentleman on stage, he gives the floor away to countless attendees who share their experiences and expertise. An even greater pleasure is being in his wife, Carol's, presence. I don't know if she is Irish or not, but her beautiful, unlined skin blossoms with rosy color, underneath a sprinkle of freckles. Kindness seems to exude from her presence. Also an MSW, she gives us the pragmatic advice to get certified in hypnosis another way, which she has done.

For me, it is a week of trance and new, close associations. I am amazed and relieved when Brian tells our friend with the Mary Magdalene memories that historical figures such as the apostles have dispersed multiple capsules of energy that people can cue into. I trust that it means the same occurs with other large historical figures, like the American revolutionaries.

With this past life regression business, it is pretty clear to me that we need to have a big tent, and invite everyone who self-identifies to the party. It is too hard to understand the rules about how souls choose and divide into next lives, for anyone to set themselves up as an expert or arbiter of anyone else's experience. Sometimes New Age topics seem like a Manifest Destiny land grab as they are introduced, where the first person to claim a homestead becomes the owner of the premise. But like homesteading on the frontier, brutal new experiences can arise and wipe out a claim in a heartbeat. It is through networking and mutual support we will grow strong in these new frontiers of spiritual endeavor and expansion.

Besides, I am ever hopeful someone else will self-identify as the "other" Mary and I can hand over some of this responsibility. I am always so relieved when the facts check out and I give accurate historical information.

In November, 2008, the month after Brian's training, I have written my research project and am coasting to graduation. Claes and I take a trip to Mexico where he will get some dental work done. I take a candle to light as I think this will help me perform my duty in automatic writing and getting the story Jesus wants me to tell. One afternoon when Claes rides the golf cart-as-taxi downtown near the cathedral to the dentist, I dim the lights in the room. I light the candle in front of the mirror, thinking that will enhance the energy, with notebook and pen at the ready. I count myself backwards.

I am on a boat with a baby and a small blond boy with curly hair. I am wearing robes that are blue along with a white headdress with a decoration on the edge. Jesus is sailing the boat.

Next:

I am on a pier in the same clothes. I am waiting for the boat to come back for me.

My rational self interrupts. "There is NO POSSIBLE WAY you were on a boat with Jesus. You lived in Macedonia. He just came to visit you and the boys sometimes. You are an unreliable channel."

I blow out the candle and toss it in the trash, close my notebook and leave the room. I latch the door firmly behind me. I head to the beach, where I watch pelicans dive into the ocean like Kamikaze pilots.

4

Centering

*Being still and connecting with
something larger than SELF...*

I pretty much spent the years from 2003-2008 learning to stop struggling against whatever place I currently found myself in. I employed my previously acquired learning of **cleansing** and shifting away from the busy-ness around me and noise in my head. I added to it the practice of layering my energy in the environment, or **centering**. I also learned to heed the directions from the voice inside my head, and in fact, completed a course of graduate study based on its recommendation. And while I was still uneasy about it, I entertained suggestions from Jesus about how to tell his story.

What the spirits tell me, and what is reinforced by my experience in my current and past lives, is that people require rooted-ness to thrive in any real aspect of soul development and making a connection with universal wisdom. It's similar to how trees require roots to receive nourishment and remain upright. My sense is that **centering** establishes connection to our roots and helps us feel attached and secure, like we have an occupied space where we belong. This can apply to family trees and genealogy as well. Additionally, we appear to leave traces of our energy in specific locations over life-times to which we can reconnect later, like homing devices. This is also similar to how a dead tree becomes part of the earth again. Having the ability to **center,** then, really helps us to gain informa-tion from, connect with, and feel protected by our environment.

I know that I told you in Chapter 2 that it was important to disconnect when **cleansing.** And now with **centering**, I am telling you to re-connect. But the point is to disconnect from noise, cre-ate an open space and then choose to re-connect with the envi-ronment. After I cleanse and create an opening from which to shift into a different consciousness, I like to meld my dimensional-ity with the physical world around me. As a kid, on summer days when there was no one to play with, sometimes I lay down on our freshly cut lawn. After at first being keenly aware of the slim, sharp grass blades cutting into my skin and the smell of cut grass, my mind began to unravel while watching the clouds shift into dif-ferent shapes. Eventually, after first plying my energy into the soft summer breeze and sunlit air, I felt my body begin to merge with the earth slowly rotating beneath me. I didn't know it then, but it was a great beginning to the altered states I experience now. I was open (**cleansed**) and connected (**centered**). From that state of consciousness, it is really easy to launch personal energy out ward into a variety of altered states.

To further illustrate the importance of **centering**, the following are excerpted from the sessions where Jesus and I shared past lives that fully explore the phenomena through connecting with the envi-ronment. The **Greek Soldiers** life came pretty early in the series of the "learning to *receive*" past lives. After experiencing it, I was left with a poignant longing for connection to the earth, like a craving.

The **Abrum** life follows **Greek Soldiers** in the chapter. **Abrum,** a Greek, Jewish shepherd, helps to rescue his village when he heeds his instincts, slows down his life, and connects to his environment. This past life was important to the process of telling this story for a couple of reasons. First, we had two facilitators for **Abrum**: my husband Claes, and our friend, Sue, so we delved into many ave-nues of questions. By March of 2011, we had a group of readers who wanted more depth in the transcripts. They felt more satisfied by the completeness of the information we developed in **Abrum**. Second, **Abrum** was a character we all could admire. He stood for something. He had wisdom. His ability to **center** in the midst of grave hardship is a story I re-read for guidance in my own life when I am seeking a shift in perspective and how to hold my experience.

Last, there is a discussion about the differences between grounding and **centering** from **Chain Gang II.**

Greek Soldiers, 1312 B.C.
Excerpted from Number 6, February 19, 2011

Me: I have brown sandals on my feet and I have hairy legs, with black hair.

I have a white tunic on with a skirt and a breast plate with a red cape coming off of my left shoulder.

Q: Are you a man or a woman?

Me: A man.

Q: Your hands?

Me: My hands are big and spatulate-looking and they have black hairs on them.

Q: Is it day or night?

Me: It's in the afternoon. I'm outside standing in some dust. There are trees and a field.

Q: Are there people around?

Me: Yes, there's a farm house nearby, and I am with other soldiers. We have horses. I hold a horse.

Q: What is the date?

Me: 1312 B.C.

Q: What country are you in?

Me: I'm in Greece.

Q: What are you doing there?

Me: I think I am going through training with my troops.

Q: Is this a period of war?

Me: I have an overwhelming feeling of being tired of war. I don't think we are currently involved in a battle.

Q: You said there were other soldiers there and you were at a farm. Is there something significant about the farm?

Me: We sleep in the barn. We practice during the day. There are eight soldiers. At night we play a game similar to dice. I think it's one of those other lifetimes with Jesus and he's in this platoon with me.

Q: So this is a shared lifetime.

Me: We talk a lot about life without war. What would that be like? We both are tired of war.

Q: Is he enlightened in some certain way?

Me: Neither one of us is very affluent. We are just foot soldiers. Maybe we take care of the horses.

We are near a farm that grows vegetables. I'm seeing turnips that are grown on this farm. We both have longing to be connected to the earth. Instead of being on the road all the time, and always being vagabonds. We're soldiers but we feel like we aren't really connected to a cause or a significant mission. We wonder, "Why are we doing this? What's the point?" We long to be connected to the earth. War doesn't make sense to us. It seems like an endless string of destruction. Neither one of us is important, connected or even very intellectual, but we see that it's wasted energy, motion and efforts.

Q: How do you think you...?

Me: I feel like I was conscripted.

Q: What is the significance of the scene?

Me: It's significant because it's one of the lifetimes I had with Jesus, and it helps to prepare us for the life where there was the culmination of Jesus the Christ. We didn't understand, why war? We thought there must be a much better way to employ people than this process of death and destruction. We both have this longing to live a fuller, more connected life. That's what is significant about it. It's how we developed.

Q: It's part of the development of the knowledge?

Me: Yes, we had this longing to be connected to the earth and we thought life could be a much more satisfying existence. We weren't particularly educated or philosophical. We didn't have high ideas in that life. It was a very simple life. But it felt wasted to us. And so that's how it was significant. We felt it would have been much better spent connected to the earth, producing something versus wasting things. How it fits in to the overall scheme is that it was one of the "learning to receive" lifetimes. It was one of the lifetimes where we became familiar with the longing to be better centered, yet we didn't have the philosophical acumen to know intellectually what we were looking for. We had the visceral sense of wanting to be connected to the earth.

Abrum, 475 B.C.
Excerpted from Number 8, March 14, 2011

Me: Looking down at my feet I have sandals on.

Q: Can you describe the sandals?

Me: Yes, they are brown leather, with a strap across the toe. I have on a white robe, it's belted. Sometimes I wear an over robe, but this has a long vest. The robe is cream colored. I am a blond man with a beard. I have a man's hands.

Q: Do you have a name?

Me: "Abrum" is what's coming.

I have a crook. I am a shepherd. Right now there are a lot of sheep. I can see up the rise to the top of the hill. I have mostly white sheep and some other colors of sheep.

Q: Are there any other people?

Me: No, I don't see any right now.

Q: Do you have a sense of what year it might be?

Me: 475 B.C. maybe?

Q: Do you have a sense of what country you are in?

Me: Greece is what's coming. I'm seeing southeastern main-land Greece on a map.

Q: Anything else interesting to note about this place?

Where are you?

Me: I think I am outside of a village.

Q: Do you know the name of the village?

Me: I am getting A-B-R-I-S.

But it's not a very big village. It is white-washed.

Q: What time of year is it?

Me: It's autumn. And I think we want to get the sheep in for the winter and shear them, slaughter some, and then sell some. But we don't want to slaughter them until the weather begins to cool some.

Q: What are you doing right now?

Me: Right now I am just sitting outside with the sheep.-- Feeling the sunshine on my face. It feels like it was a good year. There were a lot of lambs and they were healthy.

Q: Why did you come back to this place?

Me: I am asking why I am here. I'm in a resting phase in the life. I have a lot of nightmares with torches and faces at night and burning buildings. It was earlier in this life, but I am feeling happy and peaceful now. At some point earlier there was tumult and turmoil. I don't feel like I am in exile. I feel like this is my home and has been for a long time.

Q: Do you have some family here?

Me: Yes, I think I have a daughter. I am seeing a young woman with long dark hair. She has a baby. But what I am really seeing is angry crowds with sticks and torches.

Q: What are they mad about?

Me: I think there has been a betrayal. They've been taken advantage of somehow.

Q: Was the anger toward you?

Me: No, I witnessed it. I was there. I don't think I was angry. I am a very peaceful person and I believe that I have sadness because it didn't happen a better way. I am sad because there was an angry mob and I am seeing soldiers with spears and shields. They aren't attacking the crowd yet. It was a year when there was a bad drought. There are soldiers keeping the crowd from the water. There will be people who perish. The crowd came at night to challenge the soldiers so they could get to the spring. It's the only water for that year that anyone can access.

Q: So the soldiers are from the same people?

Me: They're from the government. They're from the king, I think. They are keeping the peasants from the well which is the only source of water for the year. I am bereft because that I know I can sustain myself on far less. I am always a contemplative one and I know a physical hibernation process, like a bear. When there is a year of drought, I take the sheep high in the mountains and live off of dew on the tree leaves. I am reclusive and husband my energy. It is tragic, because I know that people think the only way they can live is with the water from the well. They stand in terror because they think they will perish if they don't have water soon. But I go and live high up in the hills. I know the higher I get the more likely I will be able to find a little bit of water to live on. I take the sheep up there, too. Some of the really weak ones are lost, but the other sheep are able to forage through the forested floor. I can see the sheep eating pine needles that have dropped. That's how I am keeping the flock alive.

Q: Do you have a wife or family at that point?

Me: My wife is gone. My daughter is young, maybe 10 years old. She goes up in the mountains with me in this period of drought and she is OK. She is charming and fun and flits around like a little butterfly. Somehow she is OK with the living conditions, and for that I am very grateful. She thinks it's a great adventure to look for pooled moisture in the bottom of a leaf during this time of drought. I think I am Jewish. I don't live among the townsfolk. They are derisive of me. I would share my knowledge of how to subsist in this barren summer. I am an outcast.

Q: Are there any other things going on in the village?

Me: Well, I think this is the important part. It's one of those lessons about how to go within. It's one of the lifetimes when I learned about how to live successfully on the planet. I learned how to live through the seasons when they were harsh and unforgiving. Always at the root of the message is to be very still whenever you have an upsetting time when you feel out of control or terrified. Your impulse is to protect yourself on a physical basis and you get angry. This lifetime is about how to deal with turmoil in life. It's about how to find resources. The first step is always to go within. And then the universe will always work to help you find solutions if you will listen to it. So that's what I did as this shepherd. I went up to the mountains because I wanted to be cool.

When I would awaken, I would find there was dew around myself and I was able to survive. It was a tragic summer for those in the village.

Q: Is water a metaphor for survival?

Me: It's more about the lesson that the first step is always to go within and to find stillness. Then it's about how the universe will find an opening to communicate with you about how to survive, when you find the stillness. So having been an outcast and Jewish all my life, with my young wife who died early on and a young daughter, I always was within. I have only had my own thoughts to reflect on. There wasn't a big Jewish community. I was the last of my family dying out. I am not allowed to own land. I am a shepherd for someone else. The lesson is to find solutions, to be still and go within.

Q: Is this one of the lives that you lived with the Jesus soul, or is this a life where you lived separately and started learning this information?

Me: My little daughter who went to the mountains with me eventually ended up being the Jesus spirit in a later life. That makes sense because even in that horrible summer, she was still a light body who channeled joy, flitting around like a little butterfly.

Q: Are there things that you taught her?

Me: We spent a lot of time talking about the wonders of nature. She helped me forage. We were excited every morning when we found a little moisture. She knew she must protect her energy. What I am seeing is that eventually, at the end of the summer, there was a huge downpour. We were weak, even in the mountains where we survived. It was a pelting rain. It was such a joyful occasion because we knew we had made it. We had survived. There was a time toward the end of the summer where she lost some of her vitality and I was quite concerned for her. But it was such a magical summer and we were able to sit so quietly that the bunnies would come and sit with us. So the other part of the lesson is that there's still magic in horrible, overwhelming challenge.

Q: You mentioned a couple of times the joy about that summer. Is that important, like finding the joy in the little things?

Me: Absolutely! I'm getting tingling through my body. I'm getting that flooding. Absolutely, the joy is in the small things. When you quiet yourself, that's the point. That's the point of hardship, so we will learn to center, so we will learn to find the joy in the small things. It is so amazing when you are so still that birds light on you, or bunnies come to sit near you to get the warmth of your body in the cool evenings. I'm seeing we spent a lot of time under a big stand of pine trees that summer. Even when it was dry and the needles were underneath us--I can see them dry and crackling--it was much cooler than any place else we could be.

Q: When you entered this trance you were much later in that life. Was there something of importance in the later life, besides looking back at this?

Me: You know, eventually, when we came back down the mountain they thought we had perished. They didn't know what had happened to the sheep. When we came back down the mountain I was hailed as a hero because there were so few people left in the village. They'd experienced such hardship. The soldiers who kept the people from the water, the people who perished, it was such devastation. The physical exertion and anger depleted them. It destroyed everyone. When my daughter and I came down from the mountain, they thought we were a miracle. And we came of course, right after the rain. They associated the rain with us arriving with the sheep. I now live like a wise man in this village. People come to me to seek my knowledge. They understand that I have some of the keys to universal wisdom. My daughter, who grows into a beautiful young Jewish woman, ends up marrying one of the more affluent townspeople. It's almost unheard of for a gentile to marry a Jew. The community celebrates us and the birth of their child.

Q: And then you become a wise man by sharing this knowledge.

Me: Well, yes! They thought it was such a miracle that we survived that whole summer and we came back with such a large part of the flock. Nothing grew that summer. Everyone, even the people who had some water, were so weakened by the end of the summer. Here we came, my child and I—maybe her nickname was Barushka?—she and I came down the mountain and brought this still-substantial flock of sheep with us. We really saved the day! Everyone was able to eat well then, and over the winter. We brought food back with us. While my life is still very simple, I live very well at the end of my life. I have helped save what was left of the community.

Q: The sharing of the knowledge with the townspeople, does it become a foundation of their lives going forward? Does it become part of their lives?

Me: Oh, yes! I'm getting chills about that. In fact, it becomes a model community. It becomes known for the health of their livestock. They learn to listen with me. They learn to respect the rhythms of the earth. And actually it turns out quite well for the community. I'm seeing that it becomes a special place to visit and a place of legend.

Q: So this information travels out from your village?

Me: Yes, what happens is that because the villagers learned to live through it, they then learned to be more receptive. Outside people understood it was a miracle, but they didn't understand it was human participation that helped create the miracle. They thought it was something that God just intervened about. They (the outsiders) didn't understand that it was a relationship between the villagers and the universe. A lot of people think that when a miracle happens, it's a one-sided great gift, like winning the lottery, that it just happens and it has no connection to anything. But the other piece of this lesson is that you are always in continual relationship with the universe. Nothing "just happens." Things happen because there has been a relationship developed. Universal energy that's received often becomes a reflection of the physical that's manifesting at a certain level on the planet.

Q: So the people outside of the village didn't even know there was a lesson to be learned?

Me: Right, they just said, "Oh, those people were so lucky." The lesson in this regression is about the responsibility we have in our physical beings to check in with the universe and to find what the universe has for us. The universe is just waiting for that relationship to occur.

Q: Is there any lesson to be learned from this life about how to check in, or is it just that the stillness needs to be achieved?

Me: You know how when you sit in a bed of pine needles, you can layer your fingers into them? There's a way to connect with the earth. The most important thing is to check in with the earth with all of your senses. I am seeing that that summer as Abrum, when I awakened one morning, I knew in my heart to go to the top of the mountain. I knew it would be cooler because I had already had that experience. I hadn't yet made the connection that when I awakened at the top of the mountain, I would have dew on my face. And so that's what happened. My daughter and I both were covered in dew one morning. It's again about paying attention to the small things, but often the solutions are right there for us if we check in. I had the instinctual message to take my little daughter and go to the top of the mountain and then we received these hidden gifts right along the way. Once you start living in the cycle of the earth, the gifts come to you. It is important to notice the little gifts and be grateful. Sharing is really important. When we found moisture, even if it was only a little bit, we shared it, and we would make sure the animals around us had moisture, too. The sheep would lick these leaves—I don't know what kind of leaf it is. You know how holly leaves are shiny? It wasn't a holly leaf. It was more of an oval and it had kind of a point at the end. But moisture would gather in these leaves, and we noticed that they weren't very permeable. We would get the sheep to where the leaves had fallen, and then they would have some moisture to subsist on.

Q: You just mentioned the importance of sharing. Is that also a lesson? Being still, paying attention to the universe and sharing?

Me: Sharing is the lesson that Jesus taught with the loaves and the fishes. We think that when there is only a little bit that we must have it, because it is only a little bit. We erroneously think, if we share, we won't have as much. We get this lesson over and over again that when we share we create such a network of goodwill, we create hope with the destitute. Those that we share with understand how hard it is, when we only have enough for ourselves, when we share it with someone else. They understand that they are receiving a huge gift. It brings up so much good will when everyone is suffering together, to share everything that you have. That's the basis for the lesson in the future when Jesus had the miracle of the loaves and the fishes. He and I both had that experience. Sharing creates such a better energy and such a better intentionality. As Abrum, only my daughter and I were cued in and listening. We survived and had enough to share with this whole group of people. Like I was saying, the universe is in relationship with us. Then, when we arrive at a point where everyone comes to the core level of yearning and meditation, it really increases the ability of the universe to communicate with us and show us the way. Another piece of this lesson, like I was saying, is that God doesn't occur in a vacuum. It doesn't just happen. It's a reflection of the hope in all of us and the positive communal feelings. It's what we can create together. Together we can create such a better God than one person with one faith.

Q: How do we begin to access information from the universe?

Me: The universe will speak to you if you are still enough. The universe is always waiting for us to be listening. The universe longs for relationship with us, just like we long for relationship with it. The universe longs to cradle and cherish us. First we have to have an opening. The best way to have an opening for universal energy is stillness. And then, of course, noticing coincidence. There is no such thing as coincidence. If you start to follow coincidence in your life, the universe will start to send you more coincidence. That's its way of letting you know there is a place of awe and hope and cherished-ness. When you experience a coincidence, you experience all of that, that awe, "Wow. How did that happen? This is so amazing!" Sometimes it just tickles us to death. But when you start to follow coincidence, the universe knows it is being listened to. I'm seeing that the universe becomes joyful, too, as a reflection of the awe we are experiencing. We can help to create a lighter universe when we follow the cues that it gives us. The universe doesn't exist separately from us. It is mostly a reflection of the highest expression of our goodness and it seeks that in us.

Q: Is there a procedure or a protocol where you can get yourself quiet?

Me: As we knitted our fingers into the earth, into the pine needles, at the end of the day, we experienced gratitude for making it through another day. As we touched it, we found the earth was cool and not so dry under the pine needles, and dug into the earth and experienced such huge gratitude for the day that we had been given. What happens with hardship is that it slows the day down so much, that you are listening so intently for any message. Then when you have made it through the day, and are so grateful, the universe smiles too. It's been an accomplishment. That's why parties are important. Celebration is important, because it recognizes gratitude. It recognizes the gifts of the universe. And the universe really likes nothing better than for us to gather in celebration and homage to one another. It makes the universe really sad when we take advantage of those who have less than we. The universe works hard at finding those of us who are joyous so it can reflect and compound and multiply that joy. When the universe sees sadness, smallness and pettiness, it becomes sad. When we don't understand that we are so big, that we can create so much with its help when we open to it, then the universe is sad.

Q: So the stillness. Is it more powerful when there are many together?

Me: Oh, absolutely, absolutely. It's an exponential experience. I'm seeing a Muslim community, when you have everyone bowing to Mecca at the same time. It's a huge pooling and outpouring, of energy and universal joy when that happens. Because it's the humility in the face of God, and it's the asking to be influenced by the energy of God, so it's that opening. What I am seeing is many people bowed on a square. Maybe it's Morocco, because I am seeing those Moorish buildings. What happens is it is such a multi-faceted occurrence: you are relinquishing control, you are asking for an opening, you are waiting to be filled, and you are all giving homage, all simultaneously. I'm also seeing an algebraic equation. It creates huge energy because of the tremendous interaction that is occurring. It is compounded by the numbers. Islam understands that if you all stop and pray at the same time, it is tremendously powerful. Do they do that twice a day?

Q: Five times a day.

Me: Oh my God. That's a tremendously powerful occurrence. It builds such energy. It's the humility in the face of God, being filled by universal energy. It's the gratitude that comes from being filled. Such a wonderful thing occurs with that.

In the little village where Abrum lived, the village finally began to work together. The people who had been guarding the water understood after nearly all of the villagers perished. They would have had a chance to have a greater village if they had just shared the water that they were protecting.

Q: So not only the villagers, but the guards learned the lesson.

Me: The guards were sort of like family members. It's like what happened in Egypt recently where finally the military wouldn't attack the people, because they were the people. In this case, a lot of people had to die before they realized their mistake. There was enough water for more than the people who were allowed to use it, and it should be shared.

Q: If you don't want to answer this it's OK, but are there parallels between today's and Abrum's situation?

Me: Absolutely, absolutely. We keep getting opportunities to learn this really important lesson about sharing. It doesn't work for all the resources to be held in the hands of a few. Those few become very attached to the status quo, and they aren't original, they don't find solutions, and it is ever thus. Challenges are wonderful because they help us find solutions and strength, but the solutions and strength don't come from husbanding the status quo. The old guard will always be toppled until that lesson is learned. We must create environments where people can learn, create and live in harmony, sharing.

Learning to receive is the hardest part, because so many of our judgments get in the way. That's why it took thirteen lives. In the culminating life, when he was Jesus, the seeking and the sharing was the easy part. The hard part was learning to be open to universal energy.   We think we know how it has to be. The stillness is always the first step because it opens us. It allows us to get away from judgment a little bit.

Me: Abrum's life is a metaphor for the stillness is what I'm getting. As Abrum, I was always held apart and I was Jewish. I became very self-reliant because I was so often alone. After a while when I was outside with sheep, all that filled my head was the light of the day. I didn't even smell the sheep anymore. I had only the light of the day in my mind. In isolation, it is far easier to become one with the environment. Finding the stillness is a matter of sitting by your self and asking. I'm getting, "It's no big deal. You just sit and you ask and it will come to you." It takes desire, discipline and an opening. The best way to do it is to have a certain time of day when you say, "OK, I'm going to be still now." And if it's only even for 20 minutes, and you practice and listen to your breathing. Or if you're on a hike, it can be the process I do with the meditation. We end up with the healing light in the solar plexus, and then we send it out, out, out, and take it out to our skin and then to the environment. There are many ways to achieve the stillness.

Q: I asked because our time has very little stillness. Always something is being done or watched. We think there is no point in stillness. I wonder if learning that is important to our time.

Me: It will save us, so it's important for that reason. The universe comes only if it's asked. Everybody has spirit guides that will help direct them to the place they need to go. So if you are a person uneasy with stillness--and there are a lot of people like that--you still have spirit guides and you still have instincts. Another way to achieve your ultimate purpose or your highest calling is to listen to your instincts. So many people listen to society, listen to their parents and listen to everything except their instincts. The other thing that's kind of funny about how the universe works is that for the people who need noise, the song will come on the radio that they need to hear. The lesson in hardship is that stillness and consciousness has the ability to save you. So the people who are always busy and always have to have noise going on, kind of like a hum, then it becomes like stillness.

Q: White noise.

Me: Yes, when you have so much white noise that it helps focus because there's that hum going on. This information is for seekers.

What I have learned in past processes is the reason they are asking me to channel this is because there is so much longing for this information. I'm unlikely to be stoned in this lifetime for sharing this. There is some agreement that there is a place for it.

Q: How do you check in to this knowledge? What would be a process? Is there a way to learn the words to help somebody to go to that place?

Me: To find the stillness? I'm feeling there are layers and layers and layers of ways to find it. What I am getting is that it is the sensuous piece of us. The beginning is when we start to honor our sensuality, and I'm not meaning this in a sexual way. When you feel the breeze lift your hair, it helps to acknowledge the sensuousness of that experience. That's the most basic form. Does that make sense?

Q: Can you explain that again?

Me: When you feel the breeze lift your hair to say, "Oh that feels so good! Oh, I'm feeling this interaction with nature." It's the process of having a moment, maybe even just for a split second, where you orient your consciousness around that. "Oh, I'm feeling the air lift my hair and it feels SO good," and notice it. That's the very beginning, the very best beginning. Or when you put a bite of food in your mouth and you let it sit there. That's the mindfulness that Jon Kabat Zinn talks about when he says put a raisin in your mouth. You don't know if you even like the raisin. We eat mindlessly. It's that mindfulness of noticing what's happening around you. That's the first step. I'm seeing when you sharpen a pencil, you know how it smells? How you get the mix of the graphite with the pencil shavings, and you notice that smell. Just take that split second to acknowledge the smell of that pencil. It's the process of opening your consciousness to sensory information. The first step is sensory information.

Q: So it can be just a little thing.

Me: Yes that's the first step. That's the most basic piece of it. That's how you do it by yourself. That's why they told me to take art classes for a year, because when I would get caught in the grocery store line and would feel irritability rising up inside of me, "I have to get this done, I need to go." What happens is we don't understand we are in the perfect place for ourselves for that moment. Now when I am caught in line at the grocery store and think, "I'm late, oh, God, what am I supposed to do?" I consciously root myself exactly where I am. Sometimes I envision tree roots coming out of the bottom of my feet to acknowledge to myself that I know this is where I am supposed to be this very minute. I slow it down so that I start noticing every-thing. If I'm caught in traffic, I do the same thing. I start asking, "What's here for me that I need to look at?" And sometimes I figure it out and sometimes I don't. Some-times it's just, "Oh, I'm out of practice. I need to look at the light reflecting off the windshield of this car. See how it makes the chrome look." Sometimes it's just a reminder to be appreciative.

Q: Live in the moment.

Me: Yes, be here now. Living in the moment and apprecia-tion are huge factors. "WOW, this is awesome!" It's sort of like skiing when you are out on the mountain. You see the reflection of the sun on the snow and feel it in the back of your eyes, and you think, "Oh, my God, I am so glad to be alive!" You can get that same sense when you are sitting in the car in traffic and you absorb the feeling of the reflection of the sun on the chrome. There are all sorts of little treasures waiting for us.

Q: When you say that, I hear, "Pay attention. Be joyful." Like Abrum and his daughter were for the little things. That's the start of how you get to the stillness? Is that correct?

Me: Yes, absolutely. And it is also the beginning of the conversation with the universe. The universe knows you are listening to it. Once you have started a practice of conscious sensing, you are in communion with the universe. The universe starts sending you more messages. When you follow your intuition you get more of it. When you follow the sensory information, you get more of it. It almost gets to be like a little game you play with yourself. "Oh, I wonder what secrets of the universe I am going to learn today?"

Q: From the last channeling, why is what you're wearing important?

Me: When we learned Past Life Regression, it helps to center a person in the scene. It's like someone will say, "Anything else?" And I'll say, "Well, I'm wearing this." Plus I started taking writing classes last year, and my writing instructor asked, "Well, are you going to show the story or are you going to tell the story?" So I always do that to help create the scene.

The facilitators and I evaluate the channelings and look for gaps in information. Sometimes ideas and concepts totally blow by me. That's one of the reasons we like to present the channelings in the Q & A format, so readers understand the give and take among me, the spirits, the experiences and the facilitators. Sue, one of the people who helped with the Abrum session was perplexed by the differences between centering and grounding. I was using the terms interchangeably. It's one of the reasons we like to open up this conversation and why we appreciate readers' participation: to fully explore the meanings of topics presented. Additionally, when people are in the room with me when I go into trance, to some extent they, too, are achieving an interface with different levels of knowledge. Things that we inherently seem to know while the trance state is occurring don't always seem clear to me or other readers after the recordings are transcribed. While we're on the topic of being in the room during the channelings, the people who are with me invest their energy in the process and are often more exhausted than I am. There is something about the interface with this knowledge that requires preparation. It relates to our later discussions about creating and maintaining structure.

We asked about the differences between centering and grounding and this is the answer we received:

Chain Gang II, 510 B.C.
Excerpted from Number 23, August 4, 2011

Me: Let's ask about grounding and centering.

What Jesus is saying is grounding is a centering process, but you can center without grounding. Grounding is the idea that you put your roots into the ground, you put your hands into the earth. He is saying it is the most expeditious way for people to get the idea of centering because you feel it right away. You can feel part of yourself and your energy melding with the earth. Water is the natural cleansing feeling. If you lie in a pool or the water, you feel supported and cleansed. If you put your hands into the ground, you feel centered.

Earth is such a wonderful tool for grounding and centering purposes. I use a technique in my meditation practices where we take our energy out to the horizon and back. That's a centering process that uses the air. It's the idea that of energy pulsing outward, like radio waves, among the energies of the air, going out, out, out. You feel then, lighter.

With water, you feel buoyant. With centering in the earth you feel grounded. When I am walking I don't center using the earth because I don't think I will get very far. I use the air one when I am hiking because I already feel grounded touching the earth, but I don't imagine roots coming out of the bottom of my feet.

Q: Right, we're on a walk.

Me: Did that answer the question, what's the difference between grounding and centering? You can do all of the different processes which include cleansing, centering, creating a structure and cultivating awe with all of the four elements. However, for the novice, certain elements lend themselves to different processes more effectively. When you are in flow of water you can feel yourself being washed through. When you put your hands in the earth or touch the ground with your bare feet, you understand viscerally the idea of being grounded, and hence, centered. Those are easier relationships to understand for the novice.

5

Devotion

...developing a practice because I am worthy...

How many times have we heard the adage, "Practice makes perfect?"

In Chapters 1 and 3, I recount my experience of learning to **cleanse** and **center**. What becomes apparent, though, is that tremendous breakthroughs occurred in my life upon serious and consistent application of those principals. I experienced divine love and Jesus started talking to me after I had established a daily practice, and after I decided it was boring to make that daily practice solely about me. Jesus asked me to tell his story after I committed to years of art classes and graduate school. I was so totally immersed in the tasks that I was near to the end of graduate school before I asked, "What is this for?" I had to be willing to serve and to be guided, and make a commitment to both. I also created a devotional practice around **cleansing** and **centering** simply because I liked doing it. The experience of them was my goal.

Devotion is a complete experience. It is satisfying and rewarding to **cleanse** and **center**, **cleanse** and **center**, **cleanse** and **center**. Learning those two steps performed in repetition invited infinite

Confessions of a Closet Mystic

amounts of peace, patience, guidance, and connection to universal wisdom and divine love into my life. Additionally, those two steps performed in repetition, where the same or similar behaviors are performed over and over again are what comprise ritual. The spirits tell me ritual matters. Ritual creates pathways. Like stair steps or ladder rungs, devotional ritual consistently takes our awareness to a higher level of consciousness.

A devotional ritual also creates a protected space into which universal wisdom and divine love can flow.

What follows are excerpts from regressions of previous lifetimes with the pre-Jesus and pre-John the Baptist souls. They illustrate the practice of devotional life, where **cleansing** and **centering** are incorporated into everyday actions. Devotion deserves its own chapter. What the spirits are saying to me is discipline is necessary for going forward from this point. If what we are seeking is the ability to live a life in constant communication with universal wisdom and divine love, or grace, it isn't something that just magically appears one day. It comes from developing **cleansing** and **centering** practices in our lives to the point where they are part of the fabric of our being, where we know we can't live without them. It's the way we commit to saving ourselves. We have some skin in the game.

In addition to how they illustrate devotion, I love **Egyptian Priestess I** and **II** for their commitment to the divine feminine. I think it was a grave oversight of the people crafting the Bible to disenfranchise half the population. I know it is said to be divinely inspired, which I believe, as I have been divinely inspired to share my messages. But what I know intimately is that messengers, as hard as they try to take it all in, are severely limited by their own filters. Given that Jesus, Mother Mary, and the apostle Peter talk to me, it is difficult to believe that the Bible is the last word on Christianity, or that faith was ever meant to be anything less than fluid. As long as humanity is expanding its ability to perceive, perceptions of what universal wisdom entails and how it translates through Jesus will also be acquiring new definitions. It's abundantly clear to me that the intentions of the spirit trio informing me are to increase their connection and broaden their relevance to present day societies. Being stuck in a mindset 2000 years old is not the way to do that.

After **Egyptian Priestess I** and **II,** is **Italian Farmer**, where the pre-John the Baptist soul experiments with prayer and devotion as a way to grow better crops. He creates a structure over his property in which to compound energy. During the session, the spirits also tell me I need to learn to build a structure over the ridge where I live in Colorado Springs. Jesus was not in **Italian Farmer**, so it is not one of the thirteen prior lives. I also chose to include it because it begins to open us to the contemplation of what a production the "culminating" life was. I find it incredible and fabulous that so many amazing souls were drawn to participate in that time 2000 years ago.

Egyptian Priestess I, 200 B.C.
Excerpted from Number 6, February 19, 2011

Me: When I went through the door, I became a new person. I am an Egyptian. I have really dark hair.

Q: Do you know approximately what the time is?

Me: About 200 B.C.

Q: Can you describe the setting?

Me: It seems like it is near the water. It seems like it is really dry. I see a pyramid and the Sphinx. I have a headdress with a snake.

Q: Is there any significance of the snake?

Me: I'm getting Isis. I am a temple priestess that worships Isis and I practice rituals.

Q: Are there people around you right now?

Me: I have other young women with me who celebrate the rites of the Goddess Isis. I think I am a high priestess of this temple.

Q: Is there something special about this time, this incarnation?

Me: It's a time where I practiced collecting knowledge. It's a time leading up to the birth of Christ. I think I knew Jesus' previous life person in this life.

Q: You weren't married to him?

Me: No, I never married in that life. Temple priestesses don't marry.

Q: Is there knowledge being gathered?

Me: What I am learning to do with this life is to focus, to dedicate my spirit, to learn to dedicate physical body and spirit to a practice of worship. I am learning how to learn to be available to universal energy. When I went to temple as a young girl I wasn't really interested in this. I think my family was poor. I was a pretty girl and they could give me to the temple. I would be taken care of. It was a life where I began to learn to still myself and to learn to put energy forward toward devotion. I am seeing in this life Jesus was a warrior. He wore those outfits with the skirts and breast plates. I think he was my brother in this life. He was learning about dedication to a cause, being a warrior.

Q: Is there anything important to know about the study of the Goddess Isis?

Me: It was important also for the reason that it was a practice of exalted women which has often been lacking in history, where women are not appropriately revered. I learned what it was like being purely proud and invested in the divine feminine.

Q: Anything else that is significant in this lifetime?

Me: I had a cream-colored chiffon dress with a gold key design that trimmed it.

Q: I assume the temple was…

Me: It had a lot of white marble with columns.

C: Do you recall how old you were?

Me: When I was a temple priestess? I started living there when I was about 12, and I lived until I was about 80. I didn't have any children. I remained a temple priestess.

Egyptian Priestess II, 200 B.C.
Excerpted from Number 11, April 29 II, 2011

Me: Walking through the door I have on gold sandals on women's feet and I think I am Egyptian.

I have on an Egyptian robe. It's white. I think it is my priest-ess life, where I was a priestess at a temple in Egypt.

Q: Was Isis involved?

Me: Yes, it was the Isis Temple--The Goddess Isis--I think I am 20 and I have an interesting neck collar that has some significance. It's deep and made out of bone, maybe aba-lone, really thinly sliced, but there are some dark pieces. They are maybe dyed bone. Because it is a cream colored and black collar. I have sleek black hair that is shoulder length, and I have bangs.

Q: You have been to this life before.

Me: Yes, it's the concept of woman as a goddess that is important. It is part of what I refuse to trade on in this life, woman as goddess. Women are goddesses, and they always need to remember that. I was really coming into my prime at 20 in this life.

Jesus was my brother. He was in the military. He was my older brother by just a couple of years. And we were both learning the lesson of devotion and discipline in this life.

Q: In this life of devotion and discipline, did you live to be old?

Me: Yes. This life is also about how women support one another. We need to support each other in our strengths, discipline, commitments to a cause and in maintaining boundaries. The many lives I've had as a warrior are important. But you have to have women in devotion to a similar kind of cause, where you develop the kind of boundaries making the divine feminine the most important thing. It's where you don't take on male energy, you just revel in the divine feminine. There are some altar practices that are important for ritual.

Q: When you worshipped goddesses?

Me: We were at the Goddess Temple in the service of Isis. We lived in this temple sort of like a convent. We had a garden. We served the sick. We had spiritual devotion. We educated and trained young women in music and the arts. We had schools for young women. Comportment was stressed. We also developed spiritual identities. When the young women didn't stay as priestesses, they still were imbued with the strength of the divine feminine to carry with them. I'm getting that somehow kohl is important. I'm confused about how that is ritual.

Q: Could you explain to me who Isis is?

Me: [I am thinking "Oh, shit"] I don't have any current knowledge of that so let's see if I have any ancient knowledge of that. She was a goddess important for fertility and harvest. She was really important in the way of the Greek goddess Demeter, but I have no idea if I am making this up. Demeter was the goddess of the springtime. Isis, I'm getting, is the fertility goddess like Demeter for the spring when you plant. She is also the goddess of the harvest. The way we worshipped her, she was in charge of the growth cycle of the crops. This included planting, cultivating the crops, and then the harvest. And then we put up the produce that we grew. We also made wonderful mead, beer. During the dormant periods we spent a lot of time in devotion, where we would take requests from the people in the cities and farms around us. We spent time working out and considering how we would perform our rituals. We had the same feast days as the Wiccans, like the equinoxes and the solstices. We often spent the time from the Winter Solstice to Vernal Equinox in devotion.

Q: In devotion meaning prayer and quiet.

Me: I'm getting this picture that it is sort of like an astrology wheel. I always teach astrology wheels like a progression and the last quarter of the wheel is similar to the last section of the year and has the same meaning as the cadent houses. The cadent houses are when you spend time learning and planning for the future. You are husbanding resources,

117

taking inventories, assessing your strengths, and figuring out what you need to develop for the future. That's what winter months are for. It's like the lunar cycle after the ▫ moon, just before the new moon. The new moon relates to the Spring Equinox. The full moon relates to the Autumnal Equinox. We lived our life in the earth cycles as we are supposed to, in lunar and seasonal cycles.

Q: OK. Do you see yourself in this time?

Me: Yes. It's a hierarchy. When I first came I was 12, but some girls are as young as eight. We started out doing different jobs around the temple. There's a difference between those of us with a full devotion and those who are just at the school. I liked this life. I never did have a husband. I devoted my life to the temple. I liked living my life in those seasons. My brother who was later Jesus was learning devotion through the military. We shared strategies and supported one another.

Q: Are you able to see any of the ritual?

Me: Oh, well, at the harvest, we didn't sacrifice animals. At the harvest, we would bring the most luscious produce, the biggest pumpkin. And we would give them as a devotion to the goddess at the harvest. And it's also the life where I started my great love of food--food as sustenance, food as beauty, food as homage to universal energy. I am seeing the inside of a pumpkin and rubbing it on our foreheads--food for the spirit--that was the third eye connection.

Q: Was it like the ash?

Me: No, different. It was the same place on the head. This was about nurturing the third eye. It was sustenance for the energy to spiritually seek. We put this pumpkin on our foreheads because it would help us seek. This is weird to me. (Plus I looked up pumpkins and they are thought to have originated in the New World, so perhaps this needs further clarification.)

Q: That was the harvest.

Me: We played around with putting an apple slice on our heads before we went to bed. We did a lot of different practices to see if it gave us a different dream or spiritual experience. It was all for the sustenance of spiritual seeking. It wasn't for bi-locating. It was for the purpose of growing and sustaining our spirits. We sought to learn how to grow the divine feminine and how to nurture that source. When we offered the most beautiful piece of produce, we received the blessing from the Goddess Isis. We bestowed it upon ourselves. We were saying that we were worthy. In many families, the best pieces of meat, the best food, the best meal was saved for the male. In this practice, it was saved for the women. It was for the divine feminine. I was the embodiment of the divine feminine that planned for the successful harvests. I had a snake on my headdress when I was high priestess of the temple. A snake represents regeneration. A snake sheds. So every year with the harvest we created ourselves anew. We also made perfumes from the oils of the skins of the produce. I'm not really getting how you get oil from the skins. We made essences and essential oils.   And we used them for healing. And for some reason, pumpkin was really, really important to us.

We defined the different healing properties of the harvest. We made wonderful ales, beers and mead. We made essential oils. We were spiritual travelers.

Q: So the lesson learned in this life was the creation, the rejuvenation every year through the harvest. As the year went through, and worshipping the female divinity. If Jesus is there, is there something he needs us to know that he learned in that life? How did that relate to his service in the military?

Me: He would come for unguents and oils to take with them when they were on campaign, to keep away disease. He learned through me. He would bring me seeds that we planted. When he was away and saw fruits or vegetables we hadn't used before, he would bring it back to me to plant. And I think he grew old, too. Instead of staying a warrior, he became the army physician. I was very stationary and didn't go anywhere except where I traveled spiritually. He went abroad with his campaigns and came back with new vegetation to plant. It was a foundation for the life when he was Jesus and I was the "other" Mary, where I stayed to guard the hearth and the children and he went to learn new practices. In that life, as an Egyptian soldier, he wasn't as much the anthropologist as he was when he was Jesus, where he picked up different practices and rituals to study. But it was a preliminary practice for the life where he went and picked things up and brought them home. It developed the pattern.

Q: It sounds like he was picking up fruits, vegetables, herbs, flowers and seeds.

Me: Yes.

Q: As Jesus, he picked up people, culture, tribes…

Me: Right.

Q: The preparation was in that life. It was also for devotion.

Me: Right.

Q: Devotion to the service, devotion to you.

Me: Oh, I hadn't thought of it that way before. I'm getting chills. I don't know that he had a family in that life, but we were siblings. We were building up to the culminating life. We were defining roles. What were the roles we were comfortable in, how were we going to play this out? It was a foundation life for determining how we learned to work together.

Q: Sounds like an earlier life.

Me: I think the earlier ones had more to do with learning to hold power. Like are you a victim, or are you self actualizing?

And then for this life we were past that. When he became Jesus, when he went abroad, he recognized different sources for oils. He was already comfortable with that part. During the Egyptian life, he earmarked places he wanted to revisit and study.

Q: From his campaigns?

Me: Yes.

Q: So you both lived long lives?

Me: Yes. And that life was also about working with teams. I worked with teams of young women. He worked with teams of young men. He learned to respect the divine feminine in that life. He learned to be subservient to a woman in some situations. He learned to seek my council about some things. Some men have never learned that. First they have to learn to receive it. They don't have a compartment in their brains to receive it, as it is information that is different than they are used to. Like you are saying, men favor the "bottom line."

Q: It feels like we have the purpose, the lessons learned and the preparation for the next life.

Me: I'm just questioning if we have everything about ritual we need to know. I'm getting there is something more with the snake skins, regeneration and composting. At the end of the year we finished using all of the viable pieces from the crops that we grew. We made the oils, we crushed the skins, we put up the fruit and we made our mead. All the waste that we couldn't put into some kind of yeast for the bread and beer, we did our best to use every piece, to have nothing left over. The waste we had left, we used for an earth ritual. I'm getting this other scene. Have you ever heard the story about one of the Kennedys? I think I read that one of Ethel's daughters after she gave birth did a Native American ceremony where she buried the afterbirth. I don't know that ritual, but what I am getting about this Egyptian ritual was we buried waste after everything was spent. We returned it to the earth. This is a process that is really important for returning things to the earth. It is supposed to happen after the first frost, before the ground is frozen solid. You bury the spent remnants of the harvest and ask for guidance, wisdom, success. The process of the ritual is extremely important, to have used everything. After you finish a race, after you finish a project, after you finish something major, like a degree, and you have spent so much of your physical, emotional and intellectual capital? To take a moment to regenerate what is left, give thanks and regenerate. That's an important end of the cycle ritual.

Q: The lesson for us today, after spending emotional crops, the nurturing the harvest,

Me: And then the making of the bread or the mead…

Q: Creation.

Me: After you have spent all of the capital and finished the process, it is really important to take whatever is left. Take all the remnants and bury them in the earth with gratitude for the completed cycle, before planning for the new cycle. It is a closure piece. It needs to happen before the Winter Solstice. Around November, but after the first frost, before the ground is hard.

Q: Should people today look at this ritual along with the New Year? It feels like people start new but don't end?

Me: Yes. Remember talking about the tear in an energy field after a trauma? We have to close the tear, we have to complete the cycle. We charge off on new projects before completing the old, so we are letting our energy loose wildly. There is sort of a seasonal contracting process. Bears hibernate. I'm getting that we need to practice this going within, burying what's left, so that we are familiar with the process of closing a cycle and experiencing gratitude. That was a great and lovely thing. To return whatever is left to the earth and to express gratitude.

Q: It's the recycling.

Me: Yes, and whatever doesn't go into the compost goes into the earth. Everything needs to be accounted for. Everything has a usefulness, even the thing that seems like it doesn't. Bury the stem of the pumpkin. Bury ash after burning. It's important to bury after the first frost but before the ground is hard, as then it will be sealed in when there is a hard freeze. The sealing is important for mending the tear, completing the cycle. I'm wondering if there is a ritual for that? The answer is: USE YOUR CREATIVITY.

Italian Farmer, 300 B.C.
Excerpted from Number 24, September 26, 2011

Me: As I opened the door, the light under the door was blue—it was Mother Mary blue. Beautiful periwinkle. As I come through the door, I have on a long, one-shoulder dress. It is white and it has pleats along the skirt. I think I am Roman. I have dark curly hair with a headband and I feel like I have some kind of a gold neckpiece on. I am outside.

Q: Is anybody with you?

Me: A little boy with curly blond hair. There are beautiful trees in the distance. We are dressed very well. My little boy has on beautiful red shoes. They are very soft leather. He is two-and-a-half. He is my son. I am taking him to the stables to ride his pony. His father is blond and broad-shouldered. He is at the stables and he has a very tame pony for my son, Bobo, to ride on. I'm getting the year is about 300 BC. My husband isn't Jesus. I am thinking he is the pre-incarnation of John the Baptist. I have chills. He is so golden. He looks like pictures we see of Apollo. He has amazing curly hair and our son looks just like him. I don't think Jesus is in this life right now. Even then, this husband of mine was really, really interested in water. He was really, really interested in its healing properties. We have something between a full river and a stream that runs on our property. We are in Italy, maybe between Florence and Venice. We have a lot of money. My husband is a lord, but he is a farmer. He isn't very political. This is a very rooted life for him. We have olive groves and other crops. We grow wine, olive oil and tomatoes. He's a very tall man, unusually tall, like 6' 4". That seems too tall for then. They are telling me to just tell the story. I am not even to his shoulder. He is VERY tall. So they are saying to me they have to take me here first before they take me back to the culminating life, because it is too hard for me to have the attachment to John the Baptist in the culminating life. They have to build the foundation for me with this life we had that was very peaceful and pastoral. (crying) They want me to have that memory before they take me to the culminating life where we develop what the relationship was like. It was a very simple—simple for us because we had some servants—life. I hope we treated them well. It seems like we did.

He was really interested in using the concepts of fertility and how to imbue the earth with greater productivity. He always had the best crops. I am seeing an enormous tomato. He always had a flourishing estate because he was conscious of using energy to imbue his crops with healthy growing properties. He found that different water sources had different capabilities. I am seeing water from the mountains had better minerals.

He spent a lot of time studying that. And then he did experiments where he prayed over crops and created a protected, prayerful enclosure for the estate. He often found that praying and creating an enclosure was more productive than using the water infused with the better minerals.

Me: Should we ask questions? It was a life where I learned and experienced devotion. It was this really lovely non stressful life where I was cherished, honored and adored. They are saying, "Absolutely Julia, you know what that feels like and have that connection and identity that you can share with people." I have experienced it on this plane and other planes. They are saying I need to cultivate the space the same way I did previously. My husband, in this **Italian Farmer** life before he was John the Baptist, visualized an invisible shield around the property and he cultivated the refractions of energy inside the shield. That is what they are saying I need to do now: to create a bigger shield over my ridge when I do visualizations at night and in the morning, where I build it and the energy inside of it.

They say we are worrying too much about what results people will have. They say when people start following the practices, they will have results. But the other issue is sometimes the goal is simply cultivating awe. They are saying to me cultivating awe is enough: where you can just appreciate where you are in this moment, knowing it is a miracle. It isn't a journey where people will be physically healed per se. OK, what they are saying to me is: taking the example of my client with the eating disorder who needed to control me the minute she got on the phone with me. People who have a preconceived expectation of what the healing looks like are not coming from a basis of faith. They need to accept the healing that is available to them and establish that they are capable of receiving awe. Just experiencing a state of awe has to be enough. Sometimes that's all there is. Sometimes the best you can do is to find awe in a shitty circumstance. Those people who expect the overnight healing aren't getting it. If you can surrender your expectations to cultivating awe, then miracles can occur. But you don't get to choose how that happens. They are saying to me, "Even Jesus didn't get to choose how that happened." **He worked tirelessly to create the space to receive whatever the universe wanted to give him.** There is reciprocity. You don't get to control another person in a relationship. You don't get to control what the universe gives you. You only get to control what you create yourself. In that way the universe works for you, no matter what. I think I get that. Working with people in this process, we have to be able to kindly say, "I am going to be a mirror for you. The reflection I am getting is you have a need to control this process. And guess what, it's about faith. We want to absolutely support you in this process, but the process is about learning to unwind that faith for yourself."

Q: Is it a removal of expectation about, "Who are they to decide what will heal them?"

Me: Yes, that's exactly the point. The universe sees all. It sees everything. Sometimes what they are healing isn't from a current situation. Sometimes it's healing something from a different dimension. The faith is: that the universe knows what is the best order in which the healing can occur. So our participants may not feel healing happening at this exact moment. "Oh, I had cancer growing all over my body, and now it's gone!" but maybe the healing needs to occur from a far removed situation about which they don't currently have a memory. It can be at some basic cell level that they have carried for centuries and lifetimes. And healing that is enough. Sometimes the best thing we can do is to accept. That's what faith is: to know it is perfect exactly the way it is. What the universe is giving us is exactly what we need in our lives for our creation to occur. It's always about faith and awe. That's why they are giving us very specific instructions about how to cultivate awe. It's for learning to play in the continuum, the realm of awe. Sometimes death goes along with that. Sometimes it is the best way for it to develop. They always say it in such nice ways. I don't know that I can com-municate it in the nice way that they are telling me! That's one reason why I need to build this container over my ridge, to help me develop patience.

Q: Do they want to talk about the devotion model?

Me: I was going to orient the chapters in the order of: Cleans-ing + Centering = Devotion. They are saying that Cleansing + Centering doesn't actually equal Devotion. What needs to happen next after Cleansing and Centering is for a Devotion to occur using those two processes before anyone can go forward. There has to be a discipline of cleansing. There has to be a discipline of centering where you check in. You do the best you can to create a space to receive. You set judgment aside. You allow yourself to be a pure vessel. You are holding onto and melding yourself with the fabric of your environment. There is a need for a practice to be developed before you can actually hold a structure.

It's the devotion that helps hold the structure when you are creating a boundary. Like they are saying to me I need to build this shield around my ridge to build the energy inside.

They are showing me synapses between neurons, somehow encapsulating that space. I am seeing a super-imposition of a capsule around the synapse. The capsule encompasses the receiving end of the nerve and the sending area of the nerve. They are saying this capsule surrounding the synapse allows all the serotonin to be held there. Ease and good feeling both come from serotonin flooding into the encapsulated area. Devotion (synapse) creates the space where connection to universal energy (the firing) can occur in a safe way. And when the connection occurs, divine love (serotonin) can flood in.

Q: It is up to the person to have faith, where it is something they were performing, a habit, turning into something they believe.

Me: And let go. I always see it like a suspension. It is the lack of. The place where there is nothing.

I received this message on September 26, 2011. I took seriously the task of building a shield over the ridge where I live in Colorado Springs. A friend for whom I had given a reading was given a similar task in May that year—she was one of the friends who turned me on to Wayne Dyer, got me in to meditation with Jackie and persuaded me to do past life regression. So I thought, "OK, we're all getting this lesson." When I did her reading, the shield I saw she was supposed to develop looked like the faceted roof of the Milwaukee Arboretum. It was really gorgeous! The shield I saw for myself was not nearly as good looking! It looked like the glass top to the indoor grill we have at our house. Low, flat and smooth! Pretty homely! Plus every time I drove up the hill to my house, I thought, "It's too big. How am I possibly going to do this?" When I tried to stretch my energy around it, it felt queasy like the vertigo I sometimes get when looking down from the top of a tall structure. Then one time in meditation, I saw angels waiting to help me with this project. A multitude of angels were hanging around outside the house waiting to be asked for help! Wow! When I asked them for help, they showed me how to build the energy. They held flat black rectangular boards in their hands that looked like big, unmarked dominoes. They bounced the energy back and forth among each other using the face of the rectangular shapes. In some ways it looked like an airborne multiplayer tennis game. I began to feel the energy around me lighten, and then coat the whole ridge under the shield that looked like the lid to our indoor grill. After that, whenever I meditated I would visualize the angels being occupied in this way, thanking them for help with this job that seemed so big to me. Now, instead of feeling vertigo when I practiced this new discipline, I felt light and effervescent.

It was simply another devotional practice. This time I learned to encapsulate and grow energy on my ridge. I didn't ask what the purpose was of this practice. I understood it to be a worthy endeavor on its own. I did not understand the task as one meant to be applied in the material realm of paying forward good deeds or predicting outcomes.

On June 26, 2012, the Waldo Canyon fire came down the mountain face, in some places less than a half mile from my home, and destroyed 347 homes and vast acres of National Forest in its path. Embers that were carried more than a mile in 65 mile-an-hour wind gusts caused the fire to jump and burn indiscriminately. The ridge where I live was untouched. We have amazing firefighters for whom I pray every time I hear a siren or see a moving truck. That night was a living hell for them as they watched houses ignite that they could not reach fast enough. They remained in perilous conditions to rescue as many of the homes as they could. Eighty one per cent of the homes in the neighborhood near my ridge were saved. Our firefighters are true heroes. We owe then untold amounts of gratitude. The embers they couldn't control did not burn the ridge where I live. I am not sure what to make of this. I do know I developed the devotion of building a shield around my ridge as I was directed to do, and that my ridge did not burn.

I am not impervious to challenges. I am living a real life, just like everyone else. For instance, we have never sold a house in less than a year, even in strong markets. We have had misunderstandings with renters who we hoped would help us cover our mortgage when we had two houses. Also, Claes and I are both self employed. While Claes almost exclusively contracts with banks, they often think they are immune to the agreed upon terms for paying invoices. They pay at their convenience, not ours. We scramble to meet the mortgage when invoices are "misplaced" on the desk of the accounts payable department. So it isn't that I or my family is dancing through life unencumbered. We have debt. Some months we struggle to pay college tuitions or Christmas bills. Like any couple, Claes and I have disagreements. And, if given half a chance, my kids will tell you about all my glaring inadequacies as a mother.

Just like you the reader, I am receiving the opportunity to stretch. Just like you, I am receiving the opportunity to connect with awe, even when circumstances are shitty. Just like you, I have the privilege of learning to surrender to the universe.

6

"Why IS this happening to you?
You ARE such a good person."

...I claimed the space of my life as my own...

"Julie, maybe you could surrender it to the universe."

"Surrender what, Grandmother? To whom?"

"All your troubles. Just give them away. Think of yourself handing them over."

"I'm not really getting this, Grandmother."

It's 1985 and I'm sitting at the folding table tucked in the corner of my very small kitchen so that I can talk on the wall phone with a very short cord. The table is disguised with a gaily colored striped cloth. I'm sitting in a canvas deck chair. It's not very comfortable, but it's what I can afford. One of them has already had the arm wood split apart. I'd rather be lying on my bed talking on the phone, but I've got eggs cooking. The last time I was lying on my bed, talking on the phone with eggs cooking, I smoked two or three cigarettes too many, stubbing out the butts while emphasizing a point. It's a funny smell, blackened, rubberized hard boiled eggs. I can't decide what that extra odor is, combined with the burnt sulfur smoke wafting out of my kitchen. I know I don't want a repeat.

My little son is already safely tucked away in his crib. It's a long day for him when he gets up to shower with me at six a.m. He can't bear to be away from me. He sits at the foot of the tub. We stick the dampened plastic shower liner to the wall tile to keep the warm air close to him. I angle the nozzle a bit to the side so that he receives a gentle spray while he plays with his stacking rings. He is the world to me. Once I thought I could sneak away and shower without him. Hair dripping in pools around me, my prickled skin was a memory of the warm spray behind me. Gently urging him away from his tirade at the door, I edged it ever so gradually open, without any little fingers getting caught. Oh, my. Such a big hug soaked his jammies, as his shuddering sobs subsided.

When I was born in 1958, Grandmother had already taken the Queen Mary to Europe with her father. It was a gorgeous trip, stopping in Mallorca and ports of the Mediterranean. Photos show her laughing at the dining table in a floral off-the-shoulder gown and lipstick so dark it looks black, tinged as it is with sepia. She arrived home resolved to tell Granddaddy she would leave him and take everything he owned if he didn't stop drinking. Thank goodness he did, or this story might have a much different ending. Some scant years later, Mom, my brother and baby me, showed up in Atchison, Kansas, basically at the doorstep of their stucco and brick Tudor slung with ivy. We were escaping the brutality of my biological father.

It was a match made in heaven, me and Grandmother. Driving her golf cart, lunching with her blue-haired friends, swimming in her pool. I would fall asleep in a wet swimsuit on her best chintz sofa next to the hum of the window air conditioner. I was a bright light in her life as she pulled the pieces back together and Granddaddy became sober.

After Mom married Daddy, and after we moved to the suburbs of Chicago when I was in first grade, Grandmother and I planned our time together from a distance. There was always a pool party in my future with hoards of neighbor kids and grandchildren of her friends. She would surprise me when I arrived with a new card game, sitting cross legged in front of the black marble fireplace on dense, grey green carpet. We endlessly sought new verses of "Heart and Soul" for intrepid rounds on her upright, mahogany piano, gaily laughing all the while. And there were always lots of books.

Grandmother was on the board of the Atchison library for decades. I was reading pretty well when we moved to Chicago. Every birthday and Christmas was celebrated with a fabulous new outfit, and the best recently published books from Grandmother.

About midway through second grade, she called me and said, "And now, Julie, you must write me letters. I want you to tell me what is happening with your life and how you feel about it. You must describe the details of the events."

Writing was still such a laborious process, with thick graphite crossouts from the pencil riddled with bite marks. For the first time, Grandmother was a stern taskmaster. "Don't worry about the smudges on the page, or misspelled words, but I want you to tell me more about the skating pond. What does the air feel like on your skin? When you are skimming across the ice, what do you see? What are you thinking?"

She was every little girl's dream of a fairy godmother, that devoted mentor, expectantly awaiting everything profound or not, bubbling up from my spirit. What she didn't plan for, I am sure, is the gaping hole left in my life when she was gone.

Grandmother had a reedy soprano most of the time when she sang. However, on occasion, when I'd dress up in one of her old black satin slips, with crisp, deep lace that bit my chest and the backs of my calves, she belted out "Saint Lou-wee woman, with the diamond rings" in a low, almost guttural voice. Even when I was at the age of seven or eight, her voice transported me to smoke filled rooms, the sound of clinking cocktail glasses, and the languorous murmur of voices in an elegant lounge scene. I slunk around her living room in white, cotton ankle socks. I have never felt more glamorous or intrinsically, dangerously feminine, than at those moments.

As I grew up, there were so many events celebrating lush sensuality, in ways perhaps only a grandmother can teach. On moonlit summer nights, we crept back to her pool to skinny dip, the under water lights distorting the color and shapes of my legs, as diving bats skimmed the tops of our heads. The air was always thick and fragrant with slumbering blooms from Grandmother's garden. One winter especially, I remember my horror as she presented me with old, fur lined, zip-up-the-front ankle boots from the back of the front hall closet. She was persuading me to walk with her through the snow to the river and I hadn't brought boots. "Come on Julie, no one will see you," she laughed. As we trudged through the trees dripping with melting snow, dark wet leaves stuck to our boots. She stopped suddenly and said, "Here it is. This is the tree. One winter I was out walking by myself. I looked up at this tree and it was filled with bluebirds. The whole tree. In the middle of winter. It was a miracle." Wearing a bold plaid wool serape with hood rappelling down my back, and white, straight-leg jeans tucked inside her goofy boots, I could see my reddened nose as I looked up at a beautifully shaped, leafless tree. "That's amazing, Grandmother," I said, not knowing whether it was, actually, amazing or not. But I knew it was a cherished event she was sharing with me. And suddenly I sensed the deep loneliness of a woman waiting years to tell her sixteen-year-old granddaughter of an incident that changed her life. She had never expected to be the recipient of a miracle like that.

Grandmother was a very private person. She had been a shy child, with two older brothers, growing up in the Kansas side of Kansas City, near where the Country Club Plaza was built when she was a teenager. Her father was a pharmacist who developed a chain of drug stores. Her mother, a school teacher, had Quaker heritage, but turned to Christian Science as Grandmother grew up. She loved being a Pi Phi at KU where they drew her out of her shell and corralled her to parties. Living in Atchison, she had become quite an accomplished hostess and one of the original foodies. All the time Grandmother was alive was one great journey for the perfect thing to eat. When she picked me up from the new

Kansas City airport, north of town, we'd drive away from Atchison, into the city to pick up her new favorite imported havarti cheese. Her asparagus bed was legendary, and plentiful all through June. Nothing was better than finding that last hidden stalk, slyly grown fat, under the draping tendrils of stalks gone to seed. Mom always complained bitterly about Grandmother's failings as a parent. Even my sweet uncle said once that Grandmother wasn't the kind of mom dying to know about your day at school. But one of his friends did say at her memorial service she once loaned them her new Cadillac to drive to Atlanta to come see me, my brother and Mom while we were living there. Oh, that kind of mother.

She did the twelve-step program through AA with Grand-daddy while he was getting sober. An aside about Granddaddy: his drinking may have wreaked havoc on the family business, but he was an excellent sober alcoholic! Every holiday, there he was, at whatever AA location was in the area, helping others stay sober with him. I beamed in adolescent pride, holding his hand at the North Shore Unitarian Church at the Christmas Eve Ser-vice, while he loudly sang off key. And, from far away in Califor-nia, where she had moved after Granddaddy died, Grandmother enveloped my fragility with faith after the calamity of my failed marriage.

For a girl without many dates in high school, I was shocked that my first husband even looked at me. Later, I asked my dear friend Tom, "Was I too chubby? Was I not cute enough?" He said, "Jules, you were just too smart."

I had a death grip on the marriage that I knew, deep in my heart, was not a match made in heaven. What kept me there, despite my misgivings, was my ex's mastery of effortless exuber-ance. My favorite early memory of him was on a beautiful, warm spring day in Champaign, Illinois on the campus of the University of Illinois. Music blared from the second floor of his fraternity house as he threw a football on the front lawn. The sun caught the flash of his broad smile and a red hue in his hair as he easily shook his slim hips to the music, his extended arm releasing the ball in a perfect spin. Late into our marriage, after many mutual betrayals, we could still find a spark of gladness together and wildly dance far into the night.

When it was over, even knowing that it hadn't been a good fit didn't help the feeling I had of being sliced open from my neck to my nether regions, with all of my entrails hanging out. It was this enormous cesspool of a wound. It was a pain so deep, so intense. Was its cause my stupidity at bringing my sweet son into this situation? Was it from being rejected for another woman in my last waddling weeks of pregnancy? Was it from the shattered dreams that were never going to come true?

Regardless of its source, pain preceded me into a room and stayed until after I left. I became a beacon for disaster. In the twelve months after my son was born, I moved three times in two states and had three jobs.

Just before he was born, when she learned trouble was brewing, Mom marched herself up to Green Bay to stay with me as often and long as she could. She and Daddy had just been to see Sonia Choquette for a reading, who told them shortly they would receive an unexpected house guest. Little did they know it would be me, their 26-year-old daughter with attendant tiny child. Each day I walked our golden retriever two miles down the nearby river path, kicking through the autumn leaves, with damp air on my face and the often billowing sulfur smell from the paper companies. I held my nearly ripe baby tummy and asked for forgiveness. Even then I knew that I had to learn everything I could from this situation, so it would never happen again.

My soon-to-be ex didn't want me to leave, yet he couldn't see a future without his new love. I began to lose a dangerous amount of weight and arranged for him to stop talking to me. One of my sisters-in-law called to say, "Watch out, he's planning to cut you off financially, any way he can."

As I was finishing the crib skirt and bassinet cover on my sewing machine, it turned bitter cold before my son was born. Mom said repeatedly, "I keep seeing little penises. I think you are having a boy." In tribute, she bought a beautifully blooming Christmas cactus at the grocery.

He was born in early December. As soon as we could leave, my parents whisked me back to Libertyville in the comforting folds of my family. Most of my siblings showed up for all or part of the holidays, protecting me, protecting my baby. One of my younger sisters came home from college and made us her project, awakening with me in the middle of the night to help with feedings, holding the baby when he cried, so that I could sleep. When she had to leave, my other younger sister came and filled her space. There was so much love and promise for this new life! From the moment my son was born, he was an outburst of electrical energy. He kept us all endlessly amused with his energy and cleverness from the moment he wakened until he fell asleep at night.

In my first postpartum job, for which my son and I moved to Milwaukee, a colleague sabotaged me. In disbelief I searched for event forms I knew I'd filled out, and evidence of meeting rooms I knew I'd booked, at the large hotel where I was working as a convention services director. I wasn't feeling strong enough to mount any kind of a defense. Then my son's sitter went on an alcoholic binge and no one could find her. Moving to Libertyville for the second time that year, I next took a job at a private country club. After working split shifts, eleven-hour days, six-day weeks with weekends, all summer and fall, I was fired with two weeks' severance. The club manager was very apologetic as he informed me the board voted to find a man to fill the position instead. The absurdity of my life grew as the headhunter with the ill-fitting toupee who'd found me the job, as well as one of the club members, started hitting on me!

The day before I was fired, my ex called me at the club. It was the first or second of November, 1985. It was almost a year to the day after that fateful night when he blew off a birthday party a friend in Green Bay was having for him. She showed a movie I watched but didn't see, as we waited in vain for him to appear. He neglected to phone to say he'd instead chosen to spend the night in another town with his new secretary. A full year later, while I looked out the wide expanse of glass, past the pool to the still green fairways, golfers took in a few last rounds. He said, "I'm moving in with her." As unwelcome tears erupted on my face, I whispered, "I hope you will be happy now."

Finally, in exhaustion after my second failed postpartum job, I filed for unemployment and took a position as a lunchtime waitress (me with the cum laude economics degree) so that I could stop, breathe for a minute, and spend better time with my son. I was waitressing in a happening restaurant at the mall, with many colorful Tiffany lamps and brass accents. I felt almost jaunty in the rugby-striped navy and white polo, navy chinos and paperboy cap of my uniform. One of the restaurant owners was young, handsome, single and interested in me. Things could be worse, and then they were. Soon after, my ex's girlfriend and a friend came into the restaurant and were seated at my station! "How did she get HERE, three hours away?" I was stunned in my disbelief. I am sure I gave my table to someone else as I watched her from behind a potted palm. Had I met her before? I can't remember. I recognized her because she looked exactly like a taller, thinner, younger version of me.

After Christmas, I picked up my son from his father in Tucson, and took him for the first days of the New Year to La Jolla with Grandmother. Spending windy days playing in the sand at the Beach Club, I finally broke down and asked for help. "Nothing is going right, Grandmother, I can't work hospitality anymore. The nights and weekends are too hard with a small child. I am spinning my wheels and I am so tired." She agreed to loan me money so that I could pay rent while earning a paralegal certificate.

Nuggets of despair burrow deep when disaster metastasizes. Finally, thinking I had some luck going my way, I was quickly reminded it wasn't going to be that easy. For Christmas, my ex had bought my taller, younger, thinner version that tropical vacation he had never bought for me. But he did it with MY American Express card! With a part time job, evaporated unemployment benefits, occasional child support, the credit department at AmEx was really unsympathetic when I said it wasn't my charge. Weak in the elbows and knees, trampled in spirit, in anguish, I sank to the threadbare brown carpet in my mediocre apartment and exclaimed, "Why is this happening to me? I am such a good person!"

What happened next was the most pivotal moment of my life. In the kindest, quietest voice imaginable, I heard the universe echo back to me, "Why IS this happening to you? You ARE such a good person!"

Suddenly, I had access to a new, deep understanding, and I started laughing! Really, really laughing with the joy of it! And somehow, seemingly by osmosis, I knew what I had to do! I could feel a flexing that needed to happen. I understood the flexing was supposed to be configured within a clear shield just out from my body, maybe eighteen inches. Sometimes it was closer and sometimes it was farther.

The best way I know how to describe the flexing is that it is like when I learned to wiggle my ears as an adult. Sometimes I could feel yawning making my ears wiggle. When that happened, I focused on where, exactly, that muscle was in my ears. Eventually, with a little practice, I could make them move, barely perceptibly at first, but when I kept at it, Dumbo, beware! When my son was little, before he could talk, we had special signals like wagging our tongues at each other when I'd leave him in his car seat to pump gas. It's amazing how soon babies will respond in kind when you wag your tongue at them! Later, when he'd be sitting in my lap at the driver's license facility, or some other endless wait, we'd wiggle our ears for each other. I can still feel his little hands clawing my ears as I wiggled them for him, his baby milk breath engulfing my nose as he laughed. Oh, man, party in a can! We thought we were hilarious!

Back to the flexing, I focused my attention on the shield, especially above and beyond my solar plexus. I fanned it out, concentrating on making it strong and impervious. I started practicing it all the time. When I did that, my life shifted. Like magic, things started going better for me. My ex paid his bill. I received honors in my paralegal course and had several job offers. One of the offers was from the school where I took classes—people who had gotten to know me wanted me to work for them. That was a huge boost to my self-esteem after the humiliation of being fired from the country club. I did start working at a Mexican restaurant until I finished my certificate, because it was awkward dating my boss at the restaurant where I had been waitressing at the mall. I did have to reimburse a lady for her cleaning bill when I accidentally dumped a bowl of salsa in her lap, but five bucks was a whole lot better than the eleven hundred AmEx had been badgering me for.

Reflecting back on flexing, I know now that it helped to enforce the shield that protected me. I have never been a person who saw auras, but my sense of what happened with my divorce is that I grew a big tear in the protective energy around me. And with that tear, all sorts of bad energy was allowed in. Additionally, anything good I could produce kept seeping out.

Personal space boundaries had been such a confusing concept since I was little, tiny. It was never quite clear to me what rights I had as an individual. I still spend immense amounts of time thinking about personal space, and where the individual stops and the group begins. So much that sometimes I have been accused of being aloof or uncaring. I've had a couple of memorable experiences where people interpreted my remoteness as something other than deep, inner reflection. One was particularly ironic.

I was totally enthralled with the college boyfriend who invited me to all the dances at his fraternity. There was always a gorgeous invitation, a corsage or wristlet of flowers and, after, a photograph of the event. He was such a gentleman! Once he took me out to eat Chinese at the nicer restaurant near campus. After he took me home, I called my parents, incensed. "He ordered for me!" I protested. Mom and Dad said, "Honey, it's OK, he was supposed to. That's what gentlemen do." Oh, good to know.

Because of that boyfriend, my sophomore year at U of I was one dance party after another. For the Christmas formal, one of my neighbor friends from Libertyville and I spent days researching bus routes going to all the different shopping areas in Champaign/Urbana, looking for the perfect dress for me to wear. Finally, we found it! It was a black-on-black diagonal-striped halter dress with a matching butterfly sleeve jacket that tied in the front.

Skimming that dress across my skin was a whisper of the promise Grandmother had sung about—the femme fatale alter ego percolating under my skin since I was seven! Some months after the Christmas formal, one of my date's frat brothers commented on the magical way I moved across the hotel ballroom in that dress, so apparently Grandmother had woven a potent spell for me!

We had drinks before the dance in the standard, red-carpeted, Ramada room. I sat gingerly perched on the side of a bed, admiring my red rosebud wrist corsage. It festooned the hand holding a plastic cup filled with wine, while I chatted with other girls until the dance started. While we were waiting, the guys were off huddled near the bathroom doing something with cards. My date seemed very pleased with himself as he tucked my hand in his arm and we walked down the Ramada hallway to go to the dance.

Later I learned it was rigged so that my date won the draw to stay in the room after the dance. As he cryptically told me about our good fortune, he gave me that calculating look as he spoke. "Oh, so we're not going home right after the dance?" I asked. He shook his head. "Is that OK?" he asked. I must have shrugged my shoulders, because he then said, "Nothing ever fazes you. Does it? You just take it all in."

Sometimes life holds too much satire to be believed! That fall of 1977, a psychology graduate student named Linda had posted fliers about an assertiveness training she was doing for her research project. A group of about eight other young women showed up and Linda coached us on assertiveness. If a guy approached you at a bar, and you wanted to rebuff his actions, you could firmly say, "I'm having a drink here by myself and I don't want to talk to you." We had permission to say that! It was different than being aggressive, "No, you jerk, get away from me!" or submissive, having a drink with him even when you didn't want to. Then, for Linda's research, we kept a journal about a situation in our lives where we wanted more assertion. I chose the relationship with my gentleman fraternity friend. As much fun as I was having with him, we never talked about feelings or the status of our relationship. Was I supposed to be exclusive? I had a boyfriend from home that had been at U of I the semester before. He was now going to a different school, but would come hang out on occasion. We'd dated in high school and had one of those really close, honest relationships, but I didn't see him all that often. And how did my fraternity boyfriend feel about me? Was I just someone to pass time with, or did he want to know me a long time?

I didn't come up with the confidence to ask him those questions until after a bunch of us took a road trip to visit him in Arizona over spring break. He was doing an academic exchange for the semester. When I returned from the trip, frustrated not to have any answers, I wrote him a letter. By the time I received the reply, which included none of the answers I sought, I had fallen hard for the man who became my husband and my son's father. They happened to be fraternity brothers.

His comment that nothing ever fazed me has stayed with me a long time, though.

It was reprised when I was working at the country club, the infamous only job from which I have ever been fired. I stood at the stainless steel counter in the kitchen while blood spurted from my left index finger, which I had cut instead of the bialy in my hand. Chef said as he tightly wrapped, then butterfly-bandaged the wound when the bleeding subsided, "You know, when you first started working here, I thought you were an unfeeling bitch because nothing breaks the mask on your face."

Wow! That was some amazing feedback to hear when I thought everyone could see my entrails hanging out! It was all I could do to show up places. I didn't realize that I was still so vacant that I hadn't brought my internal essence along with me.

There's a place I go to inside myself that is way removed. It's a space of deep reflection, where answers are not immediately forthcoming. It's sort of a waiting space. It's a break in the action, a yawn in awareness. Layers on top of it handle the grocery list, what to wear and what needs to happen next. Both those men remarked on the "nothingness." "Nothing" fazed me and "nothing" broke the mask. I think they put the wrong emphasis on the word. It's a space where there is "no thing," and they were able to pick up on it. Perhaps it was so apparent because it more easily surfaced through the gash in the protective shield around me.

Simultaneous with my epiphany about flexing, a number of events and concepts began to converge in shaping my life.

When I was living in Milwaukee, one day Mom brought me a bottle of Nature's Plus Stress Tabs. OMG! What convinced me of how necessary they were was how crummy I felt when I stopped taking them. The volume of my anxiety grew tenfold. I am a committed vitamin taker now. I've always been one of the people who loses weight under stress. But then, I was nursing and my hair was falling out, so I was basically a tired and anxious flat-haired bag of bones with big boobs. I learned that what I was putting into my body mattered.

Next, six months later, when I was back in Libertyville, Mom handed me, *Getting them Sober.* It is a fabulous book about disengaging yourself from an enabling relationship. The advice I found most helpful was how to re-write the narrative of my life. The book said, "If you have trouble doing this, pretend you are someone you feel is successful in areas where you desire success, and say, 'Would so-and-so settle for this treatment? How would so-and-so behave with these challenges?'" So I set about pretending to be a good friend of mine, who always seemed like she had her life together. Additionally, I began to notice my standards for my son were far higher than they were for myself. I was still so heavily into guilt for the mess I had wrought in my life. You could have told me I was responsible for bad weather and I would have taken that on. Guilty people think EVERYTHING is ALL THEIR FAULT. "Oh, sure, that, too is my fault." It really helps to provide for an endless source of wallowing.

I knew I was the bitch who had driven my husband away, into the arms of another woman. No problem. I took that on like I owned it. It was my cloak of identity. But at least I was developing a consciousness of the identity I had created for myself.

One day I was talking to the Brown County clerk's office in Green Bay. The child support representative was telling me what my choices were in claiming the child support my ex still thought was optional. I said to her, "I just don't want to be a bitch about it." That lady was the greatest. She said to me, "Bitch has nothing to do with it. This is a business contract and he is in default!"

"Thank you, thank you, thank you," was all I could think, after I soaked that in. It took a while, but it ranks with the top ten pieces of advice I've ever been given. To this day, I wonder if that lady knows what a gift she gave me. My spirit felt so light when I was finally able to embrace her words. It wasn't personal. It was a business contract.

Most of my family, including my ex, did the *est* training a few years prior to my divorce. Mom and Dad were heavy into est seminars in the city during the period I was a single mother. Because they found it so valuable, they watched my son if I wanted to go to seminars for socialization. I was desperate for a more engaged and healing life, so I went.

Est trainers were always so dynamic, with bigger-than-life energy and personalities. I would just go to listen, still pretty vacant inside, looking for ways to fill the void. I was tickled that one of the seminars was at a purple hotel in Skokie. It felt nice to be tickled by something. Plus, once I was there, people smiled at me. I felt safe, knowing they were searching, too. We all had the *est* training in common. It was a start. Some weeks into the first seminar I attended, it dawned on me that the trainer of the seminars kept talking about this idea of "intention." She stood at the front of hotel ballroom, where hundreds of people sat on metal dining chairs with vinyl cushions. I had no idea what she was talking about. Just as Grandmother suggesting the concept of "surrender" was totally a foreign concept, so was the idea of "intention." Then, about halfway through the second seminar, it finally dawned on me. Oh! Intention was the idea that I could put a desire out in the universe, and it might materialize just because I had done that! Magic! Like hocus pocus and pointing a wand!

The trouble with being raised as an agnostic Unitarian is that there is something very concrete about the intellect. Can you prove it? Can you touch it? Can you reproduce results?

But when I put myself in the mindset of "allowing" and "possibility" that intentionality required, it became very playful and fun. And, boy, was I ever ready to have some fun! "Dress-ups" had always been my favorite game growing up, so pulling on the mantle of "intention" easily became an off-shoot of that.

Also, around this time, the *Messages from Michael* books about reincarnation were very big with my folks and their friends, the self-proclaimed "Lunatic Fringe" of Libertyville. Even though the spirits in the *Michael* books spoke block letters, which made them sound so serious and intense, there was so much that they said that seemed true to me. It really helped to understand that I was responsible only for my own karma, and no one else's. I also loved the idea they promoted that Jesus was the most evolved soul on the planet, because it allowed me to buy into Christianity. I was very impressed that those receiving messages for the book were very Christian. They were reputed to be "older" souls. So maybe Mom and Dad in their intellectualized Unitarianism didn't know everything there was to know about spirituality. The book spoke volumes about characteristics of older souls. It delighted my sense of irony that the "oldest" souls were likely to live the simplest life. The *Michael* books said that the homeless person on the street was more likely to be an old soul than the success-monger dripping with wealth. I love it when things are not always the way they appear!

As I grew in personal strength and certainty, my relationship with Mom grew more strained. Mom and Dad had embraced the Human Potential Movement of the '70s with gusto. After they went away to their first encounter group with Fritz Perls, Mom and Dad decided we would have encounter groups in our family. They were Sunday nights without fail. Mom fashioned herself as the group leader. She so delighted in bald and abrasive exposés of our vulnerabilities, especially in a group setting. She gained power while stripping us of ours. With her bold maneuvers lancing all the poisons inside of us, it became a witch hunt of the spirit. We were between twelve and sixteen years old, where the worst thing we ever had done was snipe at one another! To evade her, which we all learned to do eventually, we attributed the source of all our angst and "out-of-kilter-ness" to our non-custodial parents. That, without fail, satisfied her hunger for the week, and we finally could go to finish our homework.

The thing I did that gained Mom's unreserved approval, I learned about fifteen or more years after the fact. She hadn't cared that school was easy for me, telling me when I was a child with a perfect report card, "Grades don't matter to me." So that wasn't a way to win Mom's approval. All she wanted was for us, my siblings and me, to be agents of social change.

When I was a junior in high school, a girl in the class ahead of me became pregnant. She wasn't anyone I knew, but she was hard to miss as her baby belly grew. I saw her walking through the wide, sunlit hallways of our high school, with narrow industrial red lockers, and shining white floors. I always thought to myself, "That is the most courageous person I will ever see."

Because I was on the newspaper staff, I had become close with the dean of students for girls—I know, pretty goofy, only nerds do that. But there was something about Ms. Stephens, beyond her crusty exterior that spoke of her deep kindness. Maybe it was the left dimple on her face that deepened without smiling. It was surrounded by the fringe of dark bangs of her short haircut, when she was pretending to be stern. Anyway, I would stop in to see her sometimes, just to chat. She sat behind her desk in an orange plastic chair next to the window that opened up to a bare courtyard, One day we got to talking about that girl, the pregnant one who I thought was so brave. The rumor was she had gone up to the bars one weekend in Wisconsin, where the drinking age was 18. She met a guy there, and had become pregnant. I said to Ms. Stephens, "That shouldn't happen to girls in Libertyville. We should have better resources and better knowledge of what to do." Ms. Stephens called some people and I talked to some friends, and we started sex ed at LHS. We'd meet before school in the driver's education room with some PE teachers and a guidance counselor. Maybe Ms. Stephens thought she was too old and too single to be a credible resource to us kids, because she didn't go to the meetings. Still, whenever I wanted help with anything, I went to see her first.

"Why IS this happening to you? You ARE such a good person."

So, years later, I'm having lunch with Mom and Grandmother at Little Szechwan in Highland Park. I've remarried, my son is in school, and his cherubic little sister with red gold curls and a dimple on her left cheek is sitting in a high chair next to the table. Four generations of the matriarchy, right there, the smallest with smashed, sodden saltines, covering her face and fists. Tai-tai, the hostess, always says, "So cute, so cute," whenever we bring the children in. I'm sure we're eating Kung Bao Scallops, as that is Grandmother's favorite. We're close to the front of the restaurant, near the big fish tank. Maybe it is my birthday, because Mom isn't psycho-analyzing Grandmother and me within an inch of our lives. And Grandmother says, "Julie, I've never known your mother to be as proud as when you started sex ed at your high school." Mom is beaming and nodding for once. I had forgotten all about it.

"So that's what it takes," I'm thinking.

In 1986, as my life grew more positive, conflict with my mother grew more intense. I had a good job with a big law firm in the city and thought one day I might go to law school. But days were long with the hour commute to Chicago and back. I was so lucky to have a fabulous sitter for my son. She took in a bunch of other cute kids, in a safe neighborhood. I was always in such a hurry to get both my son and I showered, dressed and out the door to catch the train in time. More than once, I didn't pull the emergency brake all the way up in my late model, metallic blue Mustang, as it rolled backwards down the sitter's drive. The slow crunching of snow under the tires alerted me to the impending disaster. I'd run back around the car and jump into the driver's seat to brake the car. My son and I laughed wildly while cold sweat beaded on my skin. My time with him was precious, with twice or more weekly trips to the mall in cold weather to get exercise. There was a long diagonal ramp outside of Marshall Field's where, over and over, he ran to the top, only to come careening back down to the bottom, jumping into my arms. Finally he pooped out. Running to the grocery after I picked him up at the sitter's at 6:30 p.m. became a ritual. First we went to the cookie aisle and opened a package of Archway Oatmeal Raisin cookies because we were so hungry. It was the truest definition of "Eat dessert first." I reasoned if he didn't know cookies were the dessert, the scrambled eggs we went back to eat at the apartment after shopping could as easily be designated the more desired food.

Having incurred some debt while obtaining my paralegal certificate, I eyed my parents' often vacant town house as a way to become financially whole. Daddy was working as a consultant regularly in Long Beach, and Mom spent much of her time alternating between being with him there and at Grandmother's in La Jolla. They were only in Libertyville about one or two weeks of the month. With my long hours, I reasoned, my son would have more adult contact when they WERE home, and when they weren't, we'd be saving rent. I recognized the risk of having my life dominated was great when Mom was home, but decided my straitened circumstances were worth it. That part turned out pretty badly, actually. We moved into their townhouse in the fall of 1986.

I was so grateful for the extra time Mom spent with my son. A former elementary school teacher, Mom had begun selling Discovery Toys soon after he was born. My son received all of the benefits from trying out all the new toys with "Giggi," as he called her, as soon as the boxes arrived. There were sculptures and games and books. The counting books were my favorite with the big, green blob of a monster for whom body parts were added. One day we sat in bed reading "one body," "two eyes," and in his newly two-year-old voice, he recited the rest of the book as I turned the pages! Whatever the down side of living with my parents was, the up side was great. It suited Mom to pick him up at 4 p.m. on occasional days. Once or twice after my train came in, I made the mistake of running into the grocery before coming back to pick him up at Giggi's house. I thought, "OK, no problem, fifteen extra minutes." Mom reminded me that wasn't part of the bargain. I needed to come straight home to pick him up to go to the store with me. And when we returned, I needed to remember to park my car in the far space from their unit, not the closer one reserved for guests. My son and I trudged back to their townhouse, carefully through the snow, from the furthest parking space. Holding his hand, along with bags of groceries, the weariness sat right between my shoulder blades, as the sky became fully black.

That Christmas of 1986, when we arrived in La Jolla to see Grandmother, my son had an ear infection before we landed. He wailed with pain as we taxied into our gate at Lindbergh field. After we finally got him settled with medication, fresh jammies, and into a soft comfy bed, Grandmother and I poured a glass of wine in her white-tiled kitchen that always smelled vaguely of Comet. We spoke of what my life was like and where to go next. It had been an eventful year for me with many changes and accomplishments, since Grandmother had funded my new venture as a paralegal. We stayed up past midnight, thinking my son would sleep late the next morning.

At seven the next morning, Mom, with Daddy trailing behind her, marched straight into the bedroom where I was asleep without knocking. It was the back bedroom of Grandmother's house. The paneling was dark, as were the blinds, so it was a lovely place in which to slowly awaken, groggy with the weight of nearby sea air. Mom was up early and had a list of things for me to accomplish that day. She was never one to be awake by herself. She always had a plan that included one or more of us doing her bidding. This time was no different. She came in ready to direct the rest of my day.

That's not what happened. I snapped. Once I started yelling, I couldn't make myself stop. I probably ranted and raved for more than an hour. All the personal violations I had felt for so many years came pouring out. "Who do you think you are?" was the most-often repeated phrase to the woman who both commandeered and protected my life. Dumbstruck, my mother's mouth formed a silent "O." But not for long. Of course, the response was that I was ungrateful. Of course, I was out of line.

When my son and I left La Jolla, in the new year of 1987, I headed toward counseling to fix myself. Daddy called to make sure I was on track with that. My mother, the tender little flower that she was, was too hurt to speak with me.

It's to the point now that I know when the apple cart of my life flips over, big changes are coming. If I can stay conscious and maintain a semblance of responsibility for my behavior, I know when the apples get back into the cart, a whole new world will be waiting for me. Whereever I am headed, it is going to be a better place.

I found a therapist who had offices both in the city where I could see her on my lunch hour, and in Lake Forest, the next community to the east. She was awesome! She said something I'd never heard before. "It amazes me," she said, "that your mother isn't more interested in your eventual independence." She thought my mother was the clingy one who couldn't let go of running my life. She said that in spite of the fact that I stressed I had been the one to move in with them. She was a woman a bit older than my mother, with grown children, so I thought maybe she knew what she was talking about. Instead of my mom, we used the man I was dating as an example for how I could create better structure and boundaries in my life. The idea was that, bit by bit, I could design a space for my own existence. Her office was in a high rise, a ten-minute walk from my cubicle at the law firm. It was small and dark. I don't remember if it had any windows.

All the time I was growing up, Mom seemed to treat us kids as though we were an extension of her. We didn't really have private lives. She seemed to view us all together as one big amoebic mass. Somehow she'd been appointed the controller of the cell nucleus. Our individual talents and skills also belonged to her.

I was totally surprised when I began having children at nearly 27. "Wow," I thought, "You are completely separate individuals from me. I will spend the rest of my life getting to know who you are." Until then, I didn't know enough who I was individually to challenge my mother's authority in my life. Once, when I was taking an *est* seminar, a man in my study group had an illness in his family which was wearing him down. He was working hard to maintain his job and other obligations. Every week when I saw him, I asked how it was going. I told him I hoped it became easier for him. He said to me one week, "Julia, your kindness has really helped me feel better about my circumstances." It was the first time I remembered anyone saying to me that I was kind. People always told me when I was growing up that I was bossy and opinionated, "just like" my mother. Yes, I am sure that is true. But I am also kind.

Chloe, my therapist, really helped hone my consciousness. She gave me Jung's book, *Synchronicity*, to read, and I learned a bit about coincidence. In late February, she also gave me, as an exercise in assertiveness, a man's phone number. "He's a former college roommate of my step-son's," she said. "He lives in Lake Forest, not far from you." I dutifully put the number in my wallet, thinking, "I will never, ever do this."

That spring, the cold shoulder I was getting from Mom was a relief, but my loneliness grew. Accepting the distance from her, I knew I had finally lain down the most significant boundary of all, with the hardest possible person. I could feel successful in that. I had the greatest little guy in my son, who took very seriously his job to delight and entertain me, with one astounding new talent after another. After I'd drop him at the sitter on those bleak suburban mornings, en route to the train, I had such a deep longing for adult contact. I wanted someone with whom to strategize with on how to grow a life. I joined Parents without Partners, thinking I could find people to hang with there. The trouble was, the only thing we had in common with each other was our divorces. Talking about that for an hour or two in the dated ballroom with the pickled smell only made me feel worse. One poor guy was a mailman, still forlornly in love with his ex-wife. He kept getting bitten by dogs.

The guy I was sometimes dating was totally involved with traveling and furthering his career. Sometimes we were just friends, sometimes it was more. He wasn't very interested in my son. Soon after I took the LSAT in June, we finally broke up for good.

Ten or more days into July, I said to myself, "I just want to go out. I accept that I may never be a person who can sustain a long-term relationship. I just want to have some fun!" And then I remembered. Chloe had given me the number of that guy. Where was it?

My heart started beating wildly. Funny, suddenly I felt it was my only lifeline! I hoped I still had it after all that time. I turned that wallet inside out, dumping the scraps of paper and change all over Mom's kitchen counter. Finally, after going through all the small piles of papers and cards, in the far recess of the last fold, I found it! *Claes Hultgren, 312-234-7650.*

7

Creating Structure

Shaping an environment for growth...

The following are excerpted from the sessions where Jesus and I shared past lives that relate to **creating structure**. In the **Innsbruck** life from Chapter 2, **Cleansing**, addresses **creating** and **holding structure** within self as well as **cleansing**. It is the best channeled example for how **holding structure** occurs on an individual basis. As I learned as a young single mother in Chapter 6, "Why IS this happening to you? You ARE such a good person," it is important to develop awareness of our internal landscape of selfhood and how best to occupy and protect it. Holding structure must occur in order to cherish and safeguard the spark of life inside of us all. The **Innsbruck** life is also the best example of **cleansing** from previous lifetimes. It was the lifetime where the peasant brewing family who were traumatized by dark people chose not to indulge in hatred for what they experienced. This allowed them to create a different future than they would have had if they had not been able to release the dark energy.

The following sessions deal more with creating and holding structure in an environment. Often more than one of the steps

153

of **cleansing**, **centering**, **creating structure** and **cultivating awe** was addressed in individual lives. There is a continual give and take among the different steps that seems directly related to life lessons. Sometimes one is emphasized more than another. Interestingly, **creating structure** came up time and time again. As the stories unfolded, it became clear that the reason it was so strongly stressed was because it has so many uses in this work.

First, it is the way to establish self. I use **creating structure** processes often with my clients who wish to feel more confident in their identities. As in the previous chapter, it has to do with occupying and defending your body with a personal sense of self. When a trauma occurs with my clients, as in the case of a rape, it seems like it becomes no longer safe for them to occupy their bodies. It's hard to heal a wound if the space is vacant. We go through the steps of creating an enclosure for them with divine light so that it is safe to re-occupy the space of their bodies.

Second, **creating structure** is a way to help develop an environment through which we, as well as others, can experience the steps of **cleansing**, **centering**, **creating structure** and **cultivating awe** in our lives. It's akin to the idea of ambience in a restaurant. What's the best way to experience this food? Is it a hotdog on a street corner in New York? Is it a grey day with damp air where the steamed bun sticks to the roofs of our mouths and the tart pickle relish drips down the side of our throats? Or is it a five-course meal with classical music, gently clinking silver and crystal, and white table cloths that we somehow manage not to drizzle with red wine and au jus? So the idea of **creating structure** gets us thinking about, "What are the best ways we can experience this life lesson?" I have a quote by Sandra Sharpe on my desk that says, "What do you pack to pursue a dream, and what do you leave behind?" Once we have developed a space to occupy, what are the traits, skills and energies we want to engender to best experience this life we are living?

Third, and this is addressed in ensuing chapters about Cultivating Awe, Passion and Jesus, once structure is developed, it provides a container for compounding energy, as well as for receiving universal wisdom and divine love.

The following sessions are not in chronological order. Rather they in the order of progressively larger contexts or environments in which we develop and hold structure as we become more adept. **Jonah** holds the structure for an environment of many goats from whom he receives total devotion. It is a simpler task than holding the structure for an environment which may be receiving challenges. After **Jonah** is **Peacock**, where a young women skilled in mystical arts begins to understand that it is a more advanced talent to learn to hold the space in which others may develop their mystical expertise than it is to be a revered figurehead. As the mother of four children, this was a very validating lesson, as it should well be for other parents who put their talents and identities on hold so their children have more room to flourish. Next is the detailed story of how **Mother Mary** creates and holds a healing environment for envoys from Rome where the apostle Peter is developing the Catholic Church. Last in this chapter is the **Nikko** life. It is the story of a Merlin-esque, eccentric recluse living deep in the woods of Japan. What's important about his life is that he did not need to participate in society to have a huge healing influence upon the animals living around him. This circumstance is akin to the monks and nuns world wide in present day society, who with their prayer and devotion create a mystical environment and foundation from which the rest of us can draw energy and launch our mystical journeys. Also, at the end of **Nikko** is the beginning of the discussion about the power of words and the Lord's Prayer.

Jonah, 610 B.C.
Excerpted from Number 14, May 2-I, 2011

> Me: I am in the middle of a pine forest. I am a woodsman, I have an axe. I think I am in the Alps. My boots are trussed leather, like we wore in the '70s but without fringe. And I have some leather sort of pants. I have a white beard and white hair, and I live in the mountains. I am clearing out old pine trees, in Switzerland, 610 B.C.

Q: Do you live alone?

Me: I am a shepherd of goats. I am a solitary person. I live very simply. I am a bit of a hermit and spend a lot of time with the animals. I have some renown for how I tend my goats. My cheeses and my milks are well- respected, because my goats are so well cared-for. Right now, I am felling pine trees and creating a new kind of barn structure for my goats for the winter time.

Q: Do you live close to the town?

Me: I live three miles to the nearest neighbor and five miles to the nearest town. I'm getting it is where Bern, Switzerland is today. I just adore my goats. I think they are better than people. I won't allow them to be slaughtered, which is why I have to build a new enclosure for them. They are my family. I have milk and cheese. I have some hens that lay eggs. They like to live with the goats in the shelters. I don't deliberately raise the hens, they just come. Some of them give speckled eggs. They are big, fat and cinnamon-colored. I won't eat them, either. I am a vegetarian. I eat eggs, drink goat milk and eat some cheese. And sometimes I eat some berries and seasonal foods in the forest. I know about mushrooms. I'm not really an herbalist, but there are special herbs I know how to find in the forest and people who know herbs will come to get them from me. I understand all about the forest.

Q: Do you know who Jesus is in this life?

Me: He is a very round woman who lives in the closest outpost. She is interested in a relationship and I am not. We are cute together. We look like Mr. and Mrs. Claus, a hearty outdoorsman Santa. She has an eye on me and I am not interested. It seems like too much trouble. I like my life to be very simple. It's one of those resting lives where sometimes you have to return to the earth and live very simply. And I am getting the message that our lives have grown so complicated in this time, in this century, in 2011. So few of us ever have the opportunity to return to an earth connection. Somehow we need to find time to do that even if it is only in our dreams. We need to find a space to create simplicity. I am a very strong man and I carry goats on my shoulders. I assist in the births of the little kids myself, and bathe them. I don't shear them, but I do brush them. The people come to get the goat hair that I collect from the brushes to make woolen articles of clothing. I don't spin or weave myself. I do trade for that. In the winter I wear articles of clothing that have been made from my goats' fur. Periodically I will allow one of my goats to go to a good family, but they have to swear on their lives that they will never allow that goat to be killed. It must be protected. I go to look at the pens another family will put the goats in. They have to take more than one, so the goats can have company. I am extremely particular about my goat family.

Q: He's lived his whole life in this way? He seems old.

Me: I am maybe in my 50s. As a youth I was quiet and lived closer to town. I have known the woman who is interested in me since I was young. She's already had a family and she's lonely. I am not lonely. I am not interested in a physical relationship. I live a very monk-like existence. I have a very fulfilled and spiritual life, living in the mountains. It's a very similar lifestyle to Abrum's lifestyle. Abrum lived with more people. Abrum had a daughter. I like this simple life. I wait until my goats die of old age and then I will wear their skins. It keeps them close to my heart. I won't allow them to be slaughtered for any reason at all. I have so many goats. I just find a way to keep them all. I am seeing that, later on, some boys come from the village to help me make the cheese. It gets to be a lot of goats, maybe 50 goats. I will allow boys from the village to help me feed them. It's a very nice life but I don't want complications. I want to live by myself, very simply.

Q: Maybe the bottom line in this life is the resting life? What is the lesson?

Me: Let's ask. The lesson is about creating enclosures. They are showing me with their hands. I, as Jonah, created enclosures for the support and nourishment of life forms. The lesson was I created a safe space and the goats flourished. Living simply is always a big message, but I am seeing them gesture with their hands. I always used squares. I understood the power of a square and the power of four. I wasn't ritualistic. I didn't have that interest, but I had a centering and focusing process where I would pound a stake in the corner of a fence. I squared those. I worked very carefully with pine and was purposeful as I did that. It's like what they tell us in exercise class: focus on the muscle you are building. It will be more powerful. It will work better. It will develop faster. I was a mindful person. As I was designing these enclosures for my precious goats, I was very mindful as I imbued the building process with protective properties. It was a discipline for me to construct these enclosures with rudimentary tools. I think the lesson of this life is about being mindful in the process of creating an enclosure, and how it is important. Think about every piece. Be very present. Your mind can be more than one place at a time, they are saying. It is wonderful for a meditative practice.

I understood the pre-Jesus woman was also a mindful kind of a cook, but she was a meat-eater and I couldn't make myself stay in her environment because she ate meat. My goats were so old when they died that no one wanted to eat the meat. I buried them, because I couldn't make myself eat them, and they were old and tough anyway. I treasured my goats. I had a whole cemetery of goats in the forest! I cherished their spirits. It was a reciprocal process where they looked after me and I looked after them. I really cultivated that energy. I loved them. They loved me. The lesson is that creating a safe enclosure is important, along with finding as many ways as you can to engage with the special enclosure. Get ready to dream. Allow yourself to create a capsule, a safe space for a dream to flourish. They are saying that this then will translate into your day-to-day existence. If you want healing, then you can allow yourself to create these enclosures for yourself, inside your mind. It includes what you visualize, and what you can sense. It can be filled with any kind of color, smell or sensory information. Building enclosures to protect ourselves and others is important and effective, apparently, is what the message is.

Q: Is this along the lines of bio-field, aura, and layers?

Me: Sort of. It's a little different. This is like film. This is where the film can run. It's like creating a screen. If you want to think of it in holographic terms, it's the enclosure where you can create a script. It's more like creating an empty space with good energy where you can create scripts of healing or scripts of how you want your life to go. It has an intentionality feature. I'm getting it's particularly effective for your dream life, where you can ask for the dream that will show you the healing or show you the positive ways to go with your future. If you are experiencing a conundrum, and are looking for direction, you can build a vessel in your imagination to employ in your dream life. I don't know all the different ways that people dream. All of the sensory information is appropriate to be included in that space.

Q: We looked today at the marcaba. Is that similar to what you are talking about?

Me: Sure, or pyramids. I particularly like to use an egg shape. I think different shapes resonate better with different people. So, absolutely, for this fellow, his name is Jonah. He liked squares. Squares were awesome for him. If you are attracted to a shape, absolutely, use that. Different shapes have different potentials. For me, they are saying, the egg shape works, because this is a creative process, it's a birth. There are many births inherent in this process. Like little Russian dolls, there are egg and eggs and eggs.

Q: Stacking.

Me: Exactly. So there are layers in that way which are affiliated with this process. Right now I am seeing Easter eggs. A while ago I saw four different kinds of eggs. One was a Russian Faberge, one was a ceramic egg. Anyway eggs are my shape, for now. If you are attracted to a shape, go for that shape.

Q: Is that part of a ritual?

Me: It's the mindfulness piece and it's the enclosure piece. Any ritual? No, but it is important to be mindful of the enclosure. People like a little safe space. People like a womb-like area for intimacy and safety. He built a lot of little squares for his goats because the goats felt the same way. They didn't want a big barn. I'm seeing twig huts my daughter built in 4th grade in her nature classroom. A sociology of the huts developed. People like enclosures. They feel safe. It's possible to have a very simple life. He had goats and some wild hens, basically.

Me (About pre-Jesus): She made these gorgeous stews and nope, he didn't like that!

Q: She was trying any which way she could to win him over but it wasn't going to work.

Me: No. He just wanted his goats.

Q: That was a different lesson for Jesus.

Me: What's funny to me is how often he is the woman and I am the man. We are often men together, and that's the initial impression I had about how these lives would unfold.

Peacock, 1400 B.C.
Excerpted from Number 17, May 3-11, 2011

Me: I am in a place where there are peacocks. It's in a garden. I have on a maroon cloak. I am a woman feeding peacocks. I feel like maybe I am in India. Do they have peacocks in India? We'll have to check. It is 1400 B.C. I am here in this garden to meet my lover. Ooh. He's my teacher. He's an older man, but he isn't gross. He is Jesus in one of his earlier lives. He has a goatee. Compared to most Indian people, he is not small. But he is smaller than he often is. We are both petite people in this life. There is a reason we can't always be together. I was thinking initially it was because he had a wife, and that's not it. He often goes away. He is so spiritual, and he's thinking it isn't much of a life for a young woman like me. These spiritual lives are mostly for men, and I am saying, "Well, this is unfair." And he's saying to me, "So far you are unspoiled and you will remain that way, but if you stay with me…" It's like a romance novel. He's saying I have to do the right thing and marry someone else. I'm seeing this other guy and I'm saying to pre-Jesus, "He's not like you. He's not dynamic…" He says back to me, "He will grow into it." He says just hold the space for him to grow into it.

All my clothes are lovely in this life. They are all silk. I LOVE the clothes here. I'm thinking, "He's leaving, but thank goodness, I have nice clothes." (Laughter) They feel so good on my skin. I am so enamored of this teacher. I feel it is so unfair that he gets to go away and live a spiritual life because I know, even then, that I am better at it than he is. I know that women are better receivers. I instead have to take a husband who is not as advanced spiritually as I am. I'm not happy about my lesson, which is to hold the space for him to grow spiritually. I'm not happy about it at all—AT ALL! I think he is a ridiculous person and "He'll never get this." But as we grow, he does actually start to get it. He turns out to be a little better-looking over time. He fills out a little bit. My life turns out to be nicer than I thought. I don't have a strong attachment to the older man who is pre-Jesus anymore. I never lose my disappointment that women are not allowed to be spiritual masters. I know in my soul and all the way down to my feet, those soles too, that I am AT LEAST as good at being spiritually connected as my teacher is. Maybe better. And here I am, left holding the space for this husband of mine, who is a little ridiculous, so that he can come along, too.

I think what I don't realize in that life is that I have a greater capacity to receive and to create a space than my teacher does. I don't understand that this talent in holding a space can be more important than being the charismatic spiritual leader that my teacher turns into. On a universal level, holding the space for others to grow is a worthy endeavor and it doesn't have to be always about me. I guess as long as I have nice things to wear…. (Laughter)

Q: That's your prize.

Me: Yes. The peacocks are definitely symbolic of this life for me because I had a peacock temperament. I had all the abilities the master did and was also born into a high family. I didn't understand why it was all about the men. They are saying to me that the reason for that was so that I could learn to cultivate female energy. In that life it was hard for me to do. I was too competitive. It was too much about me. But it was that discontent that I carried with me, and then took into the life as the High Priestess of Isis, to help other women know that they also have abilities. I'm seeing that some, not all, women in isolation get this brittle power thing going on and unfortunately it is unattractive. Mother Mary is saying to me it's a difficult balancing act to be a woman. To know that you have the power to create the enclosures for others to transform themselves, while at the same time knowing you have to find your personal highest and best use. It's a continual struggle and conflict, and men don't have the same feelings. They often don't have the urge to create enclosure feeling. Jonah was an exception, but often men do not. What a benefit it is to help create the enclosures for others. But sometimes it is also OK just to be a peacock.

Q: Do you see what happened to Jesus in this life?

Me: Oh, he just went and did his guru thing and attracted crowds. He was surrounded by crowds of adoring people. I was disgusted with him. It was a life where he developed the Hindu powers of deep mysticism that he checked in with later. I still knew I could do it, too. I was really disappointed with him. I thought he could do a better job with this. I thought, "If you have all these powers, you could start inviting women. You could challenge society a little bit with this." He chose not to. It was too complicated. He is saying to me now--we're having a little argument (laughter).

Q: I thought that might be happening.

Me: I'm saying to him, "Well, you didn't really do that in your last life either, where you made a safe space for women." He's saying to me he's backing me all the way now. I'm saying, "Well, excuse me, you're not here." He is saying to allow my faith to engage about this. He is saying that I don't have to always know everything before it happens. They are saying to me, "If we told you how it was going to turn out, you might not..." They know how I like a mystery and they know how I like putting the clues together myself. But he's not making any promises either. He's saying, "Julia, you are going to do this because you want to, because you feel moved by it. And you will create a great network and power source for women. You don't need my backing in a physical form. But you always have it." He's saying it's my chance. We had that argument always, where I said "You don't have to be the Messiah. You don't have to perform miracles. People can learn to do it themselves." He's saying it is an opportunity for me to get to teach that piece that I always argued with him about.

Q: In this life with the workshops?

Me: Yes. That's what he is saying to me. "It's an opportunity for you to make the point you felt so strongly about." (I'm thinking "Oooooh, shit!" as I transcribe this. Picture Butch Cassidy and the Sundance Kid jumping of the cliff and that's what my stomach feels like right now.)

Q: So that was basically the lesson in that life.

Me: Well, let's see. Is there another lesson about it?

They are just saying that I have many lives where I have a chip on my shoulder...that's why I often don't come back as a woman. I think, "Seriously? (Laughter) You're not going to let me do the cool stuff that the guys get to do?" And they are saying to me that it was important that I learn— I'm not competitive in that way in this life—that I am willing to take the challenge. Actually they are giving me a compliment. To do it the way I thought it needed to be done takes a special temperament. It has a lot to do with why I have the children that I have. I had to learn when it was, in such exacting detail, OK to give an opinion, when it was OK to step back, when it's OK to say, "You are perfect exactly the way you are." It's a continual balancing act for me. It takes a special temperament to do it the way I thought it needed to be done. Jesus is saying frankly, he didn't have that temperament. Well, we'll see if I do. But they are holding me, too.

Q: Are you conversing now?

Me: No, I'm just hanging out and seeing if they have anything else to say to me. Peter has kind of a green light, like the other day we saw the green lamp over a pool table? I don't know if that means anything.

Q: Is he playing with his chakra?

Me: It's something about a heart blessing for this process that he has for us. We can think of it like a green light. I'm seeing how welders have a green eye shield. He is saying he sees us through this green light.

--Anything else?

Q: Thank you so much for being here.

Me: And again, they have deep gratitude for everyone for being here.

Q: I'm glad I'm not chewing gum and I have on clean under wear.

Me: Mother Mary is saying no one ever asks if she even wears any. (laughter)

Q: What does she look like?

Me: She says we all should go to Lourdes together and then
we will nearly walk in the air because we will so resonate in
her energy. I can see us almost on magic carpets above the
ground. She says we'll be in touch with her energy there.
She knows that none of the three of us really want the ability to heal people, but if we go there we will have a better
understanding of what that is. We can cue in to it when and
if we want. I am saying, "Who is paying for this trip?" And
they are saying the opportunity will come probably within
the next 18 months. That's nice. They don't like to make
promises, but they feel pretty secure in that one.

Mother Mary was always beautiful, not to be confused with
Mary Magdalene. Mary Magdalene was very dark, like an
Irish beauty, with that translucent skin, and very dark, curly
hair. Remember Melanie in *Gone with the Wind*?

Q: She was my favorite.

Me: Mother Mary has more of that demeanor. She says she's
a little smarter than that, though. (Laughter)

Q: She never let any male energy in. (Laughter) You kept it
all to yourself.

Me: She's saying, "Good on you. You picked up on that." She has
that kindness. That always came ahead of her. She says people
could hardly ever see what she looked like because kindness
exuded from her. She has beautiful, simple aquiline features.
Her hair is not stick-straight, and kind of a medium brown. But
the thing that is amazing about her is she was careful not to give
her features too much perfection because what was important
about her was how the light shone through her. They didn't want
people to get confused about where her beauty came from. The

beauty was in the light. Her features were fine. Mary Magdalene was exquisitely beautiful. Mother Mary did not have the same kind of physical beauty. She didn't choose that beauty because she wanted people to know that the beauty was inside of her and coming out. People would look at her and say, "I don't really understand this." She chose it on purpose so that she could always discern the people who could truly see her for how important she was. That's another one of those, "Let there be no mistaking this"—How important she was.

Q: Is she shaking her finger?

Me: No, she's doing what I am doing with my hands (holding arms open). "Let there be no mistake about this." And she says, "The best of my essence is at Lourdes." Even though none of us want the responsibility of healing others, we will have the opportunity of cuing into that energy when we go there. And that we are all her beautiful daughters, so there, girls.

Mother Mary, about 41 A.D.
Excerpted from Number 5, February 9, 2011

Q: What are you feeling now? Are you comfortable?

Me: I feel comfortable. I feel relaxed. I'm standing at a bay and I can see houses across the bay.

Q: How would you describe yourself personally? How old are you? How are you dressed?

Me: I am in my 40s and I have a white robe on and a blue over-robe.

Q: Are you alone?

Me: Yes.

Q: Do you get a sense of why you are at the bay? Do you have a purpose this day?

Me: I think I have come to the fish market but I am standing and watching the boats come in.

Q: And as you watch the boats come in, do you see anything happen?

Me: I am admiring the day. I'm feeling the sunshine on my face. I can smell the sea air. The lovely warm day.

Q: Sounds wonderful.

Me: I see some young men on one of the boats. I am thinking some of them look like my sons' friends.

Q: What happens next?

Me: I go to take some fish to my mother-in-law, Mary.

Q: What is Mary doing?

Me: She's rolling dough. She is getting ready to make a fish pie.

I have brought her some red snapper.

Q: Sounds yummy. What happens next?

Me: We start making cioppino in a crust. It's an Italian seafood dish. She's using special saffron for this, and I can smell the saffron.

Q: She's a good cook, then.

Me: She's wonderful. She's a really good cook.

Q: Is she just cooking it for the day's meal, or is it a special occasion?

Me: It's a big pie. So I ask who it's for. It's for guests that are coming. They are monks. They have traveled a long way and she expects they will have a big appetite.

Q: And what will they be talking to her about?

Me: They are going to talk to her about Peter.

Q: Can you tell us a little more about Peter?

Me: Peter and his struggles in Rome. And there's one man in particular who is kind of brawny, shorter stocky, with grey hair and a beard.

Q: So they are already there.

Me: They are coming. I don't think they are here yet. But I know them and I am kind of seeing them after. I can see both at the same time (the meal preparation pre-visitors, and the visitors after arrival). Another man is taller, thinner and dark. He has a pointed dark beard. They are dressed very simply. They are part of the group that followed Jesus before, so they are part of the disciple group.

Q: Would we know any of their names?

Me: The name Joshua keeps coming up for me, and Michael. I think the third one might be new, he might be a Roman. He is coming with them.

Q: So Romans were disciples too?

Me: He's new. He's a connection with what's happening with Peter in Rome. Peter was doing Christ's work in Rome.

Q: Let's get back to what Mother Mary is going to be talking with them about.

Me: They are talking about Peter's trials. How he is promoting the church. They are saying he needs support and money. There are some Romans who are engaged in the beginnings of the new church, but they are afraid of being killed, like John the Baptist was beheaded. They are worried. The Romans are very concerned about what they think are magical practices. The followers of Jesus can't perform them.

Q: Like the Essene training? That kind of a force?

Me: John the Baptist was beheaded because he was seen to be trying to step into Christ's shoes as the new Messiah. He did have particular talents, but it was of the water. The Roman Church did eventually adopt practices with water, but Peter and the new church are still in the determining phase. They are determining what is safe, what they can promote, and what they can talk about. They want to tell the stories of Jesus and they have to be careful about who they say what to. They keep the stories about love, forgiveness and compassion and turning the other cheek versus the great--I don't want to say force--but versus the great spiritual awakening that is possible. Because it is the spiritual awakening that is so feared. It is what the Romans want to wipe out. So Peter and the new church are able to keep the development of the church on this level of kindness.

Q: That makes sense. So what happens next?

Me: These men are spiritual men and they come to Mother Mary for purification and cleansing.

Q: Because she has her own powers.

Me: Right, she is a wonderful hostess and creates a wonderful ambiance in her home. She also has grace. The light shines through her that has been developed over many years of mystical activities and behaviors. They are coming to her for solace. She can't protect Peter. In fact, I think it looks pretty grim for him. When we talked about the water before, we talked about how the water could cleanse and then supplant. She is going to use an anointing process where she puts oil on their foreheads, and then ash from a fire outside, on top of the oil. She puts the oil of myrrh in a painted pottery bowl. She puts the ash on top of that on their foreheads. The reason is to ask for clarity. The oil represents soothing the wound. The ash on top of it is meant to provide an awakening and new beginning. It's right on the forehead right where the third eye is. It is a soothing and awakening process.

They are feeling discouraged and annihilated. They are asking, "Where do we go from here with the Romans?" It isn't as easy as when Jesus was the figure-head. They are sneaking around. They have to go quietly about their business. And they are wondering is it worth it, what's the point? They are coming to her for restoration. What she is saying to them is she can't provide the answers for them, but she will provide the space for them to go deeply within to locate it themselves. I am there. I am her student. She feels it is very important to personally handle all of the food that she gives them. She draws all of their water. It's a supplication process. It's not like she is their servant. It's more that she is the supplier of their restoration. And it is all very symbolic as well as purposeful.

Q: She is their supplier.

Me: She supplies and creates their environment. She creates the ambience for them to center themselves and heal. After their supper she lights candles around the room and some incense. It's just before she anoints their heads with myrrh and with the ash. The myrrh oil is in a brass spouted pot. So while I can be there and I can help supply energy in prayer, it's important to her that she creates the environment. I went to the fish market and she spent the morning cleansing herself and being pure. She wanted to be a pure vessel to bring the energy in. She has always been a pure vessel. She is a purer vessel than I because I have lain with a man and borne his children. She bore a child from a different kind of conception.

I'm getting it was sort of like artificial insemination, but not really. I'm seeing a lot of light around this conception process. The source of the other piece of the conception is not clear to me. I'm seeing an abundance of intense light.

Q: How does Mother Mary feel about Jesus being crucified and gone?

Me: We all miss him. She knew it was a risk he was taking. We all understood that he potentially would become a martyr. He was crossing the authorities.

Q: At the end, was it planned that he leave the way he did?

Me: There was awareness that a dramatic death was one of the possibilities. There was a possibility that it could have gone well, but the chances were that the way it occurred was likely. We were all aware of that. There was also awareness that his martyrdom would help create the movement. People would hear of that. They thought the time was ripe for shift, like now, in 2012. It wasn't only the Romans who were so materialistic. It wasn't only the Romans who were creating their own downfall. It was also the Jews, where the money lenders were at the temple. Jesus felt strongly that it was time to shake things up. He knew that he was crossing all sorts of boundaries. And he knew that there was a likelihood he would be sacrificed, but he felt it was so important. He felt that people were getting too far removed from their source. It was so important to him for people to learn to center in prayer, learn to create their own serenity, their own fulfillment and their own futures. He felt strongly that the churches and the forms of materialism were taking people in the wrong direction. He always saw that affluence created a "Catch-22." People stopped seeking as fervently when they were affluent.

Q: Kind of the way they are today.

Me: While affluence is what everybody seeks, it's also "other centered." They feel warmth and full bellies and beautiful environments can take the place of spiritual grace. Jesus felt strongly that it did not. That's why he felt compelled to live such a simple life toward the end to be that example.

That was always the danger of becoming such good "intend-ers." When you have your heart's desire and it's a material thing, where is the room for the spiritual? Have you kept a space for the spiritual in that? That's why he took such great pains to live so very simply with the Essenes, to model that simplicity. It was to be an example for the people who allowed themselves to be persuaded that material goods could fill their spirits.

Q: One question, did he mean for us to follow him as a religion, even though the disciples were trying so hard to establish it? We've been told that he didn't really mean for us to start a religion.

Me: He lived in the time of Judaism. I think his intention was only to help make modifications, to help open people's eyes.

He knew he would be a Messiah. He knew he was a great messenger. I don't think he felt like he had any control over what happened to the message afterward. He did intend to make an impact. He had a message that he needed to share. The whole development of the Roman Catholic Church and Protestantism is way beyond what he ever imagined could occur. It was the future that nobody anticipated. It would be a mistake to say that he didn't act with deliberation. He acted very deliberately in putting forth his message. He was filled with universal energy that he needed to share. He could heal people, you know. He could reach into the perfect part of others and help them connect with the perfect part of themselves, so that they could heal.

He and I had a lot of discussions about whether that was a good idea for him to heal others or not and his point to me was (is), "They are still talking about it, aren't they?" We had this ongoing...

Q: Debate.

Me: Debate. My point was that they could learn do it themselves. It was better to teach them to do it themselves. He said, "How will they stay disciplined if they don't know what's possible?" His goal was always to teach the process. His goal wasn't necessarily to heal everyone. The goal was to stay centered and be loving and compassionate, and to teach. All of the things he taught had the same goal, which was how to draw universal energy into your self. Everything that he pursued in his life, all the different topics that he studied, was in the interest of finding that information. How do you invite the universe into your spirit? He felt that it had a lot to do with centering and contemplation. There were many vehicles you could use for it, like you could use the four elements as a vehicle for the centering process. You could use contemplating your environment for the centering process. He continually looked for ways to distill the process so it was simplest and easiest for people to understand, for them to feel the energy themselves.

Q: And do you think the disciples learned how to do this?

Me: Early on they all did it, and after he was crucified only a few of them remained who followed all the practices. He was crucified, John the Baptist was beheaded. It didn't seem like a very good idea to show all of the talents they had for this kind of thing. Mother Mary could do it and I could do it. But we didn't. What we did was create and supply environments for others, to lead them to the quicker route to spiritual fulfillment.

Q: I wonder if this is a good time to answer a few questions. Do you think it is a good time?

Me: Sure.

Q: Let's ask some questions about confirmation, because you've been getting some information and some messages. You'd like to know if there is a spirit group that is working with you.

Me: The word I am getting is Peter.

Q: Peter?

Me: Yes, (laughing) Peter.

Q: Peter is your messenger?

Me: I don't know. Let's ask. YES, yes, yes. The father of…

Q: Your spirit guide?

Me: The father of the Catholic Church. It came in really loud.

I have to take a moment to describe what was happening for me at this point. For the first time since I started getting messages from Jesus in 1998, I felt a huge rush of recognition. Peter was someone I knew well! Peter was my friend! I suddenly knew he was someone for whom I felt great love and affection. I was so happy to see him!

There are many things about the journey of being a messenger for Jesus, et al. that are confusing for me, such as my blatant lack of regard for dogma and my imperfection as a human being. Another of the things that has caused consternation for me is that when Jesus first told me he and I had been married, I didn't have a rush of intimate feeling for him. Yes, I recognized him and yes, I thought he was a great man and spiritual being, but he was a distant, not close-up, relationship. I didn't have the feeling of "knowing" him. When Peter appeared, on the other hand, it was like that long lost friend you hoped fervently to meet again, but never expected to. "OMG! I can't believe it's you!" It was a gigantic relief to me, that perhaps it wasn't a case of mistaken identity, perhaps I was meant to be their messenger.

What they have said to me since about experiencing and knowing intimacy with the other spirits is that they are careful about how much I can handle. The deeper we get into my experiences of the "culminating" lifetime, the more taxing it is for me emotionally. It is helpful for me to have some reserve and distance so that I can tell the story. They are afraid the pain will be too great for me to continue if I am totally able to immerse myself into those relationships and all they entail.

Q: He's the one you've been getting information from?

Me: I've been getting information from a lot of sources. Jesus talks to me sometimes. I go back to memories of the "other" Mary. But the person who is shepherding this process along with Jesus is Peter. He is doing it in conjunction with Jesus. But it's his group of guides.

Q: It's their project.

Me: Well, it's Jesus' and Peter's project. But Peter has a group of early ministers of his church who feel that it's time to create a new written history. Because, you know, it's St Peter's Basilica in Rome. And that's where all the historical information is kept and he feels it is lacking. And I'm saying to Peter, "OK, well, then I guess it's your job to make sure it gets there." I can only do my part.

Q: And do we call you Mary? Is that your name that you went by when you were married to Jesus?

Me: Yes.

Q: So he feels like the historical information that's in St. Peter's Basilica is lacking?

Me: Right, because they purged so much early on. They purged it because of the fear the Romans had of mysticism. He knew that mystics and other devotees of spirituality would always be able to find a way to connect to these universal truths. Now it is time to add those pieces back in. He feels like the Church is losing its way. They are not able to center as well as they should to go forward. The Church also needs to move in a forward direction. They are losing ground. They are losing congregation. They are no longer as relevant in today's world. Their edicts from the past where women had to have all these children, there couldn't be birth control, even condoms are bad. Peter is concerned that they are getting away from their spiritual message. They've taken on so much in interpreting spirituality for so many people. He's distressed.

I am the Ace in the Hole for the spiritual awakening process. He says a lot of people are able to find enlightenment without this information, but this is a piece of the Church's history. You know, the Church has really gotten into people's lives while forgetting about its mystical basis. He thinks it's important.

Q: Peter has been planning to use you to help the church get back to the initial work of spiritual awakening.

Me: Right. And he feels that the Church isn't serving the people any longer when you have so much poverty. He thinks that the values are skewed.

Q: Is that why they are choosing to channel with you at this time? Because of the timing?

Me: The timing has something to do with 2012, but it isn't for 2012.

Q: I understand.

Me: Because with the Mayan Calendar, it has raised the awareness that a shift is occurring and the planet is going through a certain part of the Milky Way and all of the possibilities inherent in that. Peter says there is such fervent longing for these answers and for this information to come through, that's what prompted it. He could only do kind of a guesstimate of whether it would be needed at this time. But now it's time. There are enough people who will be served by having this information available. I'm laughing that he thinks it's going to be part of the official Church record. I think, "More power to you, Peter." But I see him very explicitly. He's a very dynamic man in a white robe with a tie around the middle and a balding head.

Q: White robe with a tie.

Me: White wisps of hair on his head.

Q: Is he tall, is he short?

Me: On the shorter side. Not really round, but he enjoys a good meal.

Q: Can Peter tell us what he hopes to achieve with this? Obviously it is intended to be a book. Is that why we're doing all this? If so, how? What and how much does he want for us to tell?

Me: It is so different from what people are used to hearing. It's good to start slowly and use the transcripts with a couple of people at a time and say, "This is what I have been doing. Are you interested in taking a look at it?" And there will people who are interested and there will be people for whom it is anathema. And it's not worth fighting about. It's not worth the argument. It's like *Conversations with God* or *Messages from Michael*. It's information that works for some people and will strike a chord with them. It will be kind of a missing piece. It will be the piece they have been looking for.

Q: I think I understand everything. What else do they want us to know today?

Me: I'm seeing a bell, like a cow bell. We're being called home. The bell is calling us. There's a safe environment for us. What we have so far, we can share freely, and we can just allow interest to grow.

Q: Since Peter is kind of leading this life that we are seeing, this segment right now, when you are in your 40s, is there more that we need to know? He took you to this place. Mary is doing the ceremony with the three men. Is there more that we should get out of this session that he wants us to take down?

Me: He's feeling satisfied. He's feeling like we are on a good track. He's feeling energetic, pleased and grateful to us for pursuing it.

Q: Peter, should we try to pull in Mother Mary? Should we try to pull in some of her background? Unless he wants to tell us anything else.

Me: As a young girl, she had a lot of brothers. None of them were as interested in the spiritual aspects of life. She persuaded her father to allow her to study with the ancient women's wisdom groups in Alexandria.

There were always women who studied the Kabala and there were always women who were Sufis. They were kept separate from the men. They had courses in miracles. She participated in the mystery schools for the women that were kept very quiet and separate. She was always a buoyant, happy and light being. She was the kind of person who could go through huge setbacks emotionally and financially and never let it diminish her spirit. She could always keep her spirit separate from turmoil. She was a beacon, a guiding light for everyone who was around her, from the time she was quite small. She had the ability to engage and heal naturally and mystically.

Q: She always had that ability?

Me: Yes. She had the spiritual sense. She was born a mystical talent. And she developed it and studied deeply.

Q: And you say none of her brothers has any inclination?

Me: They were all descendants of David. In every generation there was usually a spiritual caretaker. She naturally gravitated to that role. Her brothers were big, strapping men.

Q: Was this all planned way in advance? Was she chosen to birth Jesus? Because she was a mystical talent?

Me: The whole thing was planned, yes. I'm getting that the three kings represent preparing, seeking and sharing. There was Joseph, and he was not the father of Jesus, but he was her good and dear friend. I don't think she ever had marital relations.

Q: In her whole life.

Me: Yes, she was sort of like the predecessor to how nuns are now.

Q: They had no more children after that.

Me: She didn't have any other children. She had a lot of brothers. Sometimes her younger brothers or my sons were mistaken for Jesus' brothers. He was an only child.

Q: Did the souls of Jesus and Mary plan to come into that life to make it happen? Was all this thought out?

Me: Yes, everybody did. I was not as old a soul as Jesus and Mother Mary. They had managed to catch so much light and energy in spiritual advancement that she ran into the same problem he did where she had too much light energy to hide.

Q: Too much light to try to control it on this planet. To contain it here.

Me: Yes, exactly. And they are from the same source. I'm seeing these light bodies and they come together and then they separate.

Q: You mean both of them were from the same soul?

Me: Maybe. Maybe it's not exactly that, but it is something like that. Maybe it's a pre-soul state. But they came from a common core at one point.

I'm different, and the message that I had gotten is, I am a messenger. I was always meant to be a messenger. I know that I work with the archangel Gabriel. My question was, is Gabriel part of my spirit group, and he is, but he isn't managing this project.

Q: You were meant to stay on after Jesus dies?

Me: Yes. We are developed a different way. We came from a different soul casting. The light bodies that Jesus and Mother Mary were come from a different sort of a soul casting. The messengers come from another soul casting and were part of the messenger group.

Q: I've never heard of it referred as that before. These are soul casting groups?

Me: Yes. Like with the messenger group there might be ten messengers cast at the same time. But when Jesus and Mother Mary, the light bodies, were cast, there were just two. So all that energy just went into two entities.

Q: Oh, I see.

Me: I had heard before that they were some kind of twins.

Q: I had too.

Me: And so it's not exactly that. It's not that they are the same soul. It's that they were in a pre-soul state together. Or that's what I am getting. And it may be that everybody has a different take on this. It's not where one person is more right than another.

Q: When you say that they are the only two to come from their soul casting group is that to give them more light energy?

Me: Exactly. And there are other light bodies that are cast. But that is not information I need to worry about now. It's not my task.

Q: OK. But it's interesting they were the only ones—that's how they are so powerful. They do have to split the light between many souls.

Me: Yes, and that's what happens with the light bodies. That's why he was the Messiah and I wasn't. I never thought I needed to be the Messiah, I always knew I was the messenger. And they developed over many lifetimes. But once both of them connected with the core mystical knowledge that they did 2,000 years ago, they could never pretend to be anything else. They had become source.

Q: Expand on that a little bit. I need clarification.

Me: You know what they say about the Incas at Machu Picchu? They say that they became such light bodies that they ascended? It's sort of the same thing. The universe has this vast store of knowledge and if you resonate on the same level as universal wisdom then you are absorbed into it.

Q: And you are talking about this last life they had. That's what happened in the last life they had?

Me: Yes. Well, they had choice in that life. They had to fill their potential. They both fulfilled the most potential that's available. Because they did all the things that were available to them. Mary did her mystical studies. Jesus developed his practices of healing. And they both learned to be perfect healers through different techniques. The ultimate procedure is the same. The difference is where they are able to connect. They are vessels for universal energy. They are able to pull it into themselves. They find the core in people. Remember we talked about the purest part of them? They are conduits where they connect universal energy to the perfect part of the entity they are healing.

Q: Let's just jump back. When they reach this perfect potential that is possible, they were absorbed into it?

Me: Universal energy, they became one with source.

Q: So even though Jesus is a guide to many, he's absorbed into universal source, but he's still doing work being a guide.

Me: Oh, absolutely. And it's...

Q: So is Mary, so is Mary...

Me: Yes.

Q: So it doesn't pull them into such a light that they can't work.

Me: Yes, because when you are a light being you just reflect. You don't lose energy, you compound energy. So it is this endless source of light.

Q: Thanking Peter, Mother Mary and Jesus, for coming through.

Nikko, 400 B.C.
Excerpted from Number 12, April 30, 2011

Q: Look at your feet.

Me: Let's look at the horizon. I am in a pine forest. I'm back in that area in Japan, in Nikko, where the Hear No, Speak No, See No Evil Monkeys are, but before the temple was built. It was always a sacred space.

Q: In Nikko, Japan. Do you get a time frame?

Me: I am getting 400 B.C. I think I live in the forest. I'm part of the religion that preceded Buddhism—prior to the Shinto?—I don't know what that is, but that is what I am getting. I'm in part of the forest where we still have a huge connection to animals. It's a precursor to Shinto-ism in Japan and I am a woodsman who lives there and communes with the animals. They eat out of my hands.

Q: What kinds of animals?

Me: Bunnies and foxes. Animals that learned they don't have to be predators. You can develop communities of animals that get along and there is ample food to forage in the forest. I have a little Hansel and Gretel cottage in the forest. I'm really happy to be with these animals. I'm seeing a crazy type of Merlin figure who lives way deep in the forest. He lives a marginal life. I'm still pretty civilized, but this person is magical, and he is deeply, deeply, living off the land. He is the pre-Jesus character. I find him offensive, but wise.

Q: The Merlin–type is the Jesus life?

Me: He is the pre-Jesus life. As a woodsman, I live a very tidy existence, where I feed the animals, but he lives with them. There is something about the energy in the forest that comes from him that allows the animals to cohabit peacefully.

Q: The lesson in this life is cooperation?

Me: Yes, learning to integrate. The foundation lesson is if you hold the light, if you create the space, you don't actually have to be a participant. It's what the monks have found for years. They could just be retiring in their own little cells and create this wonderful, magical realm of spirituality. This Merlin-type person who lived in the mountains in Nikko, he was able to do that. They are saying it helps to be very close to the earth. This is an earth lesson. Fruitful monks who live off the earth, who develop the earth are closer to universal energy. The most successful spiritual participants are the ones engaged with the earth element, because they are so grounded. If you toil in the earth, you have all the roots that you need to grow like a tree. To really reach into the higher aspects, you feel very much safer grounded in the earth element to go far, far, far out into ideas and realms and opening.

Q: How is this going to work for the city dwellers?

Me: All it takes is a little bit of earth. Everyone should have a pot of earth that they can touch. I don't know this personally, but what they are telling me is the plants love for you to massage the earth around their roots. That it is like a massage for them and they love to feel wrapped in that. What I'm seeing is to massage the earth around their roots, gently, communing with them so as not to disrupt their root systems. I'm seeing Bonsai trees. You can even have a rake in the little Zen gardens. You can draw pictures in them. That also is an effective habit. I'm also seeing a labyrinth. It is another way to connect the roots with the message and with the journey. I'm seeing all of that at once. It is a layer. In the Zen garden, you can develop your labyrinth. It becomes the roots and the metaphor for the journey. It can also help you branch out in the spiritual extensions your journey takes you in.

In Native American ceremonies, they acknowledge every piece of every element that plays a part in a process. Don't feel constrained by materials, they are saying. It's that malleability piece.

Q: And intent.

Me: Intention is good. All of these processes are to allow the energy to build on itself. There are different ways of approaching them. They all have the purpose of creating space in the body. In the universe, in the process of allowing perfection to grow. They are all for the purpose of core connection to the universe to allow perfection to grow.

Q: The more we connect with the earth's gifts, the more we connect with animals, the stronger our connection to spirit will become.

Me: Right, right. People who have a house cat, versus people who have a bunch of wild bunnies, they are both really good. Everyone can lead a fulfilling life, is what they are saying. It just takes a little imagination.

Q: Is this why the Japanese are so good at living so close together in such tight quarters?

Me: I have just done a little research on the Samurai mindset. The way I understand it, it sort of turns Maslow's hierarchy of needs on its head. They are always looking to master them-selves before they are looking to master other people, so "Yes, yes!" is the answer I'm getting. This isn't our line of knowledge, but it's like we acknowledged the Islam piece in the Abrum life—they have such a good way of creating energy with their devotion. The Japanese have such a won-derful way of becoming centered in their environment, look-ing inward instead of outward for their solutions. When you can look internally for your solutions instead of externally, you don't need such a big space. It's relevant but not our line of wisdom—someone else will develop that.

But being there was instrumental for this lesson with this man in the woods. I'm seeing how Einstein said time is rela-tive, when you connect with a place such as that, you can see both the future and the past. You can gain knowledge from the future. We were able to tap into that thread of knowledge the Japanese developed for one short lifetime. It allowed us to utilize some of the self-contained introspec-tion for the work we were to do.

Q: We have the lesson?

Me: We have the earth lesson, the words…They could give us the words, but the point is not to get too attached to them.

Q: Then they are their words.

Me: (laughing)--And they got into trouble with the Lord's Prayer.

Q: Please ask what's up with that?

Me: It's a powerful phrase that expresses all the right senti-ments. It's just very rigid and patriarchal. It was never meant to be so patriarchal, nor was Christianity. Christ was not so patriarchal. Western civilization, with its ego-centricity, tends to be extremely patriarchal and there is a need to shift out of that. Hence we are women. This is largely a group that will be created by women. It is a fortunate man that is invited or wants to take it on. It's an honor for them too (laughing).

Q: Are we headed in the right direction?

Me: It's a format. It's providing a structure. The receiving lives, the seeking and the sharing. This is a sharing piece. These are the ways that Jesus learned to heal. They were never isolated.

Q: Thanking everyone!

Me: Let me just see if there is anything else. I am seeing a color coming out of Jesus and it is a beautiful green and then marine blue. It's a blue circle surrounded by green, coming out of him. He is saying it is a representation of mother earth. And we can always see the blue circle surrounded by green coming out of our hearts. It actually is a globe, but he wanted me to see what was inside of it. We can do this as a way of cherishing mother earth. He would like for us to do this as something we hold close to our hearts, a globe like that that holds all the people in the earth. However we can do it, with words and our sensitivities. We can use pine and sea air fragrances. When we have this impression, we are to allow those fragrances to surround all the people on the planet--to share and embrace them with it.

8

Five Black Volvos

While living in the space of miracles....

When Jesus, Mother Mary and the Apostle Peter suggested the structure for presenting the way to connect with universal energy, I began looking at my own life for how and when the learning had occurred for me. In each of the other instances of learning to **cleanse**, **center** and **create structure** in my life, I could immediately identify the point where my life began to shift. With **cleansing**, it was setting aside the internal arguing I did with myself about my mother and sending her light and love instead. With **centering**, it was taking art classes at Jesus' behest and my almost daily practice of hiking at Ute Valley Park. With **creating structure**, it was when I remembered that I knew how to shield myself and be bold, after many unfortunate occurrences as a single mother. When it came to **cultivating awe**, I realized it wasn't "one earth-shattering moment" that was different from the one exactly preceding it that had shaped my understanding; it was instead a series of wondrous events over my lifetime, and choices about how to view them. These inspiring events haven't unfolded in an organized manner. They also haven't come every time I asked. But when they do come,

I am a supremely appreciative audience. I revere them, holding them very close to my heart and spirit. I act on them. I am willing to appear ridiculous prior to their materialization. I have patience while learning to hold possibility as it becomes reality in my life. I have always been really lucky to be a person who is awestruck by the large wonders of the world as well as small happenstance occasions. I treasured my babies' smelly sour milk necks, and allowed them to endlessly smash food through their fingers in the deep tray of their high chair. I explained to Claes, "They are having a science experiment," as they studied masticated banana subsequently squeezed through their fist, tongued it and then offered it to me. "Mmmm." I love the calm smell of air and green-tinted sky just before the tornado sirens sound. And oh, my heavens, I love weather! I love sunny days and windy days, pelting rain and hail. I am lucky to love so much.

When the kids were smaller, my busiest time of year was the space between Thanksgiving and Christmas. Sometimes Thanksgiving lands only a couple of days before the end of November. Sometimes nearly an entire week goes by before December begins. I used be able to gauge how much weight I would lose in the month prior to Christmas based on whether Thanksgiving fell early or late in the month. If it was early, I lost only three pounds because I had that extra week to finish Christmas shopping before the maelstrom of events. If it was late, I could count on losing more than seven.

Our son's birthday party always launched the month of December, with homemade novelty cakes and special goody bags themed to an athletic event for 20 boys, the first weekend after Thanksgiving. This was followed by countless charity meals for the elderly, special Sunday school projects for Advent, multiple dishes for board and teacher luncheons, cookie baskets for teacher gifts, ornament exchanges, complete holiday meals and gifts for mitten tree families, and of course, parties: parties for kids' sports, parties for kids' classes, a party for my Girl Scout troop, parties to see Santa, with special gifts for him to hand out, sneaked in on the sly, and parties to pour my seasonally slim self into fabulous outfits bought at the after-Christmas-sales the previous year. (They call them "ugly sweaters" now.) My feet hit the floor at five a.m., and I ran and ran from one event to the next until I fell into bed after eleven most nights, with frosting or other food items in my hair.

In the fall of 1998, Thanksgiving was late, so I prepared myself for a tight schedule, but loose clothes! I was still attending meditation, but was studiously ignoring Jesus, or whoever that errant spirit was! That was the year we were leaving Christmas Day to meet Claes' family in Denver and ski in Steamboat over New Years', adding to my holiday to-do list the extra wrinkle of packed gifts and complete ski attire for our family of five. This, of course, was pieced together over a year of stalking sales, determined to find the exact shade of jade or coral ski pants that matched the jackets the girls had fallen in love with that year.

1998 was also a year I needed to have my car emissions checked by December 7th. Lordy, lordy! One more thing! But the emissions station was just over in Lincolnshire, and could be handled most likely in an hour, tops. So, after picking up Kimmie to sit for our youngest, and getting them situated at home, I headed west through the patchwork of dried fields and bare, deciduous forests, in my dark green Ford Taurus station wagon. It was an overcast, chilly day. Checking my car clock, I was right on time to reach the station when it opened at eight a.m. As I put on the blinker to turn left and jog into the station, I noticed a black Volvo sedan slowing behind me in my rear view mirror. As I turned into the station, the parking lot was empty. As I came around to the entrance on the far side, the sign on the door said, "Closed. You must take your vehicle to another station." The next closest to me was on the north side of Waukegan, about twelve miles away on a non-direct route. "Damn!" Pulling my red turtleneck closer to my face and drawing up the collar of my coat, I clapped my leather-gloved hands together for warmth as I ran back to my car. And I probably said, "Jesus, F——g, Christ," which is the favored expletive to mutter under my breath when I am frustrated.

I am one of those people who schedules my day based on the length of time tasks will take. If a time slot is open, like an opening in an almost-packed suitcase, I have the activity to fill that space perfectly. Once the mother of my daughter's friend remarked to her, "Your mother must never get anything done, because she is always on time." I think it has more to do with the fact that I am a Capricorn, ruled by the Greek Titan Chronos, and in my heart of hearts feel time is too precious a commodity to ever waste. If something comes up—like the trip to test emissions that was now taking three hours instead of the one hour allotted–I replace one time-blocked activity with another. Unfortunately, given that it was December, it meant a later night.

Sinking back into the unheated tan leather seat of my car, I resigned myself to less sleep that night and turned north onto Milwaukee Avenue beginning the process of weaving through the roads to Waukegan. Glancing in my rear view mirror after the turn, I noticed a black Volvo wagon several car lengths back. "Hmm, how about it?" I mused. "Another black Volvo."

Rather than getting stuck in traffic going through Libertyville, I decided I'd swing back east on Highway 60 and then go up St. Mary's Road, on one of my all-time favorite drives. That part of St. Mary's Road is a beautiful stretch of deeply wooded five acre lots, with charming homes peeking through the leaves in the summer. But in early December, it was an Ansel Adams Mecca of swaying tree boughs and a few last swirling leaves that had escaped rigorous herding by Hispanic men with blowers strapped to their backs.

Turning left onto St. Mary's, there were no black Volvos around. That is, until I drove fully three miles with barely another car on the road to interrupt my reverie of the late autumn silhouettes. And then I passed one waiting at Rockland Road to turn in behind me. "Unreal! Three black Volvos!" I exclaimed aloud. By this time the black Volvos had my full attention. The sedan behind me turned east on Route 176, but I could hardly wait to see whether I was to meet another one on my journey!

Finishing the five-mile length of St. Mary's Road, and with it, many fond memories from my youth, I turned east on Buckley Road to cut over to Highway 41 for the last stretch north. The next black Volvo coupe caught up to me around the dark red-brick buildings of Abbott Park, the corporate headquarters of the pharmaceutical giant that'd employed my dad, among many other dads and friends of the past 30 years. The coupe turned south when I turned north. "That's four!" I exclaimed as my inner chortling could barely contain its verve.

By now my dreary task had turned into a great quest and I was wildly singing along with Jethro Tull on the radio, "Let's bungle in the jungle—well, that's ALL RIGHT BY ME!" It didn't matter that I'd gotten to the rivers and walls of dingy, cracked concrete that made up Highway 41 in that location. I couldn't wait for the NEXT BLACK VOLVO!

Sure enough, there was one more, weaving through traffic and coming to ride my tail, with the heavy-footed urgency of a city driver. Five black Volvos! Five! Augh, augh augh! I felt like the Count on Sesame Street!

"WOW! FIVE BLACK VOLVOS! This is so exciting! I wonder what it means?" I was sure it meant something. Somewhere among the five black Volvos that followed me was hidden symbolism and meaning, just what was it? For the rest of the journey to the exhaust facility, and on the way home, I felt the hugeness of my personal miracle grow and grow until it filled the car.

I was playing around in the stock market at that time. If I heard random conversations about the same stocks, my rule of twos kicked in and I'd go look them up at the library to see how they were rated. And was this the new rule of fives? So the next time a half hour time slot came up, just before picking up our four-year-old daughter at the Presbyterian Preschool, around the corner from the imitation Monticello library, I ran in to look up Volvo stock. It seemed pretty unexciting, but well-enough rated. When my daughter and I returned from the grocery to start our next round of baking, I called our broker and said, "Please pick up 100 shares of Volvo for me." And then promptly forgot about it.

That was the wild winter where Claes and I agreed to help with the history project in our older daughter's intermediate school. We were assigned the trade route from the Far East to England. We'd bought some ungodly amount of cloves to hand out to the kids, but the best part was: Claes made the trade maps and I'd committed to making and showing up in Renaissance costumes they then could keep! I know, I know, just shoot me, right? What WAS I thinking?

We stay-at-home-moms in Lake Forest ran around like Tasmanian devils, but we sure looked good while we were doing it! Many of my friends were prettier than movie stars. Even Bill Blass was quoted as saying women in Lake Forest ranked in the top five of "best dressed" in the country. I sincerely have to make a plug for the middle-to-upper- class women whose ranks I joined in 1988. Tom Wolfe minimized us in *Bonfire of the Vanities*, calling us "social x-rays," only to be outdone by the ridiculous caricature by Annette Benning in *American Beauty*. Please tell me what is wrong with listening to self- help tapes in the car, or garden gloves that match gardening clogs on purpose? We are an amazing cadre of educated, talented and disciplined women who juggle multiple check books as easily as we perfectly smash a tennis ball to the far corner of the service box, or prepare food for and hostess a five course, sit-down dinner for 20. We are an under-appreciated, untapped gale force of raw potential. Someone, somewhere would be really smart to figure out a way to marshal our forces.

Finally, finally that Christmas Day of 1998, all the presents were wrapped in suitcases safely stowed on the Boeing 727 when we headed from O'Hare to Denver. Each disk in my spine wore its weariness like porcupine pajamas, as I cocooned in the coach seat in the back of the plane, with Claes and the children scattered around me. Two and a half blessed hours with nothing really very important to do. Claes handed me the business section of *USA Today* he had purloined from a gate waiting area on the way to our plane. I opened it up, and bubbling laughter left me weak in the elbows and knees as I melted further into my seat and read, "Ford Motor Company to buy Volvo."

I didn't make a gazillion dollars on the stock purchase, as the experts said most of the price bump from the deal had already been actualized by the time I bought the stock. I never thought that was the point, really. After all, spirits didn't start talking to me until AFTER I grew bored with focusing on items for personal gratification. But what I did get out of it was something far more incredible than money. The universe and I were having a conversation. It spoke and I listened. I acted on it and it spoke again. It reinforced behaviors I have now cultivated for years, where I orient myself in the scene around me. I know without a doubt that everything in my environment is there for a purpose. Everything. Our story is being told on many different levels simultaneously, like a Dickens novel. So while there's a whole lot I argue with, I usually don't argue with what is showing up in my life, or where I find myself. I often stop and study it. Part of being a co-creator of my experience is taking ownership for being exactly where I am in every moment.

I guess I don't really want to get into the discussion about who the universe loves best, the rich or the poor. I've never met anyone who was getting a free lunch. Even if they had the biggest, most beautiful house, and garages full of expensive cars, every really wealthy person I have ever known had a gripping personal challenge. Some had children with disabilities; others had drug addiction issues, a miserable marriage or cancer. I believe, and this is completely reinforced by having studied an incredible number of astrology charts, everyone is having a life experience expressly suited for them. In this way it is true that all people are created equal.

We never know what another person's story is, so it's just better to be focused on our own, rather than judging theirs. I once remotely knew this rotund sort of man, the dad of one of my kids' Sunday team mates as we stood out on chilly fields in deeply cushioned grass. He was about medium height with straight, sandy blond hair. He had a Ferrari. But better than his Ferrari, he had about ten different Ferrari outfits in colors ranging from red to yellow to black, which he snugly zipped onto his stout frame. There was always a plethora of zippers, like my daughters' "zip pocket flares" from the Gap. There were zippers on the thigh of the pants, zippers on the pouch in the shirt, zippers on the neck and upper arms. Even before I learned his story I thought, "How excellent is THAT?" It reminded me of a two-year-old with Tonka or Hello Kitty outfits. A WHOLE BUNCH of Tonka or Hello Kitty outfits. Well, it turns out this man had five young children with a wife who had recently died a many-years-of-grueling-pain death from brain cancer. Those five kids were the sweetest kids you ever met. What's to argue with about that? We can all be distracted by the person who looks like they are somehow getting undeserved treatment, but it is simply a distraction, and a sign that it is time to start focusing on our selves instead.

There've been times in my life where I was poor as a church mouse, and other times when I had money left over after paying my bills. In both sets of circumstances, once I learned how, I always felt able to access and connect with universal wisdom, healing and love. The point for which I want to argue is, if we are measuring and judging ourselves or others based on some sort of "who has what" or "who does what" value system, we aren't connecting to awe. It is impossible for judgment and awe to exist in the same space. They are polar opposites on the spiritual continuum.

My first experiences with awe and everyday miracles were sort of random, like the time I was in high school playing pool at the youth center. Of all the fun I had in high school, so much of it was located right there, at the Butler Lake warming house, used in cold winter months to thaw out the chunks of ice my feet became when I skated. It didn't matter, though. I stayed out there from the very minute I could get a ride until lights-out. Skimming across the clear and smooth, quickly frozen ice was always my favorite thing to do, because of course I loved the feel of frigid air on my face and going very fast. I didn't even mind falling when a big crack came up unexpectedly, because gliding fast through the biting cold felt so good, as the breath escaped my mouth in little bursts of vapor. I long for ice skating. Twenty degrees was the best temperature for skating, the radio blasting Steve Miller Band and Ringo Starr from the speakers on the light poles. I was sixteen, and so was Ringo's song. "You're sixteen, you're beautiful and you're mine."

The rest of the year the warming house was our youth center. It was several miles from my house. My girlfriends and I split a six-pack of beer as we walked there on weekend nights. Our tennis shoes squeaked in the dampness of spring lawns as the fragrance of newly budded trees and moist earth accompanied us. After we walked through the residential neighborhoods of century-old houses near downtown with large canopied trees overhead, we made our final turn along the lake. Coming across the grass between the road and the lake, we saw cars pull up outside the small, blue-grey building with white trim. In warmer weather, we played co-ed animal Frisbee on the lawn. Laughter and music escaped out into the night as the door opened and closed. The smell of freshly lit cigarettes greeted us as we grew closer, from older boys smoking across the street. There was a juke box, an air hockey machine and a pool table inside. The floor, sticky from spilled pop, sucked at the rubber soles of our shoes as we entered the room.

One night in particular, a friend wanted to play pool. I had never played pool before. There were these older boys we didn't know already playing. We had to challenge them and win to gain the table. None of the boys from our grade were there yet to make the challenge for us. I was not even the littlest bit interested in making such a prime ass of myself in front of those older boys, but my friend really wanted to play. With beer buoyed confidence, we challenged them. Never have I seen such patronizing smirks on the faces of men, before or after, not even in the movies, when they had to show me how to hold a pool cue.

My turn was fourth, after the first boy hit two balls in. My friend broke them up a little bit and the second boy didn't get any in, either. Once I got hold of that pool cue, it was like I couldn't miss! I hit two in on the first turn, banking some unbelievable shots, and three on the second! And since my friend had gotten a ball in one time, I sunk the eight ball my second shot in the third round! I was on fire! It was incredible!

We gained the table. My friend and I played, and we eventually lost the table as my expected inexperience finally shone through. Still, I was abuzz with an internal strumming of energy. WOW! That was amazing! How did THAT happen?

Wouldn't we all like to know the answer to that question?

I've had other incidences like that, usually playing a game against boys, like the time I creamed everyone at baseball pinball in Lake Geneva, Wisconsin, after never having played before, or the time I bowled a 173 in Fond du Lac, Wisconsin, having been basically a gutter ball queen prior to that occasion. I especially love bowling with my kids as we always ask for bumpers in the gutters.

I frankly don't think I am any different from anyone else. Maybe I have an aptitude for altered states, but if I have angels and spirits hovering over me, and periodically reaching through me to have some fun or to entertain or help me, I am certain everyone else does, too. What I also know is, the more I acknowledge and appreciate them in my life, the more I know they are there. Sometimes I know I grow too involved with the physical and material world and don't spend enough time checking in with the realm beyond my five senses. And usually the singular focus on the physical and material accompanies some sort of disorder or chaos in my life. It is only brought back into sync when I remember to connect spiritually.

Besides the time when the universe answered me when I asked why such bad things were happening to me when I was a single mother, I have experienced some amazing occurrences after asking for help out of desperation.

Mom and Dad were dedicated Unitarians. I know one of the precepts of Unitarianism is to have the faith of conscience—to commit to ideas and live them. And actually, if you really think about it, it is pretty hard to live your beliefs. Mom definitely believed that the buck stopped with her. There were no higher beings to give her solace in times of duress, and God was just something we humans had dreamed up to answer questions that one day would be explained by science. If she ever had a spiritual moment, she never shared it with me. She was also convinced that if she couldn't have a spiritual experience, no one else could have one either. So at our church, they examined the book, *I'm OK, You're OK* in sermons. For youth group the most popular course was, "About your sexuality." Mom was so disappointed the class filled before she got

around to signing me up, but I wasn't. I couldn't imagine anything worse than talking about sexuality with a bunch of kids I saw
once every two or three months. Another time in Sunday school,
an older girl brought her dog in that she had taught to count. It
was fascinating to hear how she had taught it finger cues, as we
stretched out on top of folding tables and leaned against metal
chairs as her patient beagle sat on the cool grey concrete floor.
That's what I was learning while my peers learned Bible stories.

It was a stunningly modern church. I loved the stone walls and
pebbled aggregate floors, where it wasn't concrete. The splashy
floral-shaped stained glass windows on the deeply sensuous circu-
lar walls were designed by a Guggenheim fellow. Inside the flower
petals of the windows were really cool images like rocket ships,
Roman columns and Prometheus.

Dad, my step father, a bit divergent from my mom, was a meditator and had rewarding experiences with altered states. Every
morning when I awakened for high school, there was Daddy, in
plaid boxer shorts, smelling of day-old Aramis cologne, sitting in
the lotus position on the short-napped, green wool living room
rug. He was such a dedicated spiritualist that when Mom insisted
our family become the embodiment of encounter groups, Daddy
had leverage to get us all trained in Transcendental Meditation.
Across the street from the most elegant shopping mall on the
North Shore of Chicago, we waited on mushroom velvet sofas
outside incense-filled bedrooms of the white suburban colonial
home. Next it would be one of our turns to receive a mantra we
were never to tell anyone.

While I loved going to Presbyterian Youth Group with my
friends, it was not easily tolerated by my parents. Once when I
returned home on a Sunday night and haltingly related how I
thought the energy in the room was charged with something bigger than just a room full of kids, Mom snorted and spun away from
the kitchen table in the avocado-green vinyl chair. Daddy started
singing, "Holy, holy, holy, Lord God almighty," and Mom joined in
derisively.

I didn't go to youth group again.

Another significant miracle experience I had in high school was the summer before my senior year. One of my class mates was having a kegger at her house, out on St Mary's Road. That's where homes with five-acre lots were, surrounded by gorgeous wooded areas. During the party, where my friends and I were drinking plenty of beer, the line to the port-a-potty was slung way around her very long driveway. I wasn't sure I could wait that long. Since there were lots of tall, fully leafed bushes lining the perimeter of the property, I found a secluded area, dropped trou and went. While I was going, a tree twig scraped my eye and dislodged my left contact lens, tumbling it onto the very dark and forested floor. I ran my fingers through the leaves and dirt several times, and found nothing. Shit!

Mom believed that vanity was something truly harmful. She later told me that when I was little, she and Daddy were afraid I would grow up to be too pretty and would never use my mind. In department store bathrooms, when other moms and daughters repaired their hair and makeup, she would make a moue of distaste. Those were "shallow" people. She often remarked if she thought I was spending too much time in the bathroom, or primping in front of the oval walnut mirror above the chipped blue-painted dresser, when I finally had my own room. I had a $25-a-month clothing allowance. I made most of my own clothes, because it wasn't even close to being enough money to be able to buy anything that was fashionable.

My contact lenses were certainly not a priority for my mom. I'd gotten them the summer after my freshman year in high school, just after visiting my grandparents. While I was swimming in their backyard pool with all my cousins and the neighbor kids, Granddaddy came out to visit with us during his lunch break, before returning to the mill. Abandoning the spirited game of shark to greet Granddaddy, I stood dripping on hot concrete in my prized purple bikini. He turned to Grandmother and said, "Look at Julie's beautiful eyes without her glasses. Let's buy her a pair of contact lenses." Later that night he wrote me a check for the whole amount. For two whole years I cherished and cared for those lenses like the lifeline to my existence they were. Just before the kegger, maybe only a week or two, Mom had been reminding me to pay the $15 insurance policy for my contact lenses. Of course, I hadn't done it.

Going home with only one contact lens received very little sympathy the morning after the kegger. I was totally bummed as I certainly didn't have the $100 to replace the lens. Oh man, going back to glasses my senior year in high school was about the worst thing I could imagine.

Unwilling to face such a horrible prospect without at least seeing if I could locate that contact lens in the daylight, I drove back out to St. Mary's Road, over and over reciting in my mind, "Oh, dear God, please help me." The car inclined toward the ditch as I parked it on the shoulder, across the street from where I thought the correct bushes might be.

Crossing the street, I mentally assessed where I had been standing the night before, in comparison to the house and the yard, looking for two bushes with a small tree situated just beyond them. It had rained the night before. The ground was damp with newly fallen leaves covering the area between the bushes. Picking a set of bushes that looked about right, I began sifting gently through the leaves. Still breathing the litany of prayers, I sifted through one layer of leaves and then another, with an aching jaw and a knot in my stomach. Then, after not very long at all, to my utter disbelief, there sat my contact lens, just to the side of a slender leaf mottled with yellow and lime green! Shining in the sunlight, there it was! It was an unbelievable moment! I began blubbering my elation, "Thank you! Thank you! Thank you!" I know I checked around me to see if I was really there, to make sure it had really happened. I was certain I had been rescued by an unknown force or energy, the manifestation of which was pure kindness.

Now when I have dreams about my eyes, which I do on occasion, as I work out problems and seek answers in my sleep, I hold them with tremendous reverence as I am sure they are a message from that kind source. I know there is something I am not seeing that can be considered from a different angle. There is a solution available, maybe even a miracle. And even when I am feeling desolate and scared, I know I live in a world where that kind energy exists and wishes me well.

After I met Claes, I knew him only a short while before I began to feel like Jane and Michael Banks in *Mary Poppins.* At the beginning of the Disney movie, the siblings read their list for the perfect nanny to their father. He tears up the list, as he considers it nonsense, and throws it in the fireplace. The viewer then sees the dour nannies Jane and Michael fearfully anticipated the next day, standing in line outside the Banks' house, waiting to be interviewed. They are suddenly whisked away by a strong wind. The wind swirls the torn pieces of paper up the chimney. Mary Poppins arrives at the front door, being ever so gently settled to the ground holding her parrot-headed umbrella. She reads Jane and Michael's pieced-back-together list to Mr. Banks, who knocks his head on the inside of the fireplace looking for the torn papers. Jane and Michael achieve everything they were looking for in a nanny, and more. That's how I felt when I met Claes—that he was everything on my list for a life companion, and more.

As soon as I learned about the idea of "intention" in that est seminar so long ago, I started practicing with it. Among many other lists and plans for the future, such as going to law school and furthering my career, I drew up a list for the perfect partner. Of course he needed to be good-looking and successful. But the quality I wanted most was something I knew I had, which was the ability to talk honestly about my mistakes and claim responsibility for them. On our second or third date, Claes told me a story about himself that wasn't altogether flattering and I knew he was THE ONE. He also adored my son and vice versa. Check, check, check, everything on the list was being met and more. Plus, he ice skates.

What I think is so funny in retrospect is that my therapist, Chloe, gave me his number in February that year. I called him five months later, in July. So when people tell me they are losing faith because their prayers aren't being answered, I ask, "Are you sure?"

I always think of intention as a sort of prayer: us working as co-creators with the universe to create events in our lives. I love those

2

manifestations! But I also love the divine miracles playing out for us that we haven't asked for: tree branches waving outside of windows, the crisp and fragrant insides of red bell peppers with their seed clusters and membranes, children laughing, the mallards returning to the pond the first week of April, and yes, five black Volvos. How many amazing and miraculous stories are unfolding around us all the time? How often do we remember to even notice them, let alone appreciate them? There are awe-worthy occasions all around us, all the time. What would our lives look like if we took cues from those miracles with any sort of serious consideration? I imagine the awe would consume us, as we consumed it. The hard part is getting ourselves into a place where we see awe everywhere, even when the circumstances seem terrible. It's a behavior worth cultivating.

Sometimes I like to take a break from my intentions and just observe what is happening around me to gather clues for my existence. I have to remind myself to use the words "possibility" and "allowing" while holding my judgments and fears away from me.

What is so attractive about judgment anyway? Why do we feel safer predicting an unsavory future for ourselves and others? Maybe we feel like it is easier to manifest doom, and the hardest thing to do after a setback is to come up with any kind of hope at all? Have you ever said to a child, "Watch out, you'll fall"? What happens next, they fall, right? Pretty easy manifestation. Every witness there saw we were right. Being right and being able to predict the future feels so good, we will sink to new lows to get there.

That's why I was persuaded that writing this book was a good idea. Because I know first hand that the universe is benevolent and adores us. We are ALL, no exceptions, its cherished and precious children. It's the reason I work in the field that I do, so I can help shape people's brains and behaviors around that knowledge. It really doesn't serve us to predict doom, when if we can learn to stretch just a little bit, we can connect with the space of miracles.

Does it mean that I will never know fear or never have an upsetting event in my life? No, not at all. What it means is I have absolute sureness that I am, and you are, unreservedly supported by divine love. And I do my best to live up to it.

Let me give an example of being in a rocky situation and having divine love as a resource. After my mother died in 1997, I had a need to reach out to my other family on my biological father's side. A distant cousin was getting married in the Southeast where that part of my family has long, deep roots. It was going to be a big wedding with hordes of people from all the branches, so I decided to go and take our two daughters with me. They were eight and three at the time. Our twelve-year-old son had a soccer tournament that weekend. Claes was the designated soccer chaperone/chauffeur and had to stay home. The one fly in the ointment was my biological father, Thorpe. I hadn't seen Thorpe for more than nine years—since he struck my son and refused to back down on his right to do so. I hadn't been in touch with him since my brother and I helped a young woman he was stalking pay for a restraining order. His demand for an apology before our relationship could resume was a comfortable way to maintain distance. He wasn't supposed to be at the wedding, but there was always a chance he'd show up because I was there with my girls.

I had been meditating for about a year when I left on that trip. As the plane climbed to its cruising altitude en route to Savannah, I closed my eyes and rested my head on the seat back. I opened my heart and mind and reached up to the layers of energy around me, melding my spirit with them while I prayed for safety and success in our trip. There's a protective energetic level available for us to combine ourselves with, not far above our heads. It is really useful in times when the potential for stress is high. To connect with it, I hold myself open for support and climb into that same support, simultaneously, as I did at that time. It takes a bit of focus and intention. It helps to be cleansed and centered so that it is easier to move around in the energetic layers without slogging a bunch of old stuff. It feels like being cradled. Every time some judgment or fear arises, it is then pre-programmed to lift into that space and disperse, with the barest shrug or glance of consciousness. The judgment and fear are allowed to leave and are held away from me, in abeyance, so I am not impacted by them.

After the raw and upsetting time of my mother's death, and the opportunity to have the relationship I longed for with her was no longer possible, being enveloped in that comforting realm of family gave me such solace. Did the threat of seeing my father and the potential for a scene with my girls help me attain that wonderful and special state? Probably. It's my goal to see challenges as a stepping stone to the next level of awareness and being, and to have faith that they are taking me to a better place.

The girls and I had a healing and transcendent time at the wedding, really deeply engaging with many warm family members at a beautiful resort in coastal Georgia. One magical evening as the sun set, dolphins swam into the Inter-Coastal waterway, as the waning light shone on their rubbery, grey heads, across the channel and the red-gold autumn marsh grasses. At the wedding, my older daughter danced every dance the band played, all by her self, with complete abandon, in her tailored cream chiffon and satin dress with matching patent leather shoes. My younger daughter and her newly met cousins played under banquet tables heavily laden with wedding linens and china, overlooking the sea.

Unexpectedly, Thorpe did show up at a luncheon the day before the wedding. I was talking to my cousin's husband, a retired Episcopal priest, when a shadow appeared to my upper left, blocking the sunlight shining through the clubhouse window. It was Thorpe. Of course my cousin's husband knew the potential for discomfort with the encounter. He steadily held me with his eyes the whole time Thorpe tried to engage with me. I felt his strong, devotional energy accompany mine as he drew me into the protected space I had opened on the plane trip. I was with the perfect person if the encounter was going to happen! Not only did he know the whole wretched scenario of Thorpe's unhappy life, he was a priest! He needed no cue cards about how best to direct our energy or what role he needed to play in helping me arrive in that prayerful and loving place. It was a zone of calm. It was a safe and insulated room, not quite in my being, but one I could access.

Reaching out and centering myself in that space kept Thorpe in the periphery of my attention where he remained threat free. It was amazing! Plus it was an inviolate space that rendered Thorpe powerless because he couldn't go there with us. He walked away. That's what it is like to confront a potentially damaging situation while in relationship with universal energy.

It was almost six months later, in March of 1998, when the spirits who first came to talk to me told me they were sorry it'd been hard for me, but they'd wanted me to stretch. When I slam into situations that scare me now, I always want to remember sooner rather than later to connect to unseen realms of energy and protection. But, because I am a human being, having a fully human experience, sometimes I forget to use all the resources available to me until it becomes abundantly clear I am totally stuck and not going anywhere until I do.

Interestingly, it was an additional nine months when the five black Volvos appeared in my rearview mirror, in December of 1998. When I decided I didn't really want to have contact with the spirits after all because it was too freaky, they set about courting me in ways guaranteed to get my attention. What I have since learned and feel confident sharing is that they will go to great lengths to have relationships with us. They know us more intimately than we know ourselves, and are unerring in their ability to pick the event that will enrapture and engage us.

Jesus starting appearing to me, again, after I gave him permission to do so. The feeling I grew to have about our relationship was very like the feeling I had with my priest cousin-in-law when he guided me to the space I had opened on the plane trip. I felt led and protected simultaneously. So when Jesus says, "Julia, we really want you to do this now," I am being drawn to a point of initiation. All I have to do is choose the new behavior and incorporate the action into my physical realm and it begins to unfold.

When Grandmother was still alive, I leaned heavily on her advice. After I was married to Claes and we struggled with my ex-husband about child support and visitation, she continued in her role as sage counselor. After sleepless, jaw clenched nights, I called her with my concerns. She asked, "Can you pray for an answer as you go to sleep tonight?" Sure enough, I could do that. Sure enough, I always felt as though the weight of whatever issue was plaguing me was somehow lighter or shifted when I awakened. Maybe a different perspective would appear that had an easier solution.

As infrequently as I desired contact with my ex, once I was on the phone with him in our second house in Lake Forest—the one with the cardinal on the roof. As I looked out the east kitchen window at the large maple, he was whining to me about how limiting his visitation was. Personally, every time our son visited him, we knew we were launching him on a trip to Pleasure Island, like the one in the Disney movie, *Pinocchio*. Desperate scenes of detox from relentless video games and Mountain Dew disrupted the balanced life we were keen on developing when he returned. The whining from my ex was incredible to me. He was victimized by us? Wow, think of that. Rather than jump down his throat about his lack of non-custodial support, I tucked that little tidbit of knowledge away and chose to feel satisfied with his portrayal of me, the avenging ex-wife. I decided I could own and occupy it. It was a hugely freeing moment. And I knew I wouldn't hesitate, when the opportunity occurred, to exercise that role.

I'm telling this story because I think it shows a behavior in me not normally attributed with the Christian way—especially the "ladylike always gentle, kind, and subservient to men" behavior somebody said we are supposed to cultivate. Just saying, the spirits talk to me anyway. And, while I don't subscribe to the whole Old Testament idea of "an eye for an eye," I do believe in reparations to create balance in relationships where transgressions have occurred. And Jesus has explicitly said to me, so does he.

One thing that totally fried me about my divorce, years later, was that my ex still owed me money from the divorce. I tell everyone so inclined to get a divorce in Wisconsin because darned if they didn't go to bat for me year after year collecting past child support across the country any way they could. I didn't even have to pursue it or waste any more sleepless nights over it. It happened over the course of time when their computer programs became sophisticated enough. But there was still settlement money from business and property I hadn't wanted to aggressively pursue after the divorce as I thought it would impact his relationship with my son–more trips to Pleasure Island and the like. Brown County, in Wisconsin, couldn't go after it for me unless I went back to court and procured a judgment against him. However, once my son had concluded his relationship with my ex on his own, the idea began to form in my brain. I could do it! I could go after that money. I could be the bitch of an ex wife who hired an attorney, went back and got the money she was owed almost 20 years later. There is no statute of limitations on capital crimes or divorce settlements. Luckily I still had bank statements, account information and cancelled checks which indicated I hadn't been paid what I was owed. Also luckily, I had been a paralegal and was successful in figuring out how to access old court documents and filings on fiche.

It was an enormously gratifying and empowering experience when the judgment was entered against my ex, and when he was finally required to pay what he owed me. I used it to help reduce the cost of my son's college education instead of going on the spa week I deserved by that point. I was both virtuous and empowered as I restored the personal boundaries that had been violated. No part of Christianity says we should let people or situations violate us regardless of gender roles. As far as we are able, we must never allow people to mistreat us. It isn't good for us and it isn't good for them. It was an important lesson for me in how to occupy and defend my own space. The ability to connect to and become a vessel for universal wisdom and divine love is not a namby-pamby thing. We have to have the ability to be stalwart in our devotion, yet light and wondrous enough to raise our energy to higher levels, while simultaneously allowing ourselves to be completely open to possibility.

When I see young women with eating disorders in my practice that's often what I sense is awry with them. Personal boundaries and identity. How do they occupy that space of self? We practice I AM statements, because when we say, "I AM" that is the exact time we become co-creators with the universe. It is when we are able to claim the space of being, which is our birthright. Once we have learned to fully occupy the space of self, it is easier to connect with the energies around us, such as the energies I call universal wisdom and divine love.

I always see the quibbling over world religions as a waste of time, as well as the ridiculous wrangling over specific words of each faith. Do they make sense? Are they in the service of love for ourselves as well as others? If yes, they are worth following. If no, the messenger delivering them isn't one to whom I will give attention. It's pretty clear to me that once you or I cue into universal wisdom through mystical pursuits, the differences become pretty inconsequential. At one point, somewhere between my move from Illinois to Colorado, I started to see world religions like this: there's this really big mountain, in a range like the Cascades on the Pacific coast. On the west side of the Cascades it is very wet and rainy. On the east side, it is desert. The clouds are trapped on the west side by the height of the mountains. The people on the rainy side of the mountain develop their belief system around having a very wet climate. They pray for safety from floods, mildew, rot and mosquitoes. The universal wisdom they receive helps them address those concerns. The people on the desert side of the mountain pray for safety from drought, intense heat and scorpions, as well as cracked and dry skin. The universal wisdom they receive helps them address those concerns. Neither people, from the dry or wet side, can conceive of what it means to live like the other. Their lifestyles and practices necessarily have to be very different, as does their orientation toward faith. But periodically a journeyer leaves either tribe, from the wet or the dry side, and makes their way to the top of the mountain. And you know what they learn at the top of the mountain? At the top of the mountain, whether one is from the wet or the dry side, the view is the same.

It is my conviction that Buddha in his infinite wisdom channeled universal wisdom in the way it best made sense to his side of the mountain. Jesus did the same thing for his side of the mountain. But it is the same ultimate truth and energy they describe. It is the same universal wisdom and divine love. It is simply shared through different messengers with different filters to address a different set of circumstances. Is one messenger more correct than the other? It's not a wager I would personally put money on.

About me and my messages. We all know my faith stems from a simple practice generated from an assortment of Presbyterian Sunday school lessons along with children's movies and TV shows. That's the side of the mountain I hang out on, the one where the children are. As I began to notice that many of the examples and metaphors for this writing originate in children's media, I had the warmth and smile of an "of course" moment. As old as I am, nearly mid-way through my fifth decade, I have always cherished and safe-guarded my proclivity for childlike awe. In a moment, I have the ability to suspend all doubt, and believe that a miracle is possible. It's a practice I live and enthusiastically recommend.

9

Cultivating Awe

I chose to connect to source…

The following are excerpted from the sessions where Jesus and I shared past lives that relate to **cultivating awe**. They are: **Chain Gang I**, **Chain Gang II** and **Roman Twins**. There is so much about the following **Chain Gang** sessions that continues to be instructive for me. As with **Abrum**, the story about the Jewish, Greek goat herd in Chapter 4, I go back and re-read them for personal guidance. While **Abrum** is significant for centering in challenging times, as he did in the time of drought, **Chain Gang I** and **II** are instructive because they help inform us about who we need to be while engaged with a group to maximize our personal experience. What I like about this lesson in **cultivating awe** is that it fully illustrates the idea that we only have complete control over how we choose to perceive a situation; we are never responsible for another person's perception of their experience. As long as we're making a choice, why not choose awe? When I am feeling particularly crabby or sorry for myself, I ask myself, "What's the lesson here? How is this taking me to awe? How can I lift my energy *right now* so that I can feel inspired?" Additionally, in **Chain Gang II**, we

213

learned that connecting to joy, regardless of the circumstance, is the most powerful energy on the planet.

The funny thing to me is while I channeled both Abrum in **Abrum**, and Claudius in **Chain Gang**, and was supposed to have been them both in previous lives, they each had a different outlook on humanity. On one hand, Abrum was very generous and through his filter I heard we should simply share with people when we have what they need. He felt people would understand and appreciate the significance of the gift when in desperate times; you share what you have. On the other hand, through the filter of Claudius, his military training was evident. When the messages came through him, he indicated that the proper expectation was to keep the bar high in interactions so that people rise to the occasion. I'm not sure the messages are mutually exclusive, but what interests me is the two of them are markedly different personalities with different points of view delivering the messages. But even in their differences, their goal is the same.

In the last story of the chapter, **Roman Twins**, pre-Mother Mary and pre-Jesus are twins who are learning to handle the largeness of the energy that develops when they are together. This is their lifetime immediately prior to the "culminating" life. The lessons answer the questions: When we experience awe, what's the best way to share that experience with other people? How do we introduce and allow others to connect to the energy of healing? How do we grow awe energy in groups?

Chain Gang I, 510 B.C.
Excerpted from Number 10, April 29-I, 2011

> Me: I have a linen cloth wrapped and tied around my feet, tied up with trusses. I am getting the sense that I'm a man. I have very heavy, ropey hairy arms. I have a thick head of hair with a beard. I have a tunic which is an olive color from many washings.
>
> Q: The cloth is worn.

Me: What's inconsistent for me is that I have this really muscular body. I'm not a beggar. I am somehow extremely physical. I might be a slave.

Q: Are you feeling what your job might be or what your purpose is?

Me: I feel like I have a whip that I carry. I also feel like I have chains around my neck. I am both slave and connected to people. It seems like I am connected to some kind of a slave gang. I also have responsibility for them. I have a whip to move them along with me. Many people are connected in this group. We travel together and we are chained together. I use the whip to get people to come along and to move with me. They are all very poor. I think I have been unjustly accused. Somehow I've been made responsible for this group. I think I am a captive from another army. You know how a conquering army captures warriors from the other places in the other countries?

Q: And make them their slaves.

Me: Right.

Q: Prisoners.

Me: I know I am not with my men from the army. I'm with some other prisoners. I see people on horseback. They think it's amusing that I've been brought to the level where I'm chained with these other prisoners. I'm responsible for getting them somewhere.

Q: Do you know what the time and place is?

Me: I feel like I'm in the northern part of Africa maybe Tunisia. The conquering group is on horseback. They have gorgeous uniforms with breast plates and colorful feathers in the helmets. They think it is very amusing they have put me in this position and are bringing me low. I am OK with it. I'm not using my whip. I want to be an inspiration to these people whom they have charged me with. I want to make sure they get where they are going.

Q: Do you have a sense of what position you may have held before you were captured?

Me: I was a platoon leader. I think I had a horse. My soldiers did not. They carried spears and walked. I was ambushed when I was sleeping. I was captured in the dead of the night and taken out of camp. They think it's very amusing to chain me with this group of beggars. I think I have been good with my men. I'm legendary in some way. I'm a good motivational leader. Now my captors are saying to me, "OK, you're with these beggars. How well will you do now?"

Q: Can you tell the time frame?

Me: 510 B.C. I'm taking this conscientiously. It's an opportunity to see if I can motivate these beggar people. I want to see, too, if I can instill them with enough confidence and will to live. They are poor and some of them are missing teeth. They don't have the right footwear for this journey. In my heart, I want them to live and succeed because I am a dynamic leader. I am legitimately a good motivational person. I take it as a challenge to see if I can indeed deliver them to the place we're going, safely, with renewed confidence, with restored health. I'm taking it as an opportunity to transform the way that they carry their energy. What I learn is that it is a big responsibility to carry these men. While I also suffer in hot weather over long miles, I am an amazing physical specimen. But to carry them, too, I just can't do it. I can't encompass them in healing light, and create a strong group. What I do during the journey is to work to engage them so that we create a joint source of energy. The learning is that I can't simply bestow this on them. You know what I'm saying? I can't just do a group healing. It's too much for me to suddenly transform them. I have a Lancelot complex. Before I was captured, I thought I was a good motivational leader. I did do amazing things. I had this puffery and arrogance that I could do just about anything. What I had was troops who were well-fed and were intelligent. We had good resources. What I'm learning is that our success wasn't all because of me.

My lesson here is to honestly tap into the hearts of men. I see myself making chest-to-chest connections with their energy. Even though the men in the chain gang are broken, we create a heart-to-heart relationship. We create a new energy field. I have to do it with them. I can't just do it to them. I have to gain their trust so that they will allow me into their heart energy field.

Q: More of a collective.

Me: Yes, definitely a collective energy source. It's also an ego lesson. I learned it isn't just about me, I learned my previous troops kind of indulged me, tongue-in-cheek. They thought I was a funny and extreme character who was a vain narcissist. They liked me anyway and indulged me in feeling that way. So what the lesson was in that lifetime, you can achieve amazing things if you can connect to the hearts of men. You have to make that connection.

I'm seeing these layers of universal energy. Charismatic people, such as religious or political leaders, are able to connect with different layers of energy that allow them to connect with the hearts of people.

They think it's because of them personally. They do have charisma. It's a personality trait that is a key to the layer of energy. This level of energy is an ability to connect with hearts.

Q: It almost sounds like you need the charisma to get to that point. And the lesson needing to be learned is that it is not you. The lesson is that you are to let that self go and become part of the collective.

Me: Right, not everybody has a charisma piece. In this life, I haven't wanted charisma. It seems like too much responsibility for other people. I understand that if I connected to people's hearts like that, then I somehow take responsibility for the collective. What a lot of people who have charisma don't understand is, once they connect to those hearts, they have some responsibility for the collective. People struggle with, "Why am I not charismatic? Why am I not an effective leader?" And then they work to be an effective leader. I don't know that I have the right kind of boundaries for that.

Q: In this Julia life.

Me: In this Julia life. What I'm getting is men are often better at this because they more easily resonate with the layer of charisma energy. Women feel more responsibility for other people's lives because they have that emotional permeability.

Q: So if we can go back to the life, where you were a captured warrior, is Jesus with you?

Me: Yes, he's one of the beggars in the group. He is the one who is particularly vulnerable. He is the one that I have to struggle with the most, learning about boundaries, and trying not to carry him too much. He tests every thing. The minute I think I've got the group going, he melts. "I don't think I can do it. I want you to hold me." He is the group energy sponge. He's really challenging me.

Chain Gang II, 510 B.C.
Excerpted from Number 23, August 4, 2011

Me: I have on a toga and I am getting the sense that I am the fellow in the Chain Gang life. It's a retrospective. I see what happened. I am in the desert and I am very content. I had been quite a successful army leader, and then I was captured from my camp at night. I'm in Tunisia. We had to walk quite a distance across the desert and I am connected to seven other people. Pre-Jesus is in the center of it.

They are saying when you are an inspired leader you are connected with the awe in yourself. This comes from being cleansed, being centered, having structure, and having every moment be a miracle. When you are in a space of allow-ing and possibility, everything seems awesome, everything seems inspiring. You aren't responsible for changing the heart of someone else. Because you can never control how they will interpret something because of their experience.

I did have this question. What does it mean to connect to the hearts of men and women? Are we responsible for what comes out of their hearts?

"Absolutely not," is the answer. You're never responsible for someone else's experience or impression because that is their own personal bailiwick; it's their own personal venue. When the spirits talk about connecting to the hearts of men and women, it's always with the idea that we need to be coming from awe and inspiration within ourselves. When we come from the place of awe and inspiration, we will make a connection. We are not responsible for how people receive it. We are responsible only for our experience and delivery. That when we are acting out of it, it is coming from the honest place of inspiration. It's from feeling like life is a miracle.

I guess my name is Claudius. What I eventually came to in that life was that I couldn't control the limp noodle that pre-Jesus was, in the middle of the chain gang. I could berate him, I could pump him up, and I could show him. There were all these other things I tried to get him, the whiner that Jesus was, to stand up and walk so that everyone didn't have to carry him. In doing that, I gave away too much of my energy because I was sending it out trying to create a change. Instead, I learned the energy was better served finding awe and inspiration in myself and acting out of that. It was better to wake up each day and say, "It's a magnificent day. I feel thirsty. My tongue doesn't move in my mouth. It is so dry. My lips are cracked and my skin is so sunburned that I can't feel it any more. I still feel awe. I still feel connected to the universe and lucky to be alive. With each step I take, as my foot binding comes off and as the fellows on horse- and camelback jeer at us as we go along, I feel so inspired. I feel so lucky. I am so happy to be who I am in this moment." I stand so straight, because I have let go of the pompousness and arrogance and "I am so special" piece. I have stepped into, "I love my life, I love who I am." I have a very focused, centered, cleansed and grounded perspective on this. I have no judgment of the fellows around me. I am finally to the point where I don't even check in with the pre-Jesus limp noodle in the middle because he is an energy sponge. I hold myself strong and erect and feel honored and blessed to be alive.

It's one of those things where if you feel awe and inspiration, you don't have to say it because it radiates off your skin. You have found the portals in the air where you are moving with the flow. You feel exquisite every single moment. It is taking ownership of it yourself. It is being the co-creator of that identity. It isn't something that is bestowed on you by universal energy, or that you need permission for. It's claiming your birthright to feel inspiration and awe. It is energy you can reach up and grab. There's a difference. Is it clear?

Q: It's very clear. I needed to hear that. I was having a light bulb moment. It makes total sense.

Me: I'm getting that too. Yes absolutely, we get too wrapped up in what is going on with other people. Then we forget to claim our own space.

Q: Exactly.

Me: It isn't about being bestowed anything. It is always a choice that we are making in every moment. To choose to feel awe and choose to feel inspired. It is the point we always want to reach regardless of the circumstance. Absolutely, they are saying to me, when you are standing in the grocery store and feeling frustrated, yes, you can then take it to the next step and say, "In this moment, I am supposed to be here, and isn't it a wonderful place to be?" That's the next step. "I am so happy to be exactly where I am."

Q: Gratitude fits in there, right?

Me: Yes, it is gratitude, and it is more than gratitude, because gratitude and blessed are sort of the same limited relationship. "I have been blessed. I am grateful for how I have been blessed." The universe gave you something and you are so happy the universe gave you something. It's beyond gratitude and being blessed because it is claiming ownership. Gratitude also had the implication, "I have been given something." Instead, this is something I have taken. It is a space I have claimed for myself. I am grateful to have the opportunity to do it, yet it is also the part where I become a co-creator, and I accept responsibility for being exactly where I am in that moment. I have had people say to me, "Oh, aren't we so blessed to see" this or that? Or, "It is God's will." And yes, my personal Julia issue with religion is, people use it as such an excuse for their behavior. I always want to say, "Wait a minute. You are here. You are having this experience. You are making all of these choices, yet you want to say that the universe did this to you?"

Q: Sure.

Me: So that's what they are saying. It is the point of being a stakeholder. It is a co-creation. It is taking ownership. It is beyond the gratitude part. It is beyond the humility part. And it is OK, because it is the part where you are coming from pure awe and inspiration. So what happened was, one day I, as Claudius, woke up and said, "I am so blasted tired of this. I am stuck with seven other people. I am in charge of getting them across this God-forsaken desert, how am I ever going to do that?" And then the universe opened up for me and said, "Don't. Just be who you are. Just enjoy who you are." All the tension melted away. I had an awakening as the dawn came and the sun rose. I first awoke with an experience of dread, "Another day where I have to work my energy around these people. This is my posse. I have to be this person who motivates..." and then I got it.

It was like an egg broke open in my head. I am seeing this wonderful cartoon-ish, peacock-ish bird come out of it. It is so multicolored. Peacocks are exquisite birds. They make you happy just looking at them. Peacocks kind of have an attitude. You don't really mess with a peacock. A peacock is inspirational because it is such a beautiful creation. But you don't get the impression that a peacock is bowed over in gratitude (laughter).

Q: Right. They are feisty.

Me: It's about having and claiming your right to joy regardless of the circumstances. Regardless of what else is happening in your life, regardless of who is surrounding you, once you connect with joy, it is the most powerful energy on the planet. Kat was asking, "What IS the most powerful thing?" I always hesitate to use the word power, but they are saying connection with joy, awe, and inspiration is the most powerful thing on the planet.

Q: Wow.

Me: How about it?

Is there another lesson? I guess the rest of the story with Claudius is, he ends up in a market place and everyone arrives safely and alive. Not everyone is happy or especially joyful, but he is. He has finally understood something so important. Always before, he needed for people to admire him. Always before, he was kind of into the puffery, "I am so amazing."

Q: More of the ego piece.

Me: Right, the ego piece. Now he is so happy to be in his own skin. He gets auctioned and is a slave, but ends up in a very nice position as a head houseman in Egypt. He really loves it!

Q: He found the key to happiness.

Me: Yes. That he could simply be happy for another day. He could be happy to feel the sun on his face, he could hear the moans of the men around him as he crossed the desert, and he was OK with it. He came from the place of, "I am joyful in my own experience. I am not worrying about yours." And that was the most powerful thing. It was the best thing he could have done. It was the energy that carried them all, then. Huh.

Q: That's amazing.

Me: I know, isn't it? Claudius lived this lovely life in Egypt. He actually became inspirational for young men. He was never in charge of a military group again, but he ran the household staff and because he had found joy, it was easier for him to connect others to it, too.

Q: It's like almost you have a beacon of light, people are attracted.

Me: Right. It is like seeing a picture. Because they had the experience of his joy, they were able to understand how to get there themselves.

Q: Recreating it.

Me: Right. And it's a choice we make. How interesting. Jesus is saying Claudius liked his Egyptian life so much better that he never connected back with his more "civilized and affluent" Roman family. He just liked who he was. It relates back to the idea where we were talking about being in the flow. He was so happy to be in that moment that he couldn't bring himself to go back and wrap himself around the superficial life he had experienced before.

Roman Twins, 50 B.C.
Excerpted from Number 19, June 11, 2011

Me: Walking through the door, closing it behind me, looking down at my feet, I have brown sandals and hairy legs. I am a man. I have on short skirts. I have dark hair cut to my chin, and bangs. I am looking pretty affluent. I have a red cape. It's off my left shoulder and sometimes I have a military uniform with a full skirt, breast plate and a helmet with a bright yellow feather at the top. Right now I am simply dressed in a finely woven robe of wool. It's very simple and I still have this red cape coming off my left shoulder.

Q: When is this?

Me: 50 B.C.

Q: What is your name?

Me: I am Roman. My name is Nero.

Q: Can you tell us about your life?

Me: I live in Rome. I have a secret or a connection. I have something burgeoning out of me, like a wisdom or knowledge. I have a spring in my step. I feel optimistic and connected to the part of the Mediterranean around Israel. I feel like somehow I know that Jesus is coming. I don't know why, but I know he's coming and I feel excited about that. I have a lyre. Isn't that like a little harp?

Q: Yes.

Me: (Laughter) Am I in the clouds, you guys? Am I like the angel Nero? I spend a lot of time in altered states. I live near a temple in Rome. I live in a vast, palatial marble home. I do play the lyre. I don't know why, but I think because I spend so much time in altered states, I know there is something in the air that augurs for greatness. I am a statesman. I used to be a general. I had a black horse with a white breast and one white stocking in the front left leg. His name was Buttercup. How cute is that, a stallion named Buttercup? I have family. I have a lovely, beautiful wife. We are not very emotionally connected. She married me for my status and I married her so I could have good-looking children. She's kind of vain. I have cute, little roly-poly blond children. I think they are twins, one boy and one girl. What I am getting is, these twins are going to be the Mother Mary and Jesus in a little while, when it comes time for that.

Q: How old are you?

Me: Forty eight. I am not a particularly good looking man. I am kind of tall and slim built. I have a big nose. It is not only deep, it is also wide. I have blue eyes. I am really, really spiritually, emotionally, and intellectually connected. I have a facility with knowledge and wisdom. I am good at presenting succinct information. I am so happy. I recognize these children when they are born. I know they are such a gift. Since one is a boy and one is a girl, they are not identical, but they almost are. They do the twin thing where they have their own language. When they learn to speak regular language they complete each other's sentences. As they grow, everyone is so happy to be with them. I feel like my great accomplishment is in having these children. Their mother is always a little dim. She doesn't ever really get it, but she really enjoys these children. When the twins enter a room, they are surrounded in light. When they are together it seems like light fills the room. If one is by themselves you can see the light around them individually, but if they are together, the light entirely fills the room. They have an understanding of that. It's an interesting demeanor because it is an understanding that they are the light bodies and they accept it. They know it is their definition. They already know how to separate themselves from their greatness. It always follows.

Q: It's part of who they are...

Me: ...and they have an interesting awareness of it. It's like someone who is born wealthy, they just know. They have confidence in that. They don't sweat the small stuff. They know it's all handled. Yes, we do have some wealth, but that's not what provides them with this amazing confidence. It's that they know they are light bodies. Many people get information about who they are by how people respond to them. They have that reinforcement, and they also have this

226

knowing they are light bodies. They know when they are together, they fill a room with light. It's a cool thing that they do. In this life, Mother Mary as the girl twin has charisma, and she is able to be bigger than life. I think it is because she has a male counterpart in her brother, where the light does a winding thing. Like a twisting rubber band, the two of them together create this incredible amount of light. Of course they learn to read right away, and are just so bright and love animals. If they weren't so fun to be with it would be nauseating, because they are good at everything. It isn't nauseating because there's an inside gurgle people get from being in their presence. It helps people know there is reason to be optimistic and filled with hope simply because this energy exists. People around them can feel it, right in the middle of themselves, like a gurgling. That auguring feeling I was talking about earlier, it is the gurgling feeling from knowing one day joy will shine from every part of your being.

Q: Not only does that impact their dad, but everyone else?

Me: Yes. You see people who are so wonderful and talented and then you get tired of them because even if they aren't egotistical, it is still always all about them. Because no one ever can measure up to how wonderful they are. Somehow this is different. Somehow these two kids have that ability to immediately connect. The immediate connection happens in the stomach area, where there is buoyancy everyone feels. They have a tremendous sense of humor, everything is in good fun.

Q: They make it better.

Me: Yes, everything is light around them and yes, they make everything better. So instead of everyone thinking, "Oh my gosh, here come those nauseating twins of Nero's," people think, "Oh, here they come, it's going to be blast. It's going to be so fun now!" There is an anticipation that it is going to be magnificent. It's going to be the most fun you ever had. They are really good at it. And again, they aren't overwhelmingly attractive. They end up having medium, sun-streaked blond hair. It's kind of like Mother Mary was in the culminating life. They are physically attractive and they have regular features. If they lived today, they could take a bad picture, where their noses were too big. It isn't their physical beauty that is so appealing. It's the sense of fun and excitement when they arrive. The room starts to buzz and light up when they come into a room. I feel very worthwhile, like I have done this amazing thing, by providing these children.

They are in this life to get used to carrying energy together because it has been a while since the two of them were together in the same lifetime. We haven't gotten Mother Mary's previous lives. I know she was in Brittany and in the original cave, but I am not sure where else she has been. She is definitely in this one. It is a practice life for how to handle the energy. I am seeing women in hoop skirts. Women in hoop skirts had to learn how to walk sideways through a door. Then they had to learn to do it gracefully so that everyone didn't see their…

Q: …underpants.

Me: …pantaloons under their dress. It is the same thing. They have enormous energy that comes when they are together. They need to learn to manage that. Really, that's what their life is about. They have the regular childhood illnesses. I'm seeing that someone's little pet died. I'm seeing that the pre-Mother Mary had a little lamb. (Laughter) You guys are too funny, had a little lamb! (Laughter) They are just seeing if we are paying attention.

Q: What kinds of lessons do they learn?

Me: That's what they learn, how to handle their energy. There is a spotlight that follows them everywhere. They learn how to pull it in, how to let it out, how to multiply and increase it with each other. They are saying you can do this by yourself. It is an individual activity where you build energy. That's one of the reasons for the enclosure, so that you can build the tension with the energy bouncing off your enclosure every time. The light bounces and comes back. It creates more energy. What they are saying is there is an even greater exponential factor when there are two or more people doing it. Mother Mary and Jesus in this "twins" life were learning to do it together. And they are saying to me this energy is amazing in its healing potential. They are saying when Jesus was most potent as a healer he had just spent deep time with his mother, in the culminating lifetime. When he could direct the light deeply into people's souls to heal them, when he could heal (snap) in a heart beat, he had just been with his mother in a deep, energy-building process. He could heal by himself, but the two of them together were always magnificent.

The lesson is we all can learn to do it. It's the whole idea behind showing up at church with positive energy. Generally people are well-intentioned at church. If you show up with anticipation and a joyful feeling, and then you start bouncing it off other like—minded people, it can turn into a hot potato game. If you stand in a circle and imagine a light glowing from inside of yourself, it can become a light game where you toss it back and forth, creating an amazing environment. A good thing to do with a group is walk in and look at each other and imagine the light bouncing among each other from the solar plexus. Of course you feel ridiculous and that makes it better. It makes it feel kind of wildly dangerous in a little way. Just hanging out with being ridiculous is a very free feeling. Sometimes you can feel it in the backs of your knees or the insides of your elbows. Sometimes you have an elevator stomach. They are saying to me this is another reason I am good for this job of messenger. I don't mind a little bit of feeling ridiculous. I think it is kind of fun. It's a little daring

Q: Dangerous but entertaining?

Me: Yes. Entertaining and completely engaged. A little bit of danger and ridiculous. It's not doing anything too bad. It harkens back to the life where Jesus and I were bandits, because we didn't think what we were doing was bad. We just thought it was a lark. You do initially feel ridiculous when you see someone noticing you exchanging stomach energy. They are saying it is meant to be entertaining.

Q: Is the word ridiculous used because we want to break down the wall or the armor between ourselves?

Me: Absolutely. Absolutely! There's a huge amount of freedom in having a willingness to make an ass out of yourself, knowing you are going to be the fall guy and that people can give you holy hell, for being stupid, ridiculous or asinine. In this Julia life, I never minded being the idiot in the classroom who said the wild thing that made everyone laugh. Even though I would say wildly stupid things, no body ever thought I was dumb. It's always nice when there is someone willing to be a risk taker and is willing to engage on that level.

I'll tell you who is here today. Peter is here, Mother Mary is here, Jesus is here and they are happy to see you! They are sitting in a triangle over there. Peter is wearing white, Mother Mary is wearing periwinkle blue and Jesus is wearing red today.

Q: Like they are posing for a picture.

Me: Yes, they look really cute. It's not quite the same colors as the American flag.

Q: We were talking earlier about single versus multiple sources of energy. I think I just heard both are good, but with more people, the energy is exponentially larger.

Me: Yes. You can be conscious of shapes, too. If there are five of you, you can think of being a five-pointed star with each being a point. Or if there are six, then it can be the Star of David. And it's more than flat. It can be three-dimensional. If you have an intention with multiple people, design a dome of containment over the group. Then stand around a room in corners doing the hot potato game, and the energy will rise. It's like fireworks that come up and around the inside of an envisioned dome.

Oh, and yes, Jesus did it with the apostles.

Q: It sounds like not only is it the hot potato game but it is weaving energies.

Me: Yes. It's weaving the energy.

If you really want to build joy, if you have a whole group it's like letting everybody in on the secret. What they are saying is it gives the same feeling as an orchestra or a choir, where everyone is participating and sharing energy together. You know how music lightens energy that way? It's the same mechanism, they are saying. One instrument by itself is lovely and beautiful and resonates, but multiple instruments give such reach and expansion for the energy. The ensemble piece is fun, because the joke is on you and the people you are doing it with.

Q: All enjoying the joke together. Going forward in the life, how does it play out with the twin souls?

Me: The pre-Mother Mary has a fever and she dies, she needs to check out.

Q: How old is she when she dies?

Me: 20 or 30, closer to 20.

Q: A young woman.

Me: Yes, a young woman. She has a mysterious fever that no one else gets. She, and her brother and I know she needs to check out early to prepare for her life as Jesus' mother.

Q: So this is the life directly before...

Me: Yes, and I think we have an awareness that she is planning to be born into the family of David. I think we know that. As Nero I knew it was happening in the area of Israel, specifically Jerusalem. I don't have the light like she does, so when pre-Jesus and I walk into the room, we don't light it on fire in quite the same way. We feel like something is missing, but we are able to be joyful and be connected to her anyway. I'm getting that her name in this life is Olivia.

Q: In the Roman Twins life?

Me: Yes.

Q: So what else did we need to learn in this life?

Me: They were traveling, where they went around to hospitals to help people on their way to healing. They wouldn't heal a room full of people, but when they entered a room, they started the healing because the energy was raised. Any time you raise energy, healing begins. It was sort of like a jump start, giving a push on the swing, pulling the cord on the lawn mower, just getting it going. Until you make that connection inside yourself, you don't know what it feels like. When they walked into a room, the connection between their mind/body/spirits felt like chortling joy, is what they are saying to me. What they have said to me before is Jesus, in the culminating life, connected with perfection and expanded it when he healed people. It was an exponential expansion. He did a winding process in this earlier lifetime with his mother, when she was his twin and they built fabulous energy together. It was another way to create the exponential expansion of energy. They are saying to me it is the beginning of healing. Building energy is the most basic step of healing. Before you personally understand how it works, it helps to experience it, and then there is a knowing. They are saying you then have a knowing and can repeat it.

Q: So the twins would basically come in and show...

Me: How it felt...

Q: Shine the light on the spot.

Me: Yes. That's a good way to put it, shining the light on the spot, identifying the spot. (Snapping) It was like lighting the kindling, starting the fire, where with the little girl in Innsbruck, it is the same spark. It also relates to the cup at the Last Supper, the spark inside of you, and drinking.

This does relate to the water ritual and that's why sharing a drink with people, making a toast, builds the same...

Q: Connectedness.

Me: They are saying absolutely sharing a toast is as important as a prayer before a meal. It builds energy. It literally does, doesn't it, because you are putting all the glasses together to create energy? They are saying it is sometimes even more valid than prayer before a meal because gratitude is great, but building that energy is so wonderful.

Q: Connections...

Me: Yes, anything that builds connections is worthy in the same way, because it always has the opportunity to build energy exponentially. Where the sum of the parts is far greater than the whole.

Q: It builds upon itself.

Me: Yes.

Q: So we were talking earlier about a procession of rituals, or a bunch of rituals that produce the same thing, and you do which ever one resonates for you?

Me: Every one of the elements is capable of performing the cleansing process. A cleansing process needs to occur before growth begins, so that's the place to start. Any of the elements is useful for cleansing. It depends what you are in the mood for and what you have on hand. If you are near the ocean, and can allow yourself to be buoyant in the ocean and to envision all of your angst being swept away. If you are in the middle of bad weather you can allow weather, the wind or pelting rain to penetrate into your spirit.

Q: Does anything come first?

Me: Cleansing, and you can use any of the elements to do that. If you don't light yourself on fire, go ahead and use passion.

Q: What I think of is how they burn the field before they plant the crops.

I think that is all of the questions. Thanking everyone for being here.

10

Passion

And am free in the wind.

Passion is what is possible. It's where the fervent desire to connect with the universe turns into a joy so big it breaks through all that would contain it. Sometimes, when passion isn't well-enough centered or hasn't had the benefit of devotion, it can seriously go awry. This is what happened in the **Bandits** life.

Ute Brothers follows **Bandits** and is passion in its purest form.

These next two lives were channeled nearly back-to-back. They each left a huge impression on me in different ways. After I came out of the trance for **Bandits**, I was very sad. I was haunted by the horrifying images, but also I felt like I had let a really good friend down. I felt deep loss and pain for my comrade with his death. When I know I need to go back to the crucifixion scene to ask a question, I gird myself prior to the experience. It's never easy, either. In some ways it is helpful to know the outcome ahead of time. I know it's going to be hard and I prepare myself for it. The remorse with **Bandits** was a complete surprise and very intense.

Still, **Bandits** is an important lesson and needs telling. It reminds me of infatuated love, which also isn't grounded. In 2011,

237

the "Dougherty Gang" siblings started a crime spree in the Southeast and then engaged in high speed car racing with the authorities until they were apprehended in Colorado. Photographed in court, Lee-Grace Dougherty was on the front page of the *Denver Post* with her hair swinging wide and a huge smile on her face. The elation on her face reminded me of the initial elation I felt in **Bandits.** It was wild and dangerous. I felt intoxicated with excitement.

At the end of **Bandits** is the discussion about why children die, as well as an initial discussion on the meaning of forgiveness.

The day after the **Bandits** session, I received the **Ute Brothers** life. It contained the same elation as **Bandits** in a similar male bonding relationship, with the benefit of being centered in the air element. It had a vastly different outcome. While I was channeling **Ute Brothers**, the Christopher Cross song, *Ride like the Wind* was playing in the back ground of my mind's eye—or perhaps in that case it was "mind's ear." (*I've got to ride, Ride like the wind, To be free again.*)

Another interesting detail about **Ute Brothers** is that the Jesus soul appeared A.D., after the "culminating" life. My impression was that while he was expressing and living in a very high level of energy, he was also off duty from his job as exalted being. It was a perfectly self indulgent life. He was not healing anyone, except perhaps himself.

Bandits, 100 B.C.
Excerpted from Number 13, May 1-I, 2011

> Me: I have clown shoes on. (Laughing) it's going to be a funny day. I hope I make it down the stairs. OK.
>
> I keep seeing this Tarot card in my deck. I think it is Daedalus. (It's the Five of Pentacles in the Mythic Tarot deck.) He's going out in the dead of the night and leaving the village. I'm so attracted to that card. I feel like I am having a life like that. I have a brown robe on with a hood. I have a dark beard and am coming up some stairs from a cellar. I have on rope

sandals. I am a slim man. I am furtive. I have had moments of desperation in my life. I think this is the life where we were bandits together! Oh, I have had moments of secretiveness and I am coming out of that. I am living a life like a monk, but I am not a monk. I am living in a cellar cell of a place. I have given up the pursuit of worldly possessions. This is the life where Jesus and I, as young men, were bandits.

Q: Prior to giving up your worldly goods.

Me: Yes, and we had just a blast! I love books with masked highwaymen. We had such a blast being on the empty roads at night and would ambush these fat, drunk wealthy men. We would take all of their money. We thought it was hilarious, just hilarious. I think I got caught and thought better of it and I don't know how...I have both my hands. Maybe I knew someone. I'm seeing that I knew someone, and the person that Jesus was, didn't know someone. He was then flayed.

Q: He knew someone?

Me: I knew someone. I made it through OK. Jesus did not have the same connections I did. He was killed.

Q: Oh.

Me: As a bandit. And it wasn't so funny anymore. So I gave it up and I just lived very simply, with extreme guilt for that lifetime.

Q: Are you seeing what the lesson is?

Me: Well, I think the thing that I learned was that I would much prefer to go down with the ship. Being the survivor isn't worth it, really. I didn't ask for the connection where

I was rescued. I could have said, "I'm staying with him. Whatever punishment he gets, I get too." And I didn't have the strength to do that. Instead I lived with that guilt for the rest of my life (tearful). And I would have preferred to die with him.

Q: If you had the chance again.

Me: If I had the chance again. But it was an exercise in strength for me. It was practice for what I would soon go through, when he died again, and I would have to live again through the pain of that. I didn't have guilt from feeling responsible for his death when he was crucified. I still needed the strength to live out that life after I had to watch him die. There were other people who were hysterical when he was crucified and I wasn't allowed that luxury. In the Bandit life, when I was rescued and he was tortured and flayed, its purpose was for me to build the emotional strength to have the crucifixion life shortly afterward. It was maybe 100 years later.

In the Bandit life I had family money. I had connections. After he was killed, I lived in a cellar, in prayer, for the rest of my life. We developed a relationship after he died. He would come to me and say, "Oh, you didn't have a choice." I knew I had a choice. By then we knew about life lessons. Somehow I knew this was a lesson I had to have. He was fun, he was SO FUN! He was that dangerous, irresistible friend. I was more cautious. When he came back to me after he died, he said, "You know, I persuaded you." Because he was the light body, he was incredibly attractive and persuasive. He was not well-connected in that life. I would have done anything to be with him. We robbed my parents' friends, who didn't recognize me, who were so drunk. It was a lark. A fun, boy's lark. And we never took anything they couldn't afford. We gave the money to orphanages. When we were caught, by one of my parents' friends, they didn't think it was so funny. They were full of puffery about that. "Who do you think you are, you young punks?" It was a cruel world in those days. You didn't get to survive THAT. He was flayed. They skinned him.

Me: They quartered the skin on his body then peeled it off while he was alive. I'm seeing it and I don't really want to.

That survivor's guilt, oh, my God, that's an awful thing. We all have burdens to bear. With the way the world is set up now, we all have those burdens to bear. At some point perhaps we can shift out of this cruelty mode without having these desperately horrendous lessons to learn, but we have to shift into a different way to be. It's not a mentality; it's a way of being. We have to learn compassion. And it's enough of us going through that who say: "ENOUGH, ENOUGH, ENOUGH."

Q: Going through the many lives?

Me: Having to carry those burdens. The point of carrying the burden is to learn to set it aside. Nobody can be Atlas. But the point isn't to be Ayn Rand either, and shirk responsibility for the energy on the planet. The point is to learn grace, to be graceful and kind under pressure and extreme hardship. Then we learn to persevere. To understand that sometimes people get into circumstances where they couldn't foresee the consequences. And to understand that yes, there's a lesson to be learned, but these are human beings or whatever animal or plant they are.

They all deserve grace. That God is there to provide universal wisdom. It is there to teach us about grace. They have sadness that we don't understand any other way. It isn't about them being stern taskmasters. OK, someone asked me the question last night, "Why do children die?"

Q: They did.

Me: OK, here's the answer. It is because it's the only way we get the message. They don't want us to have to learn it this way, but we only learn grace under huge burden. They would like us to shift out of that type of learning experience. They prefer that we not have little girls who are forced into prostitution at thirteen. They prefer that we not have little boys in Africa forced to work in the chocolate factories, who are slaves from another country. They prefer that we not have electronics made in China where the poison escapes and people are injured. They prefer that we learn better than that. It is their preference that we choose to be higher beings and we get it. They will hold our hands until we learn that lesson. They haven't abandoned us and they haven't abdicated their responsibility for us. As parents, as kind shepherds of this human lifestyle, they understand that's the only way we have yet been able to learn that lesson.

Q: Through burden.

Me: Having tremendous pressure, where we go through these awful experiences, because it's the only way we can find true kindness, compassion and grace. Like with my first marriage, I was a little sloppy. I was a little enabling. It taught me to run a tighter ship. It taught me to be more discerning in my values.

In the Bible, they talk about you just give and give and give—everything you just give away. And men understand forgiveness in an entirely different way than women do. When they have an abusive husband, women sometimes feel forgiveness means and yet again they must let that man

back in to their lives, and give him the opportunity to be better if he can. They think forgiveness means they always must
give them the opportunity. That's not true. And that has been
my issue about the way people interpret the Bible and forgiveness. When you hear Wayne Dyer say, "And we should
just forgive everyone." I think, "I don't think you know how
abused women see forgiveness." They see turning the other
cheek as laying down on the ground and letting that man
walk all over them with spikes on their shoes again. There
is martyrdom, and an enabling where they give everything
they have for abusers. How women see enabling and forgiveness is my issue with how the Bible is interpreted more
than anything else. Because I have had people say to me,
"Well if you really forgave me, you would be this way…"
meaning, of course, I would give them the opportunity to
walk on me again. I have had more than one man say that
to me.

My mother was so invasive that I feel like I didn't have good
boundaries growing up. So I've had to really think about
boundaries. And then I had a husband who I enabled, and I
didn't have good boundaries with him either. I had to have
the bad experience so I knew, "OK, this is where I needed to
draw the line before." Early on in the relationship, I didn't
have a good idea of where that needed to be. How it ties
into forgiveness is: Forgiveness can occur only if there are
good boundaries. Boundaries occur when we honor ourselves. Forgiveness only occurs if it is a gift given freely with
NO strings attached. It's not a, "I will forgive you if you do
this." So it doesn't work for an abused woman. An abused
woman's forgiveness is conditional on not being abused
again.

A gift of forgiveness has to be made from strength of hon-
oring yourself. Some of us (like me) who have boundary
issues need to have the experience of mistakes. "OK, I let

that go too far. I needed to draw the line just here." And that's where true forgiveness can occur. It comes from a protected space where you will no longer allow another to hurt you.

Does that make sense?

Q: The honor is for self.

Me: Yes, the honor is self-honor.

Q: It's not for the person you are forgiving.

Me: It's an honor, boundary, and protection for yourself. I see a breast plate. I see a cocoon. It is a safety shield where only good things can come through to you. Boundaries are a shield of personal honor.

Q: IS forgiveness a gift?

Me: Forgiveness is a gift to yourself and to the other. Forgiveness truly means letting go. Forgiving is a very empowering thing to do. "I trust you to be able to make your own way in the world, without me to protect you. I'm letting you go. I'm giving you this generosity of spirit." An enabler thinks they are protecting this person from the rest of the world, as well as protecting the rest of the world from this person. I really struggled for a long time learning not to take another's energy on. It took me a long time to learn to give that up to the universe. Learning to turn that enabling piece over to the universe and letting go, setting a boundary and developing my own personal honor has been a huge life lesson for me.

Q: Is this all necessary to make sure the other person knows this?

Me: No, not at all. It's all an internal process. It's all about you. And it shifts the entire situation. So when others say, "Just forgive," I think they don't know what a booby trap that is for women. Men and women have definitions for forgiveness that are vastly different. People don't understand forgiveness in the same way. Abusive personalities play on that. They are there to teach you that boundary lesson and they will make you define that space for yourself so that you protect yourself. That's their job.

Q: I came to a place where I asked, is my responsibility or job to forgive?

Me: You will heal if you do. Personal honor is a more complex process that women need to focus on. Don't focus on other people's path. Just work on your own.

Q: So worry is needless.

Me: Oh, yes.

Q: It's not trusting that the person you are worrying about is capable of their own path.

Me: When you are with someone who is an addict, you think, "They can't hear." That may well be. What we don't understand as enablers is that we are just getting in the way of them being able to hear. Hitting bottom is when they can hear. It's when they start to ask for help. It's when they start to develop a relationship with the universe on their own. "I need help now." The greatest experience a person can have is to be self-actualizing and we never want to get in the way of that.

Q: Forgiveness is sometimes hard. Almost like a judgment.

Me: You can't let go when you are judging. You get stuck and you can't let it go. Unfortunately, judgment doesn't help us get free.

Nobody else may like this part about forgiveness and honor, but it's one of the questions I wanted to check off. "OK, if I'm going to be involved in this process, I want this answer because what it says in the New Testament is inadequate for me. I see this is a pitfall for women." I said to them, "I would really appreciate, if during this process, we could have this answer."

Q: And what does it say in the New Testament?

Me: Turn the other cheek. What does that mean? Just let them hit you again? I needed a little clarity around what forgiveness meant. I got a bit of the answer earlier in this process, when they said, "No, it means to walk away, to let go."

Q: Forgiveness is a gift you give yourself.

Me: Yes, and it's also a gift you give others. It's a completion in the cycle. It's a "bon voyage." Letting go isn't always about forgiveness. Sometimes letting go is just, "Have a magnificent journey. I know I can't go with you." Forgiveness isn't exactly the same as letting go. Forgiveness is a subset of letting go.

Q: Say the "bon voyage" piece again.

Me: Sometimes letting go is "bon voyage." When someone dies, you are not necessarily forgiving them. You are letting them go and saying, have a wonderful journey without me. It's easier for them.

Ute Brothers, around 1600-1700 A.D.
Excerpted from Number 14, May 2-I, 2011

Me: I am seeing horses already. We are Native American. We are riding them. I LOVE the horses. We are braves together.

Q: You and pre-Jesus.

Me: Yes, I think we are brothers. This is like an afterlife. This is an A.D. life. How about it? We have Appaloosa horses. I'm thinking, "Wait, we didn't have those on the American continent before Jesus was born." There are saying, "No, it was after that. He was native."

Q: You are in the Americas.

Me: Right, I am seeing him. I am seeing his picture. He has a bone breastplate on. "Crow" is part of his name. We were brothers. We felt almost like twins.

Q: You had no idea...

Me: I had no idea that he came back, but I guess he was an "anonymous" figure. Huh, interesting.

Q: So you are young braves?

Me: Right. He ends up being the chief. I am the medicine man in that life. And we have cavalier spirits like we did when we were bandits. We get to be rowdy boys together. You know like, "Well, if we have to steal someone else's horses, what's the big deal?" Again, the penalty for getting caught was a huge thing. As Native Americans, possessions were like the wind. We lived like the wind. We lived for anything that would give us the wind. We lived near where

I live now, in the foothills in Colorado Springs. I love the wind. We wanted to go fast and to ride horses like the wind. We wanted to become the wind. We had the attitude, "Yeah, who wants to deal with these white men?" They were totally unwelcome, but only because we didn't want to deal with them. We didn't want to have to marshal our resources, or struggle with them. We simply wanted to ride our horses like the wind. We were so into that. We stood up on the different ridges, to feel the wind come down, across the mountains. We LOVED it! It was a cleansing process. We had different herbs we could smoke to give us altered states, but we didn't care about that. It was about the wind. It was about feeling the air. We had families, and we had kids. It was only the two of us with this passion.

Q: For the wind.

Me: Yes, and for the air. We so loved the raptors. He wore eagle feathers in his hair. That was his "mark" when he was a warrior. I used eagle feathers with smoke for some ritual. I think I somehow read smoke. Hmm. How did I read smoke? Well, maybe it will come. We weren't especially great guys. We took care of our people, somewhat.

Q: That was other people's problem.

Me: Yes. We thought, "You can get way too hung up on this stuff—land and possessions and STUFF." We didn't ever want to get caught. As we grew older, we stopped stealing other people's stuff. Stealing wasn't very dignified. But we thought, "Oh, man, possessions, why would anybody want possessions? You just need a fast horse."

Q: Can you see a certain tribe?

Me: I think we were Ute.

Q: It's why we love the Ute Park.

Me: Yes. We had to keep up an outward façade of good will. The Ute were largely peaceful, unlike the Apache. We lived at the bottom of Pikes Peak. We made money trading with people who would come to see the Great Mountain. We were one of the home tribes. But what we really liked to do was ride horses. That's why we liked to keep in touch with the white man. To see what kind of fine horses he might have. We liked a fast horse.

Q: Not knowing that Jesus had come back, you were under the assumption that the crucifixion was the last you saw him in a physical body?

Me: I've been asked often during these processes, have I ever seen him again, and I say, "Yes, well, I'll catch a glimpse now and then." I don't think in that life we had any conception of time. Time is sort of a facile concept. That life was definitely after the crucifixion. He grew into some authority in the Ute life, but he didn't really want it. I performed some rituals, but my preference was, "If we can ride a horse..." (Laughter) It's like avid golfers today, "That's what I live for."

We were either twins or boys born the same day, different years. Women and our children were incidental. We had this passion for horses and the wind. We were lucky because largely—it was way before the gold rush—we were on the fringes of where the white man came. Mostly we hung out with other tribes who wanted to come take the waters at Manitou. At Ute Park there is a bluff, and I can see us standing up there and waiting for a storm. Sometimes lightning would come very close. We loved it!

Q: Could you see his light body in that life?

Me: He had a lot of energy. He was always moving. Yes, if he stood still long enough, you could see the energy surround him. It appeared as an excitement. He was so genuinely excited and thrilled with his life and his passion. We had a passion for one another, but it was through this experience, because we were the only ones who understood each other. How the wind felt. In this life I got this love for the wind from my step-dad. I'm seeing him as one of our little kids who followed us around. He loved a storm, too. If the kids wanted to come with us, they couldn't complain. They had to stand out in the rain and the hail and take the chance of getting hit by lightning too.

Q: It seems like passion keeps you youthful and playful throughout these lives.

Me: Oh, yes. It was one of those lives where we just could be that. The responsibilities were basically handled. We didn't have to deal with a lot of stuff.

Q: You deserved that after what you had been through.

Me: Well, sometimes our wives weren't very happy. Luckily we were born high up enough in the tribal echelon that nobody could tell us what to do. It really worked for us.

We got to do basically what we wanted. Because our joy was so infectious and we didn't ever really hurt anyone; people enjoyed being with us. We weren't substance users. We did some ceremonial stuff, but we didn't get involved with substances. We were very good buffalo hunters, but we didn't like it. We had the attitude, "Who ever gets him knocked down first, gets to be done. Let somebody else handle this." The younger braves had to get them home. Any of the kids, even our daughters, if they wanted to tough it out with us, if any of them learned to ride a horse and could hang on, they could come, too. Our wives just weren't into it after a while. It was not comfortable enough for them. Maybe we should ask if there are lessons from this life.

Q: I'm curious about the wind and the fascination with the wind you two had. Did the wind have any messages?

Me: Yes, we loved it. We could feel it go all the way into our spirits. We could feel it when we stood out and almost froze to death when it was cold, with very little clothing on, so we could feel it resonate all the way through our bodies.

Q: Was it a merging of the elements?

Me: It was all about the wind. If the rain came, and if hail came, OK. If lightning came, it was pretty exciting. We loved to feel the wind in our hair, as we stood there and let it whip around our faces and bite into us. The wind was our God. We lived in homage and appreciation of the wind. The wind kept things light in our lives. It kept us excited. It kept us joyful. What we continually did was align our energy with that of the wind. When we stood outside in the wind, we merged our spirits with the wind so that we, too, could be light and fast. When it was calmer weather, we rode our horses so we could always remember the feeling of the wind. It's like riding a motorcycle, or being on any kind of boat, actually, when you are going fast and your face is being buffeted in the wind. There are a lot of us who are attracted to that. The lesson is, absolutely, it is a valid endeavor to allow the wind to speak to you. Listen to the wind. What is the wind saying? Allow it to lift your spirit because that is its purpose. It is a lesson of the elements. They are all available for use in a transmutation process. The wind can wipe a slate clean of despair and distress. It can replace your heavy spirit with light-heartedness. I don't know that they had a ritual around it. It was just a life dedicated to the wind. There is the potential for fear. "Oh the wind is going to blow my house down. The wind is going to keep me up at night. Oh, whatever…"

Q: It's going to mess my hair. It can be as simple as that.

Me: They wanted to be the wind. Instead of avoiding the weather, they were looking for weather. They were more like storm chasers. "Oh, good, we're going to have great weather, we're going to have great wind." They grew to be able to read the clouds to see what was coming next. That's what they did.

Q: Could they do it also with the smoke?

Me: There were some herbs that they burned and feathers that they brushed through the smoke. They had a little brazier where they burned some herbs. Instead of reading it, they took a feather and drew symbols in the smoke to invoke certain energies. That was the ritual part they used. They used it for intention. If they wanted rain or needed to find buffalo they drew that in the smoke. They had different symbols they drew in the smoke. They had different herbs for different requests, like for rain or for guidance. It wasn't their primary focus. It was more like, "OK, we did it, now let's go outside."

Q: Our chore is done.

Me: That was really kind of it. "OK, done with that. Let's go stand on the ridge."

Q: So maybe part of the lesson is: When you are not weighted down with the material, this is how light your spirit can be.

Me: Yes, and when you allow yourself to follow your passion, life will support you in that. When passion brings you joy, that's the best way to direct your energy. The joyful state surrounds everyone and everything. We had tremendous honor for the elements and for weather. We had a simplistic awe for the forces of nature. It served us quite well. And, again, we are reminded it's the simple things in life. I felt the wind on my face going down into my spirit. And the hot winds in the summertime before the weather changed. The sand bit into our skin. We loved ALL OF IT.

Q: Every season.

Me: Every season. We loved ALL OF IT. The severe snow coming over the mountains gave us such pleasure and such joy. It helped that there were two of us. There is power in two or more. We had each other to share it with, which is why we were happy to share it with our children. They knew the more people who shared the joy, the bigger the energy was. We had no patience. "OK let's go." Or, "Go home with your mother, you are whining." We weren't going to let anyone else get in the way of our joy, not ANYONE else. We were implacable in our attitudes. The wives said "Oh, OK."

I'm going to ask the question, does one necessarily follow the other? Do passion and joy create a seamless existence?" What Peter is saying to me is, "When you achieve lightness of spirit, it creates a whole scenario and environment. It gives you tremendous ability to create." It gives you spiritual lightness that even in hardship will carry you. It will transport you to wonderful places. That is also a metaphor for the wind. It will transport you to magical places.

It's important to always keep our energy kind, with generosity and compassion. What they are saying is: "The people who aren't paying attention, the people who aren't living in relationship with the universe," all three of them are saying in one voice right now, "absolutely, there are consequences for living outside the realm of positive, forward, supportive thinking. If you ever use the power for something other than good it will bite you." No one gets away with anything because it is between you and the universe.

They are really grateful to us. They would like permission to speak to both of you.

Q: Is there anything we can do to be more open and receptive to them?

Me: Pick a time of day, the same time of day--give them five minutes of quiet.

Q: Do they look like we think they do?

Me: Yes. Peter is clean-shaven, he's saying, "5' 10." He has a muscular sturdy build. He has white hair and he wears a white robe not quite to the knees. He likes to be able to move. He has sturdy, strong legs and tufts of white hair around his head. He looks to be in his 60s and is dynamic. They would all like permission to be included in your lives. They appreciate your participation and support.

11
The Mission

This project has been a faith journey for me. Jesus told me, "I want my story to be told." Once I decided to enlist in the project, I literally went into trance as often as I could, whenever I could rope together an audience to help me with the questions. We caught the story as it unfolded. It didn't always make sense, where it conveniently fit into a preset pattern, at the time. Since then it has been like a multidimensional dot-to-dot coloring book, stringing all the information together. Words like "facet" and "structure" kept recurring. Then we found that they had been mentioned far earlier than our initial awareness of them had occurred. Also, after I'd write a personal chapter, I noticed that the past life sessions it seemed to fit best with contained clues that were embedded in my personal story. For instance, in both the personal and regressed cleansing chapters, the woman in training to be a shaman who gave her son Ritalin was brought up, even though they occurred far apart in my experience.

I have a sense we aren't aware of the entire scope of the project yet. Somehow I think we'll continue to find connections and meanings. The dream I had more than twenty years ago, where I was running with the minister of our church along Sheridan Road, with one child strapped to my right leg, suddenly seems prophetic in a way that didn't exist then.

Molly, my writing coach, says to me, "You have to lay it out in a way that readers can follow." And I reply, "That wasn't the way it was given to me. How will they have the sense of discovery we have had?" I am hopeful that along the way, you will have your own parallel epiphanies, helping us contribute to the network of energy that will transform the world. It's important that we develop a multitude of strong voices keeping steadfast boundaries of respect for the planet and all the lives it holds.

The following sessions are what we know thus far about our larger purpose in telling Jesus' story. Believe me, after receiving the **Caves** life, I know that humor is at the top of the list. **Caves** tells the story of the initial gathering of souls 22,000 years ago where we learned we had knowledge to develop and that deep lines of wisdom run through different locations. **Brittany** is a revisiting of the group from **Caves,** 10,000 years later, with roles in which individual souls were comfortable beginning to flesh out a little bit. They also had practices of weaving fences, fishing nets and cloth in the community, which are metaphors for weaving energy and fortifying a protected space in which the wisdom can develop. It blew me away because I "saw" standing stones in Brittany during the trance state and I had no idea if there were actually standing stones there or not. Sure enough, they have them there! An amazing number of standing stones. After **Brittany** is **Frozen Brain**. It was a life where I was an unfortunate and cruel character. I felt trapped in that life. It was a relief to get out of that body. But it was learning I needed to have so I would know to never allow myself to be that kind of person again. At the end of **Frozen Brain,** Peter explains to me that there is recognition among my spirit guides of how devoted I am to the empowerment of other people in this life, without needing to aggrandize myself, which has reinforced their decision to send their messages through me. We also have a Q and A with Peter about the particular need for Western mind development and why ego is important. Having ego and emotions that flash through us helps us all to understand the energies on the planet.

Last is a section from **Egyptian Priestess II,** where they talk about the "lightness" of the overall message I am receiving and how it fits into the scheme of other mystical messages and messengers. They again talk about the monks and nuns who hold mystical energy for us to align with. I see this as such a powerful part of the work, where we all have the ability to make energy contributions that build off of one another in an unseen realm.

Caves, 20,000 B.C.
Excerpted from Number 12, April 30, 2011

Qt: Stepping through the door... looking down, what do you see?

Me: I have square hands, bare feet and hairy legs. I feel like I am a caveman (Laughing).

Q: Are you looking around, do you see caves?

Me: Yes, I see caves. I am in southwestern France. I have on animal skins. My hair is dark and my bangs are cut straight across. I am male.

Q: Do you actually live in the cave?

Me: Yes, I do. It's a valley of caves and I live there.

Q: You said France?

Me: Yes, southwestern France.

Q: Can you come up with a year?

Me: Oh, man. 20,000 B.C., I think.

Q: What are you doing there?

Me: (Laughing) I have a turkey leg in my hand. I'm like, "Seriously?" (Laughing harder) I know I am truly in trance because my eyes are flickering like crazy. Let's ask why we're here.

Q: Who is here today?

Me: Oh, they all are here. Peter is in front. He is laughing, too, saying, "I am glad to see humor in this process." Jesus is there, and Mother Mary, and of course all the angels and guides that are part of the process. They are glad we are so amused. (Laughing again)

Q: We are, too.

Me: They are all doing the Spock hand signal where he V's his hands once then twice. (More laughter)

Q: Back at you. Now we can ask. Why are we here?

Me: There are deep roots of civilization in this part of the world. The deep, old civilizations in France contain a line of deep wisdom. It's how the messages come through these lines. It's easier to keep the information intact when it comes through the same line. That's why they use the same messenger over and over again. It is keeping the message consistent. They are saying this area of France is an ancient civilization and it helps to be connected to that area to keep the message consistent. I'm wondering why so many of my lives are in that Mediterranean region. It's to keep me centered close to that line of wisdom. The lines of wisdom originate from ancient civilizations, is what they are saying.

Q: So they brought you back to this place to...

Me: Yes, I have had so many lives in France. I have such a connection to that area. They are saying the reason for that is they have been developing this line of wisdom for such a long time. I don't know that I am the same blood line, but to keep taking me back to that geographical area and to have had multiple lives there, helps me stay connected to the wisdom.

Q: Why are you here, in the United States, then, in this life?

Me: I think it was my choice because of the workout the Constitution is getting. Our Constitution in the U.S. is really being challenged right now for future reference. Is it a workable document? Is it going to serve the people? Because I helped to craft it in the first place, I am checking back in to see how it is working. These last 10 to 15 years have been an amazing exercise in Constitutional fitness. Is it going to work for us long term?

Q: And what about this lineage and your family?

Me: Yes, it's an integration of many different ideas. We always look for simple explanations and solutions, but there are layers and layers and layers, and depth. I am seeing piano keys and stair steps. For every situation, what they like is when you take all the piano keys and weave together symphonies of ideas and emotions and experiences to create a comprehensive whole. That's why I have been positioned where I am. One of the layers is that I live up high and I can see so much, a 360 degree view, just about, and it is metaphorical and literal. I have a great position to be able to see so much both literally and figuratively. Did that answer your question?

Q: Yes. Are there coincidences?

Me: Yes.

Q: What is the lesson we are learning today with the cave man?

Me: It's about layers of knowledge and continuing the thread. It's about developing lines of wisdom. It's why sacred spaces are important, because the energy and knowledge surround them. It's a validation of keeping the lines intact. They are saying that many people think genealogy is so important, and it's a "yes and no" situation. They are saying people get way too wrapped up into who their forebears were and who they were in past lives, without considering how they are going to take it forward. The forward piece and who they are currently are far more important than anything that happened in the past, basically. But it is good to be grounded in the past and then take it forward.

Q: To be grounded in the past regarding who you were in past lives, or your lineage?

Me: All of that. Everyone has an original source, basically. It's good to connect back to that in many different ways. It's good to know from where you have come and where you are going. Lines are important in the regard of knowing where you have come from and then taking it forward.

Q: And using any gifts or opportunities that are important to this life to help keep the lineage straight.

Is this Caves life your first life?

Me: No. But it was my first connection with this line of wisdom. I'm getting that the rest is vast in the universe. This is the first life that is relevant in this process.

Q: On this planet.

Me: They really want me to stay focused on this specific process. Of course other knowledge is integrated. I'm pretty clear that they don't want me to mess with Atlantis. While some of the knowledge from the culminating life originated there, they want me to stay focused. It's not relevant.

Q: You have been there?

Me: We don't even need to go there. They say it's appropriate for me to say, "I don't have that memory," because currently I do not.

Q: The relevant piece about the caveman is this is your beginning for this process.

Me: Yes. I'm seeing there was a group of us. We gathered together and wrote on cave walls. We shared food. We had multiple families. I'm seeing many familiar faces. In fact, this group is bringing the knowledge forward.

We are all being brought forward with the different wisdoms that we've experienced.

Q: Anything else we need to know about that life?

Me: Jesus was a woman in that life. I think he was my daughter.

Q: Was that his first life?

Me: That's also...

Q: Not relevant.

Me: Not relevant. He was a beautiful young woman with lovely honey-colored hair and he was an artist who painted cave walls to tell about the hunt. It was pretty clear even then that he was a light body. Light bodies are easy to spot in a crowd. They have special charisma and energy.

Q: Were you also a light body?

Me: No, I am always a messenger. I was cast as a messenger soul.

Q: And you will always be a messenger?

Me: Yes.

Q: What about the thread of wisdom?

Me: What they are saying is there have always been practitioners all over the world who connect with universal wisdom. Those are the shamans from every tribe--The seers. They have an easier time connecting with universal wisdom. Universal wisdom is similar worldwide. The thread of wisdom I carry originates in western Europe, in that cave culture. Other threads are historical threads. We have genealogy threads in the sense of biological reproduction. We have knowledge threads, where bodies of knowledge are being developed. There are two main knowledge pieces of our thread in western Europe. One is the thread that develops into representative government. The other is the thread that develops into the Western way of spiritual association. That's a linking thread of wisdom.

It's an honor to be part of shepherding this thread of wisdom. Ha! They are pointing at me saying, "It's an honor."(Laughing) They know I don't always see it that way. It's another lesson for me.

Q: This is good we are at the beginning.

Me: I'm seeing spokes of a wheel, and you know how there is the center of the wheel, and the way that connects to the axle? I'm seeing right now I am in the center of the wheel. I am being supported by the different spokes. Each of the people in that cave community is one of the spokes in the wheel. At any given time any one of us can be the center core of the wheel. Right now I am in the center, but at any moment that could change. Any one of us involved in this process could be the person sharing wisdom and being supported. We all have it.

Q: Are we all messengers?

Me: Not necessarily. But that's also not...

Q: Relevant.

But we all have the knowledge.

Q: Is there anything else we need to consider in the cave?

Me: Oh, animals! Animals come, too. We are surrounded by animal totems, your animals in this household and my animals in my household. As you are here, my household is also surrounded by wild animals, and they all like to check into the process. In my neighborhood, I have three golden eagles and they--this is so interesting--when they fly over my house they develop a protective energy shield that only eagles can do. And I have owls with which I have had many spiritual experiences. The raptors are definitely connected to this process of bringing information and helping the channels stay open and keeping us protected.

They are saying is it's likely there will be many spin- offs of this information to make it more accessible to people. There are many people who will want to train in the wisdom.

That's why they are setting it up in such a structured but loose fashion. Have it work for us. The words are our own. They are saying for us to set up workshops where people are doing the same things so they will understand the power of group. They are also supposed to be created so that people in workshops take ownership of their process. This is universal wisdom and it has a different slant for different people, and meets a different purpose in their life. They feel like Christianity has become frozen. They want it to be a malleable working body that can continually mutate. What they want is for this body of knowledge to be more facile, to work like DNA. You know how DNA is the double helix? DNA doesn't mutate right away, but when you have an experience or an upset in your life, there is a layering process where it can be carried to your children. It doesn't become part of the DNA structure for several generations or more. The double helix exists as a core foundation of truth. Still, it is malleable. That's the way they want us to set this up, so that there is this core truth that we see. They want us to set it up so that it mutates with consciousness--nothing really big or spectacular. (Laughing)

Q: So that it guides rather than dictates, as the Church dictates.

Me: Yes.

Q: And this is just the guide. The Bible is considered absolute. It's not a parable. It's not an experience. It is fact and we have to do it that way.

Me: Right. Exactly. How many of us have had an epiphany where we said, "Oh my God, if only I had been able to see it from that perspective before." And it really opens up a whole new spectrum of emotion, sharing and community. That is the point. They want us to be able to work with this idea system so it is embracing and inclusive. It's the idea that universal wisdom shifts and mutates with us. What they are saying is that they take the highest and best inside of us and then it reflects. It's a mutual relationship. To create the best universe, we need to take the best of both and reflect it back and forth. I'm seeing it as a higher level, but it is also an internal energy--all things at once.

Q: So we are responsible for our own spirituality as opposed to being told? So we should find our own reflections?

Me: What Peter has said is that he has been upset with how frozen religion has been. Peter has a devotion to the Catholic Church. The parts that are really wonderful are the mystical parts, for the development of spiritual ascension. The monks and nuns for generations have been creating this spiritual community for the rest of us. And now it is time to open it to the masses, basically, so that we can have a shift occur. It's for the purpose of creating an outpouring, where we cherish the planet and the people in it. It's for the purpose of learning to love one another. We have to be able to identify the perfection in each of us regardless of what the experience has been. We have to heal each of us. It is going to take more energy than they have ever required before.

Me: I'm thinking, "Shit, I don't want to start a religion." They are saying, "Settle down, Julia, settle down." (Laughing)

Q: Maybe you're like the optometrist where you provide binoculars. It doesn't have to be called religion.

Me: Like a viewfinder. Like a context. They are saying, "Whew, somebody gets it!" (Laughing) It can be like a lens.

Q: Churches forget to focus on spirituality.

Me: As with the DNA issues, there is a way to integrate that. There is a better way to create a web. It is like the spokes of the wheel. One person isn't always the appropriate center of the wheel all of the time. A wheel is a network, and anyone can be at the center of the wheel any given time. Any of the people primary in this process can be asked to be in the center of the wheel at any time. I'm saying, "No problem, guys. I'd be happy to give up my space."

Brittany, 10,000 B.C.
Excerpted from Number 18, May 18, 2011

Q: Describe the door to me.

Me: It's a narrow hallway and the doors are narrow. I went past the door that had the gold light coming from it and I went past the door that had the blue light coming from it. This door has an apple-green light coming from it.

Q: As you open the door, turn around and close the door and then face the scene. What is the first thing you notice?

Me: I am seeing a rock formation, kind of like standing stones, but I don't think it is Stonehenge, it is too short. It has a cap stone.

Q: There are other places with those stones.

Me: I am getting Brittany. I don't know if they have those stones there.

Q: If you can gather a year, do you get a sense of what century it is?

Me: I think it is early--like 10,000 B.C.

Q: How are you feeling?--Content or anxious?

Me: I feel like I am near the ocean. I feel the wind. It's not cold, but it is not a warm, balmy wind either. It is a spring-time wind. I am female and I have long blond wavy hair. I have on a white robe and I am 24.

Q: What is your name?

Me: Moira.

Q: Is Moira alone?

Me: I have some little children with me. I am holding the hand of a small boy. He is maybe six. The other hand is a little girl, maybe four.

Q: Are they your children?

Me: I don't think so. We are having a picnic. I am somehow a household helper.

Q: Like a governess.

Me: Yes. We have come to have a picnic by the stone formation.

Q: What happens next?

Me: Horses. Men are on horses.

Q: Are they threatening?

Me: They are men on horses who are like guards or some-thing from the keep where we live.

Q: Where do you live?

Me: Not far.

Q: Is it a castle? Is it a home?

Me: It's a group of huts. It's fortified. There's a fence, but inside it are huts made of grass and mud. But there is a bigger one in the middle. There are little ones around. It's a pretty good-sized establishment. Maybe 200 people live here.

Q: There's a fence around it.

Me: There's farming outside the fence. The horses live inside the gates with us.

Q: So they won't be stolen.

Me: Right. People are wearing shifts. Some of them wear leggings. It's not like fancy Roman garb. I guess we have weaving. There are some cloth leggings and some buckskin leggings. And they have bow and arrow. I always hope to be historically accurate. I keep my fingers crossed. They have horses pull some of the carts. This is a family stronghold and a community well known for its warriors. We are successful. I am seeing donkeys that pull carts. There's a lady who belongs to the keep and I am getting that it is a previous life for Mother Mary.

Q: What was this lady's role?

Me: She's the female leader of the community. Her husband is a big man. He is almost bigger than life. He is a head taller than everyone else. He is very broad and very muscular. He is the male head of the keep.

Q: Is that anyone you know?

Me: He is the person who became Joseph of Arimathea. Their son becomes Jesus. I am someone who is in the household.

Q: How old is the son?

Me: He is eighteen. He is younger than I am. I watch the smaller children. I think this couple had about five children.

Q: The older boy is Jesus.

Me: Right. And there is another boy who is maybe 15 and a girl, 10.

Q: Do you recognize them as being anyone you know?

Me: I'm seeing my daughters in this 2011 life, but I feel like it is an invasion of their privacy to go there.

Q: So what else do they want us to know about this scene?

Me: It was a feudal system, but it was a jovial place, a very happy place. They developed their military prowess not out of a desire to conquer, but because they had high energy and a lot of...

Q: Testosterone...

Me: Yes. High energy and they were good sportsmen. It was a way to hone their physical abilities. A by-product of that was they were revered, respected. It was one of those lives where things worked out.

Q: It sounds like the Robin Hood era.

Me: It was more rustic than that. The cloth is much simpler. The garments are much simpler. There are either whites, or they used nuts and berries for dye and they fade easily. Whites and beiges and browns don't last long. It is early. It's way before castle systems. It's sort of a feudal system, but it is before castles. 10,000 years before Jesus was born.

The caveman life they said was about 20,000 B.C.

We lived in huts and we had horses. We lived in the coastal area of France. We had a pretty nice life. The crops came in. We had domesticated animals—goats and sheep. And we were able to weave cloth.

Q: Getting back to Moira, what happens to her as she ages? She's twenty four.

Me: She marries one of the young men in training with them. He isn't one of the keep's family sons. He is tall and blond. He has a really good arm. He can throw far with his spear arm.

Q: That's what we need is a good spear arm. That's what makes them attractive.

Me: Right. The day I have the picnic with these kids, he's been out riding around with other comrades. I guess he is courting me.

Q: How old are you then when you marry?

Me: I think about 26. I am old. I don't know why…I think I had a different situation before this. I was married young. There was some illness. I was the survivor. It was a small town nearby that was wiped out by a plague. I survived without a lot of pockmarks.

Q: Your husband died.

Me: Yes, I had some small children who died. I'm kind of a healer. I'm in that role because I have survived the plague. I was pretty young, maybe 15 or so, when I came to live in this fortified community. I learn from some of the older women. They think I am blessed because I survived. They cut me a wide swath.

Q: You have a nice life.

Me: Yes. I study different herbs with women in the community. I don't have any other children. I love to be with the keep children.

Q: Why do you call it the keep?

Me: I don't know.

Q: What happens with Jesus in that role? What happens as he ages?

Me: He marries a young woman from a nearby community. He becomes head of this, when his parents pass on. My husband and I live in a little hut. The community keeps growing. We have more fenced area. This fence is like mud and grass...sometimes we mix sand with it and sometimes sea shells. It's stronger. There are people who live with us who learn how to fortify the walls in a better way.

Q: So you keep expanding the walls.

Me: Yes. Most of us are very blond. We like living by the sea.

Q: It sounds like a tranquil life. Is there anything monumental in this life that we need to know about?

The relations with any of the people?

Me: It's pretty stress-free. It is the point that when you have a stress-free life, you flourish. Good things don't always have to come out of hardship.

The potential for this exists.

Q: The potential for what?

Me: That everyone can lead a fulfilled life. It's a community based on respect. They funnel their energies in a good way. There are many people here who were in the beginning in the cave. There are many forming bonds of people who later will network and weave in and out and end up as apostles.

Q: So even in this past life they were starting to form relationships for the future.

Me: Right. There are trust relationships forming the roles in which people are comfortable.

Q: We would like to think in the new shift on the planet, we could have lives like this.

Me: Yes. Trust is a big part of it. Trust comes in many ways from the leadership. It's learning how to funnel energy in a positive way by listening and having direction. It helps to have enough to eat.

Q: Let's ask the guides, Jesus, Mother Mary and Peter. Is there anything else we need to take forward from this life?

Me: It's a foundation piece that we built on. They are saying the people who are intimately involved in helping to deliver the material this Julia life were probably part of that early community.

We were weavers. We were cloth-makers. It's kind of a metaphor for the network. We wove nets for fishing. We wove basket walls.

The whole group that began in the cave, and were later in the keep, and are interestingly part of the knowledge base.

Q: They have stayed as a group to help bring this forward.

Me: Yes.

Q: You are saying they will come together.

Me: Yes. We will recognize each other. There will be coincidence. There will be a lot of 12's and 16's.

What I've noticed is that there are people who can't put this material down, who are so excited about it. Others can't make themselves read it. What they are saying is that people who are so excited about it, who can't put it down, who can't wait for the next installment, are definitely people who have been part of the journey. They are part of the wisdom of the thread.

What they are doing with me, is they are giving me a narrow vision. Otherwise I will get off track. I don't have the whole Atlantis piece.

As you might imagine, I have ongoing arguments with myself and anyone else who will listen in physical or spiritual form, about how it is possible for me to be this person who receives spiritual messages. Whole weeks can pass where I don't even think about my "other life" as a receiver. Those are the weeks when I am just Julia, the mother of four children, wife of Claes, and social worker intrigued with how brains can be trained for our benefit. It is very difficult for me to hold on tightly to this alternate identity. It is very difficult for me to take myself seriously. An extension of that is it is very difficult for me to take THEM too seriously. But periodically I do. At the end of the next life, Frozen Brain, Peter talks to me about, "Why me?"

I have a good friend who is actually one of the women who turned me on to Wayne Dyer and the one who said "You MUST do past life regression!" Sometimes when I am having a moment of trepidation about this work, I tell her it is ALL her fault. When I am looking for answers to the question, "Why me?" I remember how she once told me that I am a person she can tell anything. No matter how weird it is, I am still very accepting—or sometimes, even better, I am doing something weirder.

The gift my parents gave me was that of boundless intellectual searching. I am always game for a new, cool idea. It's why I am not very dogmatic, and also why I just take the parts of religious teachings that I like and forget about the rest. But I am also genuinely earnest and well meaning. I take seriously this opportunity to create a better world.

Following the session, Frozen Brain, is an excerpt from the tail end of **Egyptian Priestess II**, where another part of the answer to "Why me?" is addressed.

Frozen Brain, 1012 B.C.
Excerpted from Number 9, April 6, 2011

Q: What is your first scene, what are the details that you see?

Me: I'm a man. I'm in a tunic with a cape. I have dark hair. I have some sort of a gold leaf around my head and I have a red cape off my left shoulder. I don't have a breast plate, I have a belt. I think they call it a girdle? I have a short tunic. I am looking up at a knoll in front of me with a tree. There is big leafy tree. My first inclination is to say it is a locust or a linden tree on the top of the knoll.

Q: Do you get the feeling that you are in the armed forces? Are you dressed that way? Or a dignitary?

Me: I am a dignitary, some sort of an ambassador. Initially I thought I was royalty, but now I don't think so.

Q: If you wanted to reach out and pull a year out of the sky, what would it be?

Me: 1012 B.C.

Q: I'm guessing we're in Greece or Rome?

Me: I'm thinking Algeria.

Q: Let's describe this man. Does he have a family?

Me: He's too important to worry about the family he has. They are in Rome or Greece. He feels very important. He's a big man. He is feeling powerful and important.

Q: Let's go back to the scene. What is he doing now?

Me: I think he's planning. He has a scroll. I think he's planning to read the scroll from the top of the knoll another day.

Q: And do you get a sense of the essence of the scroll?

Me: It's something about enslavement, but that's not quite it. He is part of a group of conquering heroes and they are going to give edicts to these people in what is now Algeria. These are smaller, little darker people. He is not a very nice man, and these people are cowering. He feels very righteous. He isn't getting that it's over kill. These poor people are cowering.

Q: Let's just keep going. What does he do next?

Me: Well, he makes his proclamation the next day from the knoll. All the guards round up the people. They are taking them to work farms.

Q: So what happens after he rounds up all the people?

Me: He feels satisfied. He has come to conquer the land and he is doing it. He feels completely righteous and satisfied.

Q: Does he have to report back to a king?

Me: Maybe he's the governor. He's been appointed. Things don't turn out well. He is too harsh. He isn't kind. Of course, slavery doesn't work to bring out the best in people. Work farms don't work. He doesn't ever get it.

Q: So what eventually happens to him? Does the local group try to overpower him?

Me: Oh, no, they can't. It's a lifetime where he commands and abuses this whole group of people. He feels SWOLLEN with grandeur and righteousness.

Q: Let's ask this question, was his soul coming into this life to do this duty? Or did he totally change his path?

Me: You know, there's part of me that is so horrified. I think he is me.

Q: Well, we all had these.

Me: I understand, but I think it's about that. It's about…

Q: That you could have been that evil.

Me: It's about needing to have that experience. Through-out all my other lifetimes I cringe when I look at this one. And it's about having complete control over other people's lives. It's always meant for me to have with me as a measuring stick. How close are you to this? This is what it feels like, this complete control. When everything you say must be heeded. Yet with what you do, you wreak destruction in your path.

Q: But most souls have had those lives.

Me: Right, but it doesn't make me feel any better about it. It also is a reminder. It's one of the reasons I am so hesitant about becoming a public figure.

Q: That's why we're being shown this life.

Me: Right. I had the other life where I was burned at the stake for abusing universal wisdom. I'm really having that cold, steely feeling resonate in my body right now. It's a feeling of implacability.

Q: Let's ask about this life. Was Jesus in this life in any capacity?

Me: He was one of the slaves. I can see him imploring me to be different.

Q: Was he a leader of the slaves?

Me: He was an old man, imploring me to be kind to his people. He is so old that his back is rounded. His spine has started to curl. I ignore him.

Q: Do you have several conversations with him? Do you get to know him?

Me: He's worthless. He's beneath my notice. [I am blown away by the dismissiveness in my tone as I transcribe this.]

Q: Is there anyone else in this life that you connected with?

Me: I don't think I ever really connected with anyone in this life. Earlier I was a successful general. I crushed the enemy. Now I am the governor and it turns out to be a fiasco. We can't farm with these people who are destitute. It's a horrible life.

Q: He spends his entire life lording over this group of peasants?

Me: I'm seeing an arrow in his back. His own troops eventually kill him. I think he was in his 60s.

Q: It sounds like he must have been that way for more than a couple of years.

Me: Oh, 20, I think.

Q: Augh.

Me: Until there was almost nothing left. It's the life that was Abrum's opportunity to redeem.

Q: Was there anyone else in this life that we should know about?

Me: I think I feel pretty lucky I didn't have other people around. I wasn't always so cruel. It's one of the reasons I work now with helping people making their brains more malleable. My brain in that life was frozen in this ugly, rigid, paralysis of meanness. I couldn't change.

Q: It's like we get the amnesia and it just takes over. Maybe we could ask some questions now?

Me: Maybe I could leave this body first? I don't really like the feeling of being in it.

Q: We know what happened. Let me count to three, and you'll be at the last day of that life.

Just let me know what is happening.

Me: I'm free. Thank God I'm free.

Q: Oh, you are already gone.

Me: I think there was a spirit inside that couldn't get out. That was trapped inside that frozen brain.

Q: OK, now that we are up above and looking down, any other feelings or impressions? Anyone you want to say good bye to? Anyone you need closure with or ask forgiveness?

Me: I want to ask ALL of them for forgiveness.

Q: Do that now.

Me: (Pause). They were like little raisins of people. I can see them now filling in their grape-ness.

Q: Now let's ask Peter our questions. Are you supposed to create movement with this book? Is this supposed to involve seminars, talks and promotions? Is that how he sees you doing it or not?

Me: He knows that my purpose in this life—I'm going to cry—

Q: It's OK, dear. Do it.

Me: He knows that my purpose in this life is to teach others to become whole and to open their minds. He knows that I will balk at being a messiah. He knows it is never who I wanted to be. I never want that responsibility of directing all of those lives. He understands (breaking down)…

Q: It's OK, just take a moment. He's just showing you all the love he has for you.

Me: The process that I have been through with my children, and how I have learned to support them, to open to direction from the universe, about learning and being open is why I have been chosen…

Q: It's OK, just take your time.

Me: That my need to be pure about it, to be responsible, to be self-monitoring, that I continually refine my approach to give the people around me as much power as I can is why I have been chosen. He says I've needed to learn to adapt and change quickly. It's been important for me to accept feedback when I received new information and learned that what I was doing wasn't working. He says it isn't that I have always been perfect. We know it's not that I have always been perfect. But he says I am completely dedicated to strengthening others.

Q: How is it supposed to happen?

Me: He's saying that's why I was chosen. I will use the material to empower others. He knows I have been using the work right along. I had a fellow give me a hard time about the introduction to one of my classes (on the astrological chart of Dec 21, 2012). He said, "Seriously? There's no exact center of the universe." And I said, "I'm going to present it the way the Mayans said it, that's what I can do." And then I lectured him, and I don't usually do that. I took one of the lessons from the "other" Mary. We can take this and ourselves too seriously. We need to have a sense of wonder...

Q: Yes.

Me: ...and childlike awe...

Q: Yes.

Me: ...and playfulness using it. I said to him, "It's not my job to make sure you are open to miracles. You have that choice. I recommend that you take it." I am allowed to speak with authority about that. And what was hilarious is that the man backed down. He said, "I apologize."

Q: Am I clear that you will be doing seminars and teaching the information?

Me: Yes, we will. Yes, lectures and classes. We will be bringing it to the people. It's OK to do it in my way. I will do it to empower other people. I say to them, "You are the way." Always in my therapy practice I say to my clients, "You know way better than I do what will work for you...."

Q: We're just the facilitators.

Me: Exactly.

Q: And that's what we're getting out of these regressions is a formula that is tried and proven, that Jesus has practiced, that your close association with him enabled you to pass on, because you learned them with him.

Me: Yes. We learned together. Remember, I have that debate with Jesus where I say, "Do you really have to do all that healing and that miracle stuff?" And he says, "Well, they are still talking about it." And I say, "We could teach them to do it themselves." That was why it was such an emotional breakthrough for me, because Peter acknowledged that's who I need to be and that I had done well with the lesson to be that support person. That was such a big emotional "whoosh."

Q: Everyone's consciousness is ready to hear this where it wasn't before, the time is now.

Me: He says just be who you are about it. Who I am about it is "It's not the story that's important, it's the message."

Q: You come across as very sincere when you talk about it. You are not ego-centered.

Me: How I feel about the whole Mary Magdalene thing is we are all divine women. I am not about to sack her story. She is a divine woman. She had a part to play and she played it well. I'm not going to be at cross purposes with her in this story. We need more divine women. It's important to be supportive and to say, "Yes, you have a right to your voice, whatever that voice is. And take it, embrace it." I'd read some of the work on Mary Magdalene and to me that was a huge impediment to doing this work. I'm not about cutting someone else off at the knees because their work is contra-dictory to mine.

Q: Do you think that the spirit of Mary Magdalene believes she was married to Jesus?

Me: I don't know. It's not my issue. I so do not want to go there.

Q: OK.

Me: The "other" Mary doesn't want to either. She had this wonderful purposeful existence where she has a story to tell in her own right.

Q: You're talking about the "other" Mary...

Me: Yes, the "other" Mary, AKA Odessa Lamporopolous.-- The blond woman who carried Jesus' two sons. Her purpose is not to take energy away from anyone else. Her purpose is to encourage people to flourish in whatever way they can. To recognize that we get so caught up in "She said this...I had that..." information. And it's not important.

Q: And that's similar to there are many people channeling Jesus, with different aspects of Jesus. Most people agree it is fine. They all have a different way of looking at the energy. It's OK.

Me: We all have a different filter and a way to receive information. It isn't about being in competition. It's about filling the void in people's lives, and how we can all arrange ourselves to do that. For a while I thought I just wouldn't say who I was (in the life with Jesus). For a while I thought I could just say I was with Jesus and not have to tell the whole story.

Q: Because everyone will ask.

Me: Yes, I have to tell the whole story because she speaks with authority. She lived with him. And, she lived with the mother Mary. She lived with both of them. To see those two light bodies correspond and cross over and connect was magnificent. It was the best art, the best emotion, the best experience of energy. When you aren't as pure an energy as they were, it was like living in glory, it was like hearing angels sing, when they were both resonating at their highest levels.

It's funny because I have always said in this Julia life, when people say, "Let's give the Buddhists credit for all the spirituality." "Well the Buddhists didn't have Beethoven, Mozart or Bach." Many of those wonderful musicians channeled the glory of God in western civilization. That's what it was like, hearing angels sing when Jesus and the Mother Mary were together. Those great musicians could hear the angels sing, plus the gods and the thunder and all the wonderful emotion. We aren't just people who sit on hills and meditate. We are vibrant, physical beings who learn to deal with great power and emotion. And the power of the earth is huge--unless we know what that feels like, how then can we learn to work with it and to heal it? They are saying it helps to understand that cataclysm exists. We have to be able to allow it to penetrate our spirits and our soul. We have to be able to accept the energy. It's not necessarily about harnessing the energy, it's about…

Q: Letting it go through to our human bodies, feeling and resonating with it.

Me: Yes, absolutely. Until we understand it, I'm seeing a wave crashing through us, then we can't prepare appropriately.

Q: We need to be seeing a life where there is a ceremony of adding to the knowledge?

Me: The western piece of the knowledge is laden with ego, and truly Jesus fought ego every moment of his life. That's what the 40 days in the wilderness were about, "How do I take this?" He felt the crisis of that.

I'm getting this huge wave of emotion that we have in Western civilization. This fiery, powerful, ego-driven arrogance is necessary for understanding the planet. It's like what you were saying, when we let it run through our body, when we allow it, we can understand better how to heal the planet. And, yes, that builds the knowledge to know it is one of the steps of healing—not to bury the emotion, but to allow it.

Q: Like Jesus did.

Me: Yes, it tormented him. That's why he took it out to the wilderness. Always, then, he had different rituals for himself, to remember humility, like washing people's feet.

Q: I'm thinking this is a good place to end.

Me: Yes, this has been an emotional session for me.

Q: They needed to let you know how much they love you.

Me: Sometimes it feels like too big of a responsibility.

I was unhappy to go forward with this project based solely on having been these other people in previous lives.

Q: The message I keep getting for you is that all your friends are gathering around you, so that you can do this with all of us, so that you don't have to do these classes by yourself.

Me: I love having company!

Q: And it's to help witness. It's why we're all here for you, so that you're safe and we're letting everyone know that what you have to say is important information that they need to hear. And you just do it. And everyone with you has your back. Your family has your back.

Me: And it's OK for me to step into it. It has a lot to do with why I didn't want to channel by myself. It's a group effort. It's the women's way to do things, by consensus and in groups. And it's a way of fully expressing the divine feminine.

Q: And that's another thing coming in to the shift is the divine feminine.

Me: There's so much more to learn from building a strong network together. Thank you. Thank you!

Egyptian Priestess, II, 200 B.C.
Excerpted from Number 11, April 29 II, 2011

Me: The question I want to ask is, when they are channeling Michael, in *Messages from Michael*, and Abraham, it all seems very formal. Then there is the nun who is channeling Jesus now, it also is very formal. I'm curious about why mine is so informal. Is it a different soul group from which I am receiving messages?

They are saying this information is directed to a different audience. There is additionally the matter of a different ability to receive. It's also a different line of knowledge. This is a place of compilation--of concentration. We are drawing from many different sources for the information. You know how the Michael messages come out, they are so wooden and in block letters? I'm not sure how the Hicks' information comes out and whether they interpret it. But this is drawing from different sources, and it goes through many different filters before it gets to me. Because we are who we are, it allows for a lot of humor and a pragmatic approach.

The universe is often a reflection of our highest selves. What's the highest part of you, and that's where you will find the universe talking to you.

They desperately want to engage with us. That is the point.

Q: And I feel too that there is such a lighter audience out there who wants this to resonate with their lightness of souls themselves--with humor...

Me: And delight. I am getting a chill from that.

Q: And love...

Me: So much of religion and rules are SO HEAVY. There's a lovely slim whisper, a beckoning, a subtle nuance. If we have an allowing for it, stroke us like a feather. Delight isn't heavy.

Q: It's da light. (Laughter)

Me: It's like, "chill out," this is supposed to be a loving message.

Q: I feel like there are so many people waiting for that, because they can't take the staunchness. With the staunch, starched and strict comes fear and punishment. The fear has rolled into "You have to, you should, you must." Where's the give it to me with light and love and it will resonate with my soul and spirit so much more strongly? Than whipping, beating or scaring it into me...

Me: Or making me carry the world around on my shoulders.

Q: Exactly--or making me feel bad that Jesus died for me.

Me: I've had to wrap myself up into a pretzel to accept that concept. What he is saying is the whole conversation about "I am the way," he's saying that "I AM is the way." He knew he was going to be a martyr when he died. He couldn't avoid that. And he thought, "This could be useful for us." He knew it was the end. Let's ask Peter about that. "What was that about, Peter? He died for our sins?"

Peter is saying that it is meant to be taken as, "He didn't die in vain." He died for the purpose of showing us the way.

Q: Boy did that get twisted.

Me: Let's ask about, he's nodding his head, like, "Why the white woman here, Peter?" As in, why me as messenger? The WASP-Y woman, and not an African or Native American, or someone more ethnic, to carry this message. He's saying it's for the audience who understands what you said about lightness. It doesn't all have to be hard, heavy and grim. We, the white upper middle class women, can carry that part of the message, the light part. It's similar to how choirs are broken into parts based on vocal range.

Q: We don't come from a culture that is mysterious. I don't think WASP-Y women are that mysterious.

Me: You don't think so? Huh, amazing, just saying…

Q: Kind of surface-y. We are very deep in our souls. Look at us from the outside.

I can't wait to meet the audience, if they are as fun as we are. (Laughter)

Me: When are we going to have the laughter ritual?

Q: Spiritual seekers can be so heavy, too.

Me: Questioning is always good.

Q: The childlike piece.

Me: The wonder, the awe. You have to really scroll it way back to get to that awe. That's what is said about the mother Mary, that she was always able to get in touch with that piece of herself. No matter what the situation was, she never lost the sense of wonder and awe. That's why she was such a magnificent healer. The rest of us get caught up in the story and the drama. She never allowed herself to be contaminated.

Q: True. It feels like when you are authentic with yourself, it doesn't matter what anyone else does, you can still find your wonder and awe. When you concern yourself with what others think...you get separated from your truth.

Me: Right, and you need your wonder and your awe. There's always something inside of us that has the potential to create it, so we just need little, gentle reminders. There is something wonderful in this situation, no matter what the situation is. Awe...

Q: And finding it is just the best prize.

Me: If what we want is to evolve to the next level, we have to be clear in what our goals are. If we want a world without war, where little children are safe and women aren't enslaved, we need to have a jump shift. So, how do we do that? How do we create a life where we can all heal to that degree? How do we live out of honor and respect? This will help. If we all learn to self-heal, just a little bit, it will help to move us forward. If those of us who can, do it.

Q: So with those we refer to as the light workers now becoming more prevalent, they are able to come out because they aren't afraid of ridicule or burning at the stake.

Me: That's what this is for. It's for helping them to have more resources and tools. They will be tools that everyone can use.

Q: Tools everyone can use.

Me: Well, not everyone can make themselves read the information, but those who can, ultimately the idea is to heal. Ultimately, when we put all these formulae together, then healing can occur, as that is what Jesus did. He used all of these processes to make space in his body so that he could become a pure vessel to let the light come through and shine out at other people. He identified in an instant the perfection that was inside each person and grew that so they would heal. That is what it takes to heal, is to find that part of perfection in yourself and grow it like crystals.

Q: So to heal you need to find the perfection in you…

Me: And expand it. You have to find room to expand it.

Q: By cleaning house again.

Me: A lot of these rituals are about how to clean and how to re-supply. Aligning yourself with the different elements to fully purge. All the great spiritual seekers have a purging ritual. Sweat lodges and…

Q: To create the expansion and room and then the rituals to bring light in and this is how you'll grow, just as the plants on earth.

Me: Like the trees in the forest, if there's not enough room, then the little guys can't grow, and they might be the best ones. They have to receive light too.

Q: We have everything we need to learn these lessons...

Me: We keep looking outside of ourselves and all the answers are inside of ourselves. Peter is saying that all these mystical talents have been available to align with universal wisdom pretty substantially--monks and nuns. But the trouble with that is that integration with the public at large isn't ever required of them. That's why he's here with me. That's one of the reasons why I wasn't chosen before in other lifetimes. There wasn't the lightness. There was an arrogance... it wasn't funny.

Q: Rejuvenation.

Me: So many times in this life I have had to suck back my energy. "Oh shit. What did I just do? What did I just say?"

Q: That keeps you on the right path.

Me: It was really important for me to not go off on my own and do this--to engage my friends to help create a safe space and to feel supported--and to network. My grandmother, in this life, and I were witches together at one point. We were largely herbalists and good witches. But we were definitely using magical arts. I was careless about it. I kind of had this attitude "I can use the knowledge any way that I want."

So now I ask myself. Am I creating a safe space? How am I holding this knowledge? Even though it is light, it is also very powerful.

Q: I was going to say, integrity.

Me: Yes. I have a lot of integrity, and then periodically, I don't. And I think whoops, what was that about? I have to call my energy back. Whoops, whoops, whoops! Oooh, I think I just did a vampire thing there and sucked somebody's energy dry. Maybe I had better give them that energy back. It isn't like this is always easy for me to integrate.

12
Jesus

There are many unanswered questions about Jesus of Nazareth. Who was he as a man? What were his feelings? Where did he spend those years we know nothing about? What was it like to be the Messiah?

Along the way, we have received answers to some of those questions, and more. We know he had a very inquisitive and scholarly mind, and now know he still has an almost slapstick sense of the absurd. He is engaging, funny and exacting in his requests. It's almost as though he is continually saying to me, "There is no sense in doing anything half-assed. Give it everything you have, Julia." Maybe it's to the point of, if you are going to die a grueling death, it for sure should be worth every moment of it. And for some reason, even though religious dogma is often beyond goofy to me, I do everything he asks me to do—eventually. Clearly there's more to the essence of this story and the man than is indicated in the narrow viewfinder of the Bible. Somehow his energy has managed to grow far beyond that limiting tome, even though it holds the bulk of what's officially reported about him. I have a group of largely anti- and a-religious readers who can't wait for the next installment.

So with that in mind, let me tell you about my friend, Jesus. As I was awakening one morning in early December, 2011, he was singing in my left ear,

"Making a living the old, hard way. Taking and giving my day by day. I dig the snow and the rain and the bright sunshine. I'm draggin' the line (draggin' the line)

My dog Sam eats purple flowers. We ain't got much, but what we've got's ours. We dig snow and the rain and the bright sunshine. Draggin' the line (draggin the line)

I feel fine. I'm talking about peace of mind. I'm gonna take my time. I'm getting to good times. Draggin' the line (draggin the line)

Loving a free and feeling spirit. Hugging a tree when you get near it. Digging the snow and the rain and the bright sunshine. I'm draggin' the line (draggin the line)

Draggin' the line (draggin' the line)

I feel fine. I'm talking about peace of mind. I'm gonna take my time. I'm getting to good times. Draggin' the line (draggin the line)"

He sang all the parts. He had good range and voice. He was wearing a red robe and sunglasses.

The words were vague to me as I awakened. It took better than a day to place the song. I finally remembered the chorus and typed it into Google. Thank you, Tommy James, for such a memorable song.

So please remember Jesus is the spirit of a groovey person, too. It is important to him and he has entrusted me with the telling of it.

In the following sessions, we learned about Jesus' progression in the "culminating" life. In **Marriage with Jesus,** Jesus initiates a conversation about having sympathy for the Church orthodoxy that doesn't want to let go of the old, implacable ways of doing things because of their fear that religious pratices will be severed at their roots. He understands that modern materialsim has interepted the connection of source to the hearts of men, as it did in his day with the moneylenders at the temple.

In **Jesus at a Roman Party,** we learn more about Jesus the anthropologist. We are shown that he respected all belief systems and was always looking for ways they were similar rather than how they were different. As he grew older in the culminating life, he appreciated all the parts of life and was able to identify the perfection in everyone. He continues the conversation about forgiveness, and says that we must maintain boundaries with the forgiven and must never allow them to possess us. With regard to healers, they also need good boundaries to keep their energy separate from those they are healing. He says the foundation for healing and forgiveness is respect: self respect, respect for the energy and respect for everyone else.

Continuing the conversation about orthodoxy, he says it is only good if it remembers it originates in source, which is always kindness and love. Empty tradition is worthless. Any time there is rigidness or implacability, it is time to shake it up. He uses a tree as an analogy. A tree has deep roots, but it is always influenced by and must adapt to its environment.

He also discusses his distress with the bad rap Judas has received as well as different ways to concentrate energy within structures.

In **Oil and Ash in Turkey**, we are shown the relationship between Jesus his mother and cousins. Jesus has just returned from a trip to the hills in Morocco where he has learned the ritual of the oil and ash. His mother anoints him as head of the David family.

There is also a discusssion about the lineage involved in soul memories and how they are difficult to replicate.

Finally in a single paragraph excerpt from **Roman Twins,** the magnitude of Jesus' essence is defined.

Marriage with Jesus, about 16 A.D.
Excerpted from Number 21, July 19, 2011

Me: I am going down stone steps at a waterfront. I am wearing a white Roman toga. It is much more revealing than the usual robes that I wear. My hair is in a bun with baby's breath. Jesus has on a white Roman toga. Jesus and I come down the stairs holding hands. It is the beach and our wedding ceremony. We get married under a canopy on the beach. I am asking them, is it OK for Jewish people to get married outside of the temple and they are saying yes.

Q: Where is this taking place?

Me: The Sea of Galilee.

Q: Are there a lot of people there?

Me: About 30 or 40 people. There are Roman dignitaries there, because we are a wealthy family. We're bowing to their presence with the clothing we are wearing. We are very young. Jesus is 18 and I am 20. Before young men fill out, they have shoulders like broomsticks, wide but not deep. I have a ring on my finger that is the scarab carved out of jade. I've had a memory of that for a long time. When I started seeing scarabs at museum stores, I remembered that I used to have a ring like that. I wear it on my right hand.

Q: Why not on the left?

Me: I have just a carved band on the ring finger of the left hand. The scarab ring is something to remind me of rebirth. We have such a huge connection right away. It is a very spiritual relationship. I'm not a twin with him like his mother is a twin, but we've had so many past lives together that the memory permeates our energy as soon as we are together. I don't think we know yet where we are going with the energy, but we know we have an amazing ability to tap into universal energy. We know when we are together there is almost buzzing around us. I wonder about this sometimes, and, "Yes, there are ways to carry your energy so that it is incognito," they are saying to me. I have had people comment, "Oh, my God, Julia, it looks like you are lit from within, the light around you is so strong." I know it is when I am deeply emotionally/spiritually connected and I am not thinking about it. I've had people say that to me and I think, "Ooh." Like he and Mother Mary in the Roman Twins life needed to learn to handle that energy, I need to learn to handle that energy too, in the culminating life, because being with him is an enormous charge. We can almost feel the buzzing around us, the energy is so strong.

Q: Who is here today?

Me: There is a big group today. (Laughter) Jesus has on a patchwork robe. It has more colors than just turquoise and purple. There is some maroon and white. When he comes into your presence, his energy is swirling, so the colors around him swirl. He is saying that the swirling is a way to raise energy.

There are a lot of angels today. There are grey-and-white- winged angels. Peter is there with the angel choir and Mother Mary is there.

Q: I have been talking to her a lot.

Me: She is happy about that. She wants us to do that so that we grow the feminine energy. She is saying it is OK to be gentle and definite about it. This is for me because I have such a hard time claiming the space of being this channel. I feel like it is an ego trap for me. I dance around it. They are saying, "Respect is where you start." We must always, always insist on personal respect.

Q: That's a good place to start.

Me: It was one of those things I needed to experience so that I would claim that "respect" space. I am glad I am almost finished with it. It has been very challenging. This was one of those boundary issues I had when I was born that I needed to fully embrace and establish.

Q: What else does the scene have to show us?

Me: He could have chosen someone else. But it was Jesus the anthropologist who wanted to marry the beautiful young Greek girl. It was a heart decision as well as a philosophical choice. The philosophical choice was that I would better understand wisdom from other places he was gathering because of how I had grown up and because of our previous lives together.

He had an inkling then of how he was going to draw together all of his experiences. He had very strong issues with the Jewish Torah. It was a similar circumstance to how it is today, where the Romans were materialistic. He could see that they were creating their own downfall and he didn't really care about that. Already at 18, he was deeply saddened with what was happening within the Jewish faith. As with the money lenders at the temple, he really felt they were losing touch with their roots. Abraham and Moses were his personal heroes in the Old Testament. He felt that Moses couldn't have led all of those people without deeply connecting. He is saying that he really understands where the orthodoxy is coming from, even today with the dispute between modernists and fundamentalists. He is saying he gets where the orthodoxy of the Catholic Church is coming from, because they are afraid if they accept any of the tenets of modern society that it will completely sever religious practices from their roots. His point is that with modernism the problem is that they stop connecting to roots and stop connecting to the hearts of men. Moses could not have led the people into the Promised Land without first connecting to the hearts of men. He's saying that it is like the "Chain Gang" life. He's saying our leadership is too vulnerable to materialism and that's why this grass-roots movement is so important. This grass-roots networking, where we join together as caring individuals pulling together wonderful, loving groups. Oh, my God, I can feel it in my hands.

Q: It's getting back to basics.

Me: And connecting to hearts.

Q: I like the idea of the workshops so that you are not alone in this.

Me: Right, and that's part of the deal. The people who want to be part of it are adding themselves to the network. What they are saying is that I come with a strong bond with the people who have self-identified as being connected to the work we are engaging in. The purpose of Peter telling me late last winter to go ahead and start sharing the material was to build a support group. It is so flattering that people already do believe me, and people already are so kind. They are saying, right, absolutely, no one wants to piss them off, just in case. But it is a yearning in so many people and it is a missing puzzle piece.

Q: Absolutely.

Me: And that's what they are relating to more than me, the messenger. "Oh, my God, my heart has been yearning for this missing puzzle piece." I am a vessel for information. I almost become inconsequential. They are saying I am more comfortable with that part of the message than I am with the piece where I say, "It took me a long time to develop this ability," and talk about having any personal mastery. They are saying that the **Frozen Brain** regression, where they told me at the end is why I absolutely was meant for this process and why I have the heart for it needs to be part of the story. They want me to say, "They came to me. This is what they wanted. This is the story. This is why I was chosen. I say this with complete, honest humility. I don't feel adequate to the task. I feel like there must be some mistake, surely they mean somebody else." They are saying it is the right combination.

John the Baptist was at the wedding, but it was before we traveled to the place between India and China and had the water lesson. He was a light body.

The Gnostics, then, were the network that supported Jesus in his light body.

Q: Agnostic?

Me: Gnostic with a "G." The Gnostics were his energy network in supporting this huge and very nearly super-natural being. They are saying it's not going to happen that way again and to be suspicious of false prophets. There is an uprising. There will be many networks with many light bodies that come up from that. We are a healing group. Our message is about how to heal from the inside out. Our job is using personal energetic healing methods as well as traditional medicine.

I am seeing John the Baptist, our friend, and Mother Mary. Mother Mary could read cards. One night we learned Gnosticism was to come.

The Apostles were all part of the networking group that supported Jesus in his light body. These card nights, we started out in channeling meditations and they grew until we had that group that supported Jesus. They all had different tasks, and they were all part of the energy. And then they each started to receive the Gospels. The Gospel according to Thomas and the Gospel according to Mary Magdalene. I'm just making sure I'm keeping my Marys straight. There was no Gospel according to me, Mary. I was the recorder. Mary Magdalene didn't come in until I dropped out of the group. I don't ever see us being in the same space early on. I was the recorder. I was the person who was meant to keep it for later.

Q: So everyone who is part of this network is expected to fill a role of sharing and to receive?

Me: Not all of them will. They will self-identify. You and I were attracted to it so we stepped out.

Jesus was a scholar and he had a little ranch with horses near Galilee. His mother lived with us. He traveled whenever he learned of a new process, so there will be more of those recorded. I did go with him to more than just India. I think we went to Polynesia together and we saw the fire ritual. We had heard about that, where people walk on coals. We rode on elephants in India. He was so interested in how people achieved altered states, where it took them to a place where there was no pain and no burning. Where they could puncture themselves and there would be no blood. So whenever he heard about a healing ritual, he would go to investigate. As the boys grew older and needed more supervision, I didn't go with him so much. I did travel with him until James was about five. Then I wanted to be with the boys. I was to be the recorder. It turned out to be sufficient if I learned the technique at some point.

Jesus at a Roman Party, about 18 A.D.
Excerpted from Number 22, July 26, 2011

Me: Going in, I'm in a room where people are all wearing togas. It's early in Jesus' and my marriage and we are at a Roman party. Earlier in our relationship we spent a lot more time with the Romans. We were friendly with the Roman governor in the Jerusalem area. There are a lot of men at this party with an occasional woman. Jesus and I are there with Mother Mary.

Q: What's the purpose of the party?

Me: They are showing me this because in the early part of Jesus' life they were friendly with the Romans because they were from a high family. He did his best to be cordial and there were reciprocating social events with them. The purpose of the party: I'm getting it is around the time of Passover. Initially when I walked in the door I saw the Apollo card from my tarot deck. The party is at Passover but it is for the Roman god Apollo. Jesus was very open-minded about their polytheism. He was very interested in the idea of the different facets of higher energy. He didn't dispute that there were different facets of higher energy and that it came to people in different ways. I'm getting also a picture of cut stones with facets. It wasn't his faith. He didn't see multiple deities. But he did understand that there were different energies. It was more than respect for their culture. He was the anthropologist. He wanted to understand it. He wanted to layer those values on top of his own, like layering transparencies, to see how they fit together. He wanted to know where they were the same and where they were different. These are their core beliefs. He always wanted to know, where did the story come from? He never judged the presentation. He was always interested in how they arrived at their conclusion.

Q: What lies beneath?

Me: Exactly. What he felt was, "I'm sure at some point we share some core beliefs." They took an outward manifestation in a different way. He was so curious. I am seeing the sun god Apollo. The Romans imbued Apollo with magnificence and golden energy. Jesus being a light body could relate to that. He also would enter the room as though the sun was shining. There was a statue of Apollo which is festooned with some golden things, and then there is Jesus surrounded by light. He gets the whole Apollo thing. He is always interested in how energy manifests. Ultimately, that is his goal. He looks at the root. He understands, "This is the problem you were trying to solve and this is the solution that came to you. This is the name you put on it." Jesus definitely believes in the supernatural. He knows there are ways to relate to different kinds of energy and how they come through you. He really becomes quite an adept practitioner with those methods.

He was such a master at taking energy and refracting it through his body. He also was a person who only ever healed people who asked him. Because then he had permission. He did not invade other people's space unless he was asked. He got to the point where he could hear people ask on a non-verbal level.

Q: Right, telepathic.

Me: He felt people imploring him. It isn't just telepathic. He appeared to heal people who appeared not to ask. But they are going like this: shaking their fingers. That is not what happened. He absolutely never violated another person's space. When he saw a bilious yellow or grey guy at a party, he made a note. He was a medical intuitive, so he did a scan and then would say, "This is what I am seeing and this is where it resonates in my body." He wouldn't heal them. He noted the energy and watched for the correlation. I am seeing him send out little checking scans. "This is what I am seeing." He's saying, "After a while you know how the body works and it is a skill you pick up on without being a medical intuitive. It's because you understand what the manifestations of different diseases are. You can get to the point where you identify symptoms and can make accurate conclusions." (It seemed like homeopathy to me, as he described it.)

Q: Yes.

Me: He would feel it in different parts of his body. Early on he was fine at a party. He didn't drink much. He enjoyed being with people. He was really jovial. He told funny, raunchy stories. He was really, really a funny guy. He loved the story of Pegasus and winged horses. He thought that would be such a cool thing, to ride one of those winged horses. That's how the story in Revelations grew. Someone was recently telling me in Revelations, "Oh yeah, at the end of the world we're all going to ride a white horse." He was totally into that. He was like, "Sure, why not?" He was that kind of a guy. Yes, people took him really seriously in the *Left Behind* series. He's saying, "Sure. They are kind of like science fiction, why not?" "Why not say, 'Yes, at the end of the world, those of us who understand how to channel our energy, we're all going to ride a white-winged horse'." He says, me on the other hand, I wanted a magic carpet. "You ride the horse, I'm taking the magic carpet," is apparently what I said. He said, "Why NOT imagine that?" Because he says, "We knew there were different ways to raise energy." Yes, it was tongue-in-cheek, but it was one of those "yes and yes" answers. Because he always saw the humor in ironies, hypocrisies, and inconsistencies. When he was younger, he was angry about them, but as he grew older, he was so "I love it all," and I'm going to cry, "I just LOVE IT ALL."

He was the person who said, "Yes, I get you. I get who you are. I understand where you come from. I can see these rigid structures inside of you, and I think you are magnificent." No matter who they were, no matter what they had experienced or how awful they were, he LOVED them anyway. The thing of it was, he had something like x-ray vision. It got to the point where he could look at someone and say, "I see this happening with you and you are still magnificent. And I see how perfect each part of you can be. I can help you create it if you want. I can help you get there if you want. But if you just want to be who you are, I can adore you and see your magnificence, even if no one else can, even if you have no inkling of it."

Q: So he connected with all people on a soul level.

Me: Absolutely! And there was a, and I don't want to say 'pity,' but he would see and understand somebody's failings and weaknesses in a heartbeat: "All right, I see you are stealing money." It wasn't a pity thing, it was an acceptance and "I can see the bigger part of you, and I am going to speak to that bigger part of you." The higher soul self, the higher energy, the potential—he could always speak to the potential in somebody.

Q: That's a beautiful way to live and I think that's where he wants us and the rest of humanity to get to, that soul connectedness with each other. I think that's what he meant when he said, "Love your enemy." Not so much love the personality or what they did, but love that person on a soul level.

Me: Right. He and I have had a lot of conversations about this whole forgiveness thing. It's not like you ever allow them to possess you. You don't ever, ever invite that energy into your life. You always want a boundary from it. A lot of healers become ill because they don't have enough boundaries. They get a little inkling early on of how to merge their energies and think, "This is easy, I can heal them." But what they are not getting is there is a really, really specific protocol about how to do it so you are not merging your personal energy with theirs. It is this whole idea, "You MUST have permission, you MUST have a structure, and you MUST use universal energy. You don't use your own." It really relates back to there are so many enabling women, and women have such a hard time holding a structure. They are so intuitive and emotional, which is a good thing but they have to learn to hold a structure so that they can hold themselves apart from the mingling of any toxic energies. And they have to ALWAYS, ALWAYS, ALWAYS demand respect.

You can't heal anyone if they disrespect you. Then there are boundary issues with the vampire in your life who sucks you dry. Those are good lessons to have. You can only have healing energy if you have that wonderful structure where you are building it all the time. And if you allow the energy to be dissipated, it's like what you were talking about earlier, needing to pull your energy back in. If you allow it to be flopping around all the time like a fish, then it is not going to serve anyone. That's at the root of the respect and boundary issue. Alright, I am getting this multiple message. If you disrespect, devalue and are profligate with your healing energy, if you allow it to go everywhere, then not only are you not holding onto it and not concentrating it so it can be its strongest, but, number two you are disrespecting it. You are not valuing it the way that it needs to be valued. It is more precious than gold. It is the alchemy that everyone seeks, this ability to draw it all together and heal. It must be cherished. It must be contained in a safe, special place. It's more precious than rubies or emeralds.

Q: I put a protective bubble around me and I use it with divine energy and light. Is that what they are talking about, how I protect that?

Me: Right, right. They are not talking so much about you. You have good structure. You have good boundaries that you have created for yourself. It has a lot to do with why some of us have personal space that is invaded early, so that we do create that. "This was unacceptable behavior. I cannot tolerate that. I know I will lose my soul if I tolerate that behavior in other people."

I am seeing this cylinder structure that we all need to hold our energy in, like a silo, almost. At the foundation of the structure is respect. It is self-respect, it is respect for the energy and it is respect for everyone else. And it has a relationship to the root chakra. There is something about how it is related to fundamentalism in churches. It is respect, structure, roots and connection. The connection piece is so important because it connects them to deeper elemental energies. I had an issue recently where there has been too much rigidity in certain parts of my life with certain people. He is saying absolutely those fundamentalist, orthodox, rigidity pieces that stand in for tradition, they also become disconnected without roots. Don't just take it at face value, "orthodoxy is good." Orthodoxy is only good if it remembers from whence it came, if it is connected to source. Source is always kindness and love. Sure, we have tough situations that come from source insisting that we be our highest selves, but any time there is implacability, any time there is rigidness where no change is allowed, it is time to shake it up.

Q: Change is growth.

Me: Yes, change is growth. Respect for tradition is good. Empty tradition is worthless.

Q: Right.

Me: You have to always ask, what is its purpose and what is it standing for? When I was transcribing *Number 21*, he was saying he had some sympathy for the fundamentalists and I was saying, as I transcribed, "OK, but you can't leave it there because you have to take it where it needs to go next." And he is saying, "Absolutely. You don't just have tree roots. You have new growth and every year is different. Every year the growth changes because of the soil or the weather. Or sometimes the pests come and you need to respond to them. A tree is a wonderful analogy for the way spiritual relationships develop. You don't just have roots and this structure that never changes. A tree has malleability. It isn't the same year after year. And it is still a tree." Change doesn't cause it to lose its tree-ness.

Q: I am drawn to that metaphor.

Me: Right. If you have a drought, your tree suffers. You have to do special things to fix the drought. Or when it has too much water or not enough light, those are all circumstances that need to be responded to. That then relates back to the conversations he has had with me about change within structure.

Let's talk a little bit more about the Romans. He was buddies with those guys. He was a fun guy. He liked to be with people. He connected. Everybody adored him. As he changed, he grew more definite about how his life needed to be. As he grew into the Messiah, those who knew him as the guys' "guy" felt abandoned. The jocular storyteller was gone and they wondered, "Where is my buddy Jesus?" His take on it was, "I have to do this." That was the root of how everything fell apart at the end and he knew he was growing that, along with his philosophy. He knew he was growing the discontent in the Jewish and Roman strongholds. He became someone they couldn't count on to look the other way and be the "yes" man. There was a time he kept that need to go on his own in abeyance as he was fully grasping the energy and where it came from. And when he began to pull it all together, then he started to distance himself from them, knowing full well that they would feel betrayed. You withdraw your energy from people when you do that. He was withdrawing his energy and redirecting it a different way, so they were bereft. They didn't all get it. Some came and some did not.

Q: They took it personally.

Me: Yes, they didn't see or understand. He could see the picture. He shared with his support group the big picture that he saw. This is how I think it is going to happen. He loved Judas. He knew it was their agreement that Judas would do this thing. It is an area of personal sadness that Judas received blame for the betrayal that occurred.

Q: He does have a bad reputation because of that.

Me: He was so close to Jesus. It is sort of like *A Tale of Two Cities,* I am getting that tingling again. Where the guy steps in and says, "I'll be beheaded because I don't have as much going on as you?" He was as close or closer to Jesus as Peter was. But Peter had this whole system he was getting ready to implement, so Peter was the rock. So Judas said, "OK, I'll step in. I'll be this guy. I know it needs to happen this way." What a huge offering, what a huge gift. Judas said, "Master, I know you are going. I don't really want to be on the planet without you. I would rather live the life as the outcast." I don't think Judas was killed, was he?

Q: I'm trying to remember.

Me: It was more like, "My life is going to be in despair any-way, because I know you are going. I might as well take this hit because my life is going to be for shit anyway." I'm get-ting that he was outcast after that. There was a whole script that they had written. He left. He didn't think he could bear to be there when Jesus was crucified. And as the "other" Mary, I so longed to switch places with Judas. Rather than have to live the life I was going to have to live. All of us in that tight-knit group knew Jesus was going. We knew that we were going to have to live without him. We knew that there was such a slim chance he would survive. We had these discussions: "OK, what do we think we can live with? How do we think we can continue our lives without his magnificent presence, with this huge void?"

Q: He was like the water source, so to speak.

Me: Right. And I was lucky I stayed with the Mother Mary, because she was so healing for me. Her energy was so simi-lar to his. It was just flavored a little differently. He grew and grew and grew his light body.

Q: The healing question: Since healing is a higher energy, is it true only higher energy pursuits can access it?

Me: It relates back to the cylinder and silo. It needs to be kept in a focused structure. Because it can be dissipated and flop around like a fish. So we have to hold it in a cer-tain way so that it is direct and intense. And impervious, OK I'm getting it. That's why structures are so important to this process, so that we can learn to direct this energy like a laser beam, because the intensity is important. When it is intense, then it can't be redirected. But we have to be conscious and deliberate and focused about it. And then it cannot be redirected for a lower energy use. If we follow all of the rules it will be fine. We have to follow the rules of cleansing, centering/grounding, creating a structure and cultivating awe, developing the intensity. Those are the reasons why. It is a powerful tool. They will be helping us direct it. But we must always specify it is only to be used for the higher good.

They are saying, too, that housewives have been so under valued and so under utilized that they really felt they were such a tremendous untapped resource, so they agree with us. This is this cadre of energy that can change the world. Any time you go see these healers, the audience is mostly women.

Do we have a lesson from the life? It's about how you carry your energy different ways. How you allow other people to be who they are. How you can connect with them without enabling them. When they see that you are recognizing that special kernel of perfection in them selves, it is that poignancy. And poignancy is a little different than sweetness. It is the idea, "Oh my God, somebody really gets me." And then that draws people to you. This is what they say. They appreciate our playfulness and our willingness to just go with what they say to us. It isn't everyone who will do that.

Q: I am pretty easy-going.

Me: When I am transcribing these, I'll be thinking, "REALLY? Are you serious?" They are saying to me, "Yes, you do that, Julia, but you still show up."(Laughter)

The next session, **Oil and Ash in Turkey**, came early in the process of receiving past lives. A couple of months later, we received the **Abrum** life, which is recounted in Chapter 4, "Centering."

The message in them both seemed so strongly to speak to how important it is for us to center in the small things and go within, especially in times of adversity. After we received the **Abrum** life we began to see some themes appearing and I, for one, was hugely relieved! As noted in the introduction, it wasn't until June, 2011, when we began to learn the sequence of the categories, **Cleansing, Centering, Creating Structure** and **Cultivating Awe**. This journey has truly been one of happening onto signs as we worked our way through a dark forest.

Oil and Ash in Turkey, about 23 A.D.
Excerpted from Number 3, January 26, 2011

Q: Can you tell me where you are?

Me: I'm in a grassy area and there're mountains in the background

Q: Is there anyone else with you?

Me: The boys are here and they are little. They are playing with a dog. They are three and five.

Q: Where is the rest of your family, where is Jesus today?

Me: There're here. We are on a trip. We have a big tent. It looks like a medieval battle tent, like they used to have, with the banners, and it's striped.

Q: And how are you feeling?

Me: At peace. Happy. We've had a journey and we're going to stay here for a few days. This is our destination.

Q: So when you say, "We're staying here," is there a planned activity of what you are doing when you are there?

Me: It's a gathering of a lot of people. We're kind of on the outskirts with the boys. There aren't a lot of other little children here. There's a stream and we're under some trees. There is a bigger gathering further along, where everybody gets together.

Q: And what's happening at this gathering?

Me: It's some kind of festival. There's music, dancing and people are selling wares. I can see bright copper pots hanging and rugs in booths.

Q: Will you and the boys be at the festival?

Me: Yes, it's a family gathering. It's one of those David family gatherings. And I was always part of those gatherings.

It's a beautiful area in Turkey. It's very cool in the mountains. It's a summer excursion to get away from the heat.

We chose this location because it's a trading spot. Our family is upriver from the trading spot.

Q: And does everyone there know that you are Jesus' wife?

Me: Yes.

Q: Do you have a last name?

Me: I have a Greek last name.

Q: OK, can you spell the name?

Me: Lamporopolous.

Q: So are you Greek?

Me: Yes, I am from Pella. That's where we met.

Q: Are you with the Mother Mary quite a bit?

Me: Yes, I adore her.

Q: Is she at this occasion?

Me: Yes, she has her own tent, but she is here. She adores the boys. She carries the light with her where ever she goes. And my mother in this culminating life died when I was quite young. I was an innkeeper's daughter in Pella and that's how I met Jesus. Mother Mary and the David family are very sophisticated and I want always to please them. I'm conscious of not having the same kind of polish, although I have a sweet personality. I am beautiful and I am very fair compared to most of the people in this family, so that has a lot to do with what drew Jesus to me. Because I am very unusual-looking and he was fair, for a Jewish man.

Q: He was. He often had a red-tinted beard. Fair.

Me: When I knew him it was chestnut. Maybe when he was younger.

Q: Do you two have an affectionate relationship?

Me: Yes. Very affectionate.

Q: So tell me a little bit more about this scene. Why are we seeing the scene? Is he going to speak? Is he going to say anything? Or was it just to show us what your lifestyle was like?--The celebration with the David family?

Me: No, I think he is being bestowed an honor. It's an official ceremony that acknowledges his bloodline. His mother is anointing him. She's using special oil and she's touching his forehead. All the family members are looking on, so it's some acknowledgment of him being of the David bloodline.

Q: It has nothing to do with the fact that he preaches a sermon or gospel?

Me: You know he's really young. He's still in his 20s. We're still learning.

Q: We're seeing a scene of your early life.

Me: Yes. He was always extremely intellectual. He was a person of great moral fortitude, even at this time when he is about 25. People come to him to solve problems.

His mother was anointing him to become head of the family. It's like being a lord, a feudal lord. He spends time helping family members settle disputes.

And at night there's a big bonfire where we roast a cow. It's too big to be a pig and they don't eat pigs anyway. But it's on a big spit over a huge fire. There's a lot of dancing and music.

Q: Do you and Jesus dance?

Me: It's like Greek dancing where everyone dances in a line or a circle. Yes, and I dance.

Q: Is there anything else about this scene that we need to know?

Me: I think the fire is important and it's after the ceremony and after the banquet, the roast and feast, they put ashes on their foreheads…

I'm not Catholic, but I think it's where the Catholics got Ash Wednesday. It's relating to what I was telling you about the Phoenix and how I wore the scarab ring. It's another purification ritual.

Q: And when you say "purification," is that a ceremony that the family has made up? Or is it a spiritual purification?

Me: I think it's one he has brought to them. I think it is one that he has studied. He brings…

Q: I know he goes to foreign lands.

Me: Right. The family is educated. And he takes it as his responsibility to share information from other cultures. But I think this is from Africa. It is a Moorish practice, from back in the caves, in the hills of Morocco.

Q: So you're just showing us a really nice glimpse of our early history of Jesus and you're showing us how he helped the nation grow with traditions, with ceremonies.

Me: Well, this was something he incorporated in his practice as he grew spiritually. He was first anointed with oil by his mother and then he put ashes on his forehead. Next he put ashes on the boys and on me and everyone else. He said some words over the dying flames before he used the ashes. We're being shown this because it's part of his consciousness-raising. It is one of the steps through which he drew power to himself. This is part of the knowledge that's being held for us to learn. He is teaching me. I didn't go with him on this trip. I'm tired and I've had a lot of wine to drink. He's saying to me, "you know, Mary, you need to learn this"--laughing at me-- so I am doing it with him. And in the following days I practice. It's written on a sheepskin scroll.

Q: And you practice it then, once it's written.

Me: Yes.

Q: So he has not at this time started traveling or started making speeches to groups to help anyone in his philosophies. He's too young.

Me: He always shared information

Q: He doesn't have disciples following him.

Me: He is a very important person in his family and yes, he is taken very seriously. Some of the disciples are his family. When he started going on the road and teaching, with the disciples following him, was just an extension of what he was already doing.

Q: I see.

Me: What happened was he became a master. At this point, when he is in his mid '20s, he's collecting vast stores of information. You know he studied all the ancient wisdoms. He studied the Sufis, the Taoists, and Kabala. By this time, he'd had 10 years already of studying all sorts of different mysticism. When you are so well-versed in topics, after a while your mind starts to create its own base of information. He is at the point where he is beginning now to grow his own philosophy. It's a special event, where he has been anointed by his mother and he takes on the mantle as head of his family. It's a large, large family and they have traveled from far to come to be here. But his mother, you know, is also gifted. The line goes through her.

Q: When you say the line goes through her...

Me: The line of David goes through her. She is also mysti-
cal/psychic. She is luminous. She glows. She has so much
light coming from within her. For her to anoint him in that
way is to share her responsibility being the head of the family. She has some older uncles, but it is coming through her
and then to Jesus.

Q: So she could have chosen the uncles, but she felt like
Jesus…

Me: Well, she could have chosen the uncles, but Jesus was
her offspring. It's a very close family, and within any wealthy
family there are religious masters, and then there are some
that manage the land, and some that go to war. And the
uncles are older than she, so it's a transference of responsibility and family power. He has been groomed for this, like
a young prince, all his life. His mother has mastery. She
doesn't travel much any more. She's extremely well educated for a woman of her time. She's a wise woman and she
studied in Alexandria. For a woman, she is deeply immersed
in mysticism. Sufis kept that separate. She is the exception.

Jesus is pulling together the study of elements.

Q: So this is new.

Me: It isn't new. None of what he did was new. He didn't do
anything that hadn't been done before, before the end. What
he did was study from far regions and bring it all together.

Q: So was he starting to do any teaching with the four elements?

Me: Well, that night he did. He did a prayer of the ashes and
he put them on foreheads of those who wanted to do it. He
explained the scarab that rises from the ashes. It's the begin-

ning of his faith message. It's starting here. There's been a long drought. He's telling his family members that it's a different type of cleansing process, but it also reinforces new growth. He talks about the faith needed to create transformation and reminds everyone that they are not physical bodies. He tells them the drought, and famine that comes from drought, are to remind us that we are not our physical bodies.

Q: You mean the physical drought, not the spiritual drought.

Me: Right, right. There is a purpose to drought, like "There is a season." He says drought is a different type of cleansing. Water is an emotional cleansing like we talked about before (in *Number 2*). This kind of cleansing is about creating something out of barrenness, out of the caked earth that won't produce anything. What can you produce out of that? He's saying that you need to remove your emotional self and remind yourself that you are a spiritual being, not a physical one. He says it's a testing. "About providing for your family," he says, "of course, do what you can, it's good to find the river or the ocean where you can fish, or the animal to hunt."

He says it's a lesson for the farmers who are trying to create something out of the earth. "We are nomadic," he says, "and then it is time to let go and shift. We become too attached to the material, being able to produce and create." He says, "It's a reminder to shift. There's a process." Of course, he says you do everything you need to do to survive and sometimes that's impossible. He's saying we are lucky we are surrounded by water and there are always fish. But he says that famine isn't the worst thing that can happen, and yes, you don't like for it to impact your children, but it's a reminder that we are spiritual beings having a physical experience.

"It's time," he says, "when that happens, to return to your roots." He means that in more ways than one. It's time to move and to let go of the thing you think you have created. It's time to go within yourself and meld with the environment and send your spirit out to search. He says we panic and we get even more attached to what can happen with the material and it is misplaced energy. The ashes represent the barren earth and the way to create something from the barren earth is to shift and first go within yourself. It is something like what I do in my guided imageries, where I tell people to become one with their environment where we expand our spirit out, out, out, out. And he says it's very much like that.

Q: I missed that and I want to pick it up. We panic when we think we are going to lose the physical.

Me: We hold onto it even tighter. And the point is not to do that. The point is to go within yourself and to shift away from the material. He's telling me now, that's what he was saying that night, that to anoint with the ashes after the oil is to remind us of that process.

Q: OK.

Me: I need to start talking about what people are wearing. He has on a white robe and a red-and-white striped over robe, with a belt. I am looking at him, at that time, when we are both in our '20s. I am looking at him with horror and at my beautiful chubby-cheeked little boys and saying, "What are you talking about, that we are just supposed to ignore the famine of our children?" He gives me a smile and says, "It's easier to philosophize about this than it is to put it into practical application." His cousins are saying to him, "Buddy, let's work on this one. We can make this one better."

Q: I'm questioning if he's showing us this because our planet is going through the same thing right now? Meaning we're panicking because we are losing physical possessions, and we try to hang on to them even tighter. What we should do is let go, go within and remember that we are spiritual beings.

Me: Oh, absolutely! And we get too hung up on ownership, he says. The way to make something multiply is to give it away. He says we read that book, *The Rainbow Fish*, to our children, about the little fish who gives away all his scales, so that everyone can be as beautiful as he is. He says we teach our children those values and then we forget to practice them ourselves.

Q: How did it happen that you escaped being mentioned in any of the history?

Me: You know there were a lot of Marys. And sometimes it was a reference to me and they would say, "It was his mother," and some times there'd be a reference to me and they'd say it was Mary Magdalene. But I didn't go on those trips with him. It wasn't a particularly desirable place for a woman to be.

Q: But they just never connected, when he was back with you, that you were his wife.

Me: He didn't bring the crowd with him. He would come all by himself. It was only the last period of his life where he was a public persona. He didn't spend his life with these thousands of people. It was at the very end he started to attract crowds. He felt this burning desire to share the wisdom that he had, and he felt, somewhat erroneously, that he could just tell people to forgive and love one another, and then felt he could show people the power that would give them.

When I went to see Brian Weiss, he was saying Jesus was an Essene. I had a "No, I don't think so" gut reaction to that.

He hung out with the Essenes in Jerusalem. He slept there because it was a place for him to be. It appeared from the outside to many people that he was an Essene. The Essenes were similar to the Shakers from 100 years ago. They lived very simply. They gave up all their worldly goods. He was growing to the point where he thought, we don't need this stuff. It's not important. But he was NOT an Essene.

Q: He just studied with them.

Me: Yes. He lived in their place, he hung out with them, and he taught them. They became like a Venn diagram. Part of the Essene group became part of the disciple group. But I didn't go with him. I said, "Who wants to go there?" It was dirty, icky. And by then we knew I was the keeper of the knowledge. By then we had done our explorations together to understand that we had different roles to play. We were mystical together.

It's possible for everyone to get the learning, but these soul memories are hard to replicate. The people we were in that life, in the year 23, there's a soul memory from that.

Q: And that's what is hard to replicate.

Me: And that's what's hard to replicate

Q: To keep the lineage going because you are trying to keep the soul memory. So let me get this straight. You are the keeper of the soul memories that are hard to replicate through these many, many, many generations.

Me: Over the ages there have been purges of knowledge.

Q: What do you mean about the purges?

Me: Like what the Catholic Church did to the Gospels. Or like what Mao did in the Cultural Revolution.

Q: Where they just killed everybody and threw everything...

Me: Yes, there've always been these times where they purge vast resources. It's easier to maintain the line of knowledge if I don't have a lot of traumatic deaths. I brought one on myself when I was burned at the stake. It's easier to maintain a clean line.

Q: And would you agree that we are being downloaded with electromagnetic energy, so that we will be raised to a higher frequency, is that true? Can you talk about that?

Me: That's not my knowledge, but that's what the planets are saying. I don't know about electro magnetic frequencies, but the planets for sure are positioned for this. There is energy that comes from the planets. You can extrapolate that it's only part of the process. I'm sure it's happening on many different levels.

I think they already have been...I think you see practitioners all the time.

Q: I'm talking about a more widespread area. Many thousands and millions will be doing this whereas now there are only a select few teachers and ascended masters on earth doing it.

Me: Well, it's always over a period of time and there's always choice. There isn't going to be a group mind bending. People have to choose it. You know, the more important question is, are people going to adopt green energy? Is there going to be a planet? (Laughing)

We have to understand that when we destroy something we have to create something new. We can't keep destroying things. We have to repair damages we have done. When we hurt somebody, we have to apologize. There are many incomplete transactions occurring now. We have to learn to complete a transaction. When you take someone's power away, you have to give it back. When you demoralize someone, you have to replenish their spirit.

Roman Twins, 50 B.C.
Excerpted from Number 19, June 11, 2011

Me: The point is: nobody should underestimate the gargantuan task it was for him to learn to do this. Even being a light body, he still had lifetimes and lifetimes of training. You can by-pass (snapping) and pack a bunch of learning into one life so that you can suddenly ascend. But what they are saying is most people aren't equipped for that. You have to be able not to hold on to anything. Never to be jealous, never to be hurt, and never to feel victimized. You have to be a person continually reorienting yourself and foraging ahead. When you can do that, you are just a clear vessel. You have this, I'm seeing like a glass structure, wide at the bottom, wide at the top, a circle on the inside, but you have to be this grounded, free enclosure. That was what was so great about those Ute brothers. That's what they were. They just were channels for this wonderful energy. They pulled it in. And they put it out. That's what was so magnificent about them.

13

The Crucifixion

It all ends up here. Would Jesus have been as remarkable a practitioner of the ultimate mysticism had he not died on the cross? The man who became God sought God during an excruciating death. It's my sense that he so fully immersed himself in and melded with universal energy and divine love as his death occurred that he became universal energy and divine love. As he informed us in **Bandits**, rising above personal injury and pain creates a heightened sense of inspiration.

What we learned early on is that Jesus will answer any question. The first question, posed here in **Bandits**, "What was it like to die on the cross?" was asked by a man enduring the personal challenge of radiation treatments. Jesus further informs us that in following the path of **cleansing**, **centering**, **creating structure** and **cultivating awe** set forth here, we are getting the truncated version of his personal soul journey. He says after he created the path and as more have followed him, the journey is more easily accessed by others. He again expresses the foundational sentiment that judgment has does not belong in Christianity.

In **Chain Gang II**, we follow Jesus to Arabia where he utilizes his mastery of Talmudic law to help a sheik negotiate water rights.

In exchange, the sheik teaches him some Sufi mystical practices which he then utilized when he was crucified. (After the **Mother Mary** session, where we learned she had been trained in ancient Sufi practices, we learned that Sufism did indeed predate Islam.) He also asserts that at no point was he ever a victim, and clarifies what happened to Judas.

Finally, in **Chain Gang I,** we learn about the cloth of Turin in which Jesus was wrapped after the crucifixion. We also experience the hours after his death where all of us present strove to release the pain we carried so that the true honor of Jesus could live through us. What it takes to become truly Christian is also defined.

Bandits, 100 B.C.
Excerpted from Number 13, May 1-I, 2011

Q: The question I would like to ask, "What was it like to die on the cross?" seems disrespectful.

Me: All right, here we go. He says it was a lesson for him in learning to disengage from physical pain. He'd been practicing a long time for that. And to trust the process. He knew ahead of time what he was getting into. "Sometimes it was easier than others," is basically what he is saying. It's sort of like the Deepak Chopra tape I heard where, when he was in medical school, there were yogis who came to demonstrate, and they would put a knife or whatever into their arm. They were able to control the blood from spurting out. There would be no seepage, even. And then somebody in the front row distracted him and the yogi went into ego and the blood would start pouring out until he was able to call his composure back. That's what Jesus is saying. He'd been practicing for a long time for that. With St. Francis, who had the stigmata, it was the step beyond hair shirts, with the monks. St. Francis also was learning to disengage from the pain. It was a composure process. "I am not my pain. I am separate from this. I am a complete being without this pain." It's like Mother Mary who was able to be the light body regardless of the circumstance. She never allowed it to break her step. She never stopped being the light body that was always a loving, healing, wonderful presence. No matter what adversity she was faced with. It's that sort of seamlessness we aim for in our human life forms. How do we maintain our sense of spiritual self regardless of the circumstances we are in? How do we have a greater identity, in our spiritual selves than we have in our physical body? Everyone has a different lesson. That's the lesson he chose. "I can do the messiah thing."

And I kept saying, "It's not for me."

We all have a different purpose and there is a lot of choice in that. He signed up for that life. They didn't say to him, "Jesus, you are doing this." He said, "I think I can do it. I think it is a useful way to expend my energy."

Q: His purpose in the crucifixion wasn't to "take away the sins of the world." But his purpose for doing that was to teach us something? Or was it part of his personal lesson?

Me: Well, it was multi-faceted and that is what our whole process is about. What he said to me initially was, "I want my story to be told." And it is a multi-faceted story. There are many levels and many layers and many different permutations for this. What he wants us to understand is that he is giving us more than the snapshot version that is in the New Testament. That was just a Polaroid of a second. He's saying there are enough of us now on the planet who want to understand this information. He wants the story to be told so that we can understand. People want overnight salvation. They want overnight healing.

OK, at one point, he said, "Through me," because he lived those lives, because he had the learning. Once the technique is in place, it can be used again. We don't all have to take the same amount of time he did. Some of us can get the Cliffs Notes for this. But until he did it, it really hadn't been done in quite the same way. I think they still say his energy resonated on the planet higher than anyone else's. When it says in the New Testament "I am the way," he's holding up a lantern for us. The New Testament is the snapshot version of, "I am the way." He's saying there're all these other different complexities that went along with it.

I've known people who have the ability to read the New Testament and center their lives in it. They are gracious, wonderful, loving, compassionate people. Good on them that they can do that. I haven't been able to do that, personally.

Q: That's understandable. There are far fewer that can actually live the Word than can teach the Word, or they use the Word for their personal selfish, ego-driven uses.

Q: People hide behind the Word.

Me: But it is all a good lesson. It's their lesson. We don't have to worry about them so much. The universe will handle that. They may get to spend a little more time here.

Q: This has felt like a clarification process and bringing to modern time in language that we need now--the people who are on the earth who are ready. Instead of the...

Q: ...20,000 different versions of Christianity. You can spend your whole life weeding the garden before you see the flowers.

Me: It's still about the journey. At the very end he was still journeying. He was still a practitioner, learning a skill and a discipline. It is the discovery of it that makes life in the physical plane worth it.

The universe is often a reflection of our highest selves. What's the highest part of you, and that's where you will find the universe talking to you.

They desperately want to engage with us. That is the point.

Q: What plane do these three reside on?

Me: They are on the plane of Ascended Masters. They are saying they can hear the angels from where they are, but they don't need to live with them. The angels come to talk to them. It is just a different resonance.

There are apparently many different opportunities for us when we are out of our bodies.

Q: And one is really no different or better than the other?

Me: I don't really know. It was never anything I was ever very interested in.

Q: No, I'm asking them.

Me: Oh, (laughter), It is basically where your energy fits.

Q: A level where your energy fits.

Me: You know how atoms are configured differently? Electrons move at different speeds. They can only make a molecule with electrons that travel at a similar speed, am I correct in that?

Q: Yes.

Me: If your energy isn't at that level, your electrons aren't merging. They can't be together. They don't accept one another.

Q: Can you grow, can you graduate?

Me: Oh, sure. It isn't exactly like the table of elements, because you aren't stuck with a certain number of electrons for the rest of your life. But it is a growing process where some learning needs to occur. Basically we have the choice of whether it is hard or easy learning, is what they are saying to me. It is what the lesson is today.

Q: Is there God?

Me: I'm getting many different answers. There are a lot of different answers to that question. Everyone sees God in a different way. For this purpose, they are allowing God to be defined the way I like to define it, which is universal wisdom. And that is a collective/collaborative approach. Other people use the filters and the information they can accept. But for me, I see God as the collective unconscious. I am very Jungian in my orientation. They are happy to use that lens with me. They are saying there are an infinite number of ways to view this, but the way I like to view it, where all energy has purpose, is useful.

Q: Is there any more information we need to know from the life where you and Jesus were bandits?

Me: I guess I kept a cup that we stole. We really liked this gold cup that we took from one of my father's friends. I kept it. And that's kind of where we dreamed up the concept of the chalice, the one that is supposed to have been hidden in Scotland. We liked that cup so much we thought it would be so fun to have a legend around it.

Q: In the last life you were together.

Me: Like the chalice at the Last Supper. They love plays on words, like vessels and chalice, and so many people are actually looking for the physical artifact. It probably has some mystical power, but what they think is hilarious is how easily distracted we are by the material, and clearly the chalice is within us and has always been within us.

There is real power here. This is a salvation story. That's true. Whatever it takes to get people to salvation is what they will do. While they have considerable humor, incredible intelligence and we can play all sorts of word games about what Jesus really meant, this IS a salvation story. This is a story of how we turn straw into gold. This is an alchemical story about how we transform ourselves.

Q: Salvation in every life or at the very end? I don't know what salvation looks like.

Me: I think that's one of those things you get to co-create. What do you want it to look like? Let's ask that question, "What is salvation?"

"How do you create a world you want to live in?" is the answer.

Q: So you live your salvation. It's not what I was taught. You only got one chance.

Me: No, it's an everlasting story. It just keeps going.

The people inside my head are saying we need to take responsibility for our behavior. If we ruin something, we need to make reparations. We are responsible for our actions. There are consequences for our behavior.

Q: Can it be cause and effect versus our creator making something bad for us, as in karma? It's almost more emotional.

Me: This is what I am getting from them: "Judgment does not play a part in this."

Q: It just is. Because you hear, "He got bad karma." Karma doesn't care what your judgment is. It is just there.

Me: Everybody has a different deal they make. We get into trouble with judgment about it. "That person deserves to be a cripple in this life because they must have poisoned someone in another life and that's the way they are choosing to pay off their karma." Whatever! There's a judgment in that. The point is to tread lightly around it because our job is to only deal in kindness and compassion. And where was the kindness and compassion in the statement that a paraplegic needs to be that way because they poisoned someone in the last life.

Q: Or that the people in Japan deserved the tsunami because they poached dolphins and whales.

Me: What they are saying to me is: "DO NOT GO THERE." I am seeing that in block letters. They're saying that was a wonderful statement for you to make. There is no equivocating over this point. That's a relationship that we can never grasp on the physical plane. Our job is only to develop kindness, compassion and solutions. The minute we go there about what others "deserve," we better watch out, because in a dark corner something's going to happen. We are absolutely not to go there.

Q: Absolutely, in block letters. Thank you for the warning.

Me: Judgment takes you back to the start.

We know what he's wearing when he appears means something about the function he is performing. Who knew THAT?

Chain Gang II, 510 B.C.
Excerpted from Number 23, August 4, 2011

Me: Mother Mary is here. Jesus is here. They are all wearing blue and white today. Peter always wears white. Jesus' beard is a little longer than usual. Do spirits' beards grow? I don't really get that. (Laughter) This is what he is saying: The red outfit that he wears is right after vision quest, and when he wears the brown peasant shift that we see him in, that's his vision questing and Messiah attire, so that no one gets distracted by what he is wearing. It's that concept where you simply see his light and his magnificence. But then when he comes back from vision quest, he likes to wear red and shave his beard. This blue and white look is the scholar, land owner, the mentor. He is a mentor today. Good. That's what the different outfits mean. (Laughter)

Q: Good to know.

Me: When your beard is long, you are being the mentor.

For some reason I am seeing belly dancers and many different colors. Jesus is in Arabia. He learned a process here. I am seeing him dressed up. He's wearing brocades, sitting on a rug. He has a turban on, his beard is long. He's outside watching belly dancers. There is a fire. He's eating "sweet meats and nuts" they are saying. It is raisins, nuts and dates, all mixed together in a bowl. There is a sheik who wants to give him one of his daughters, and he is saying "No, thank you." Oh! Then the sheik then says to him, "Well..." and I am wondering why they want to give him a gift. Jesus has come to teach this sheik a language maybe? Helping him write...he already knew how to write. OK,

OK, it's helping him with negotiations. In helping the sheik with negotiations he is using, and I am getting the word "Talmud" or "Talmand" and I am getting it is an ancient Judaic law format. Jesus has come to help this sheik, who is negotiating with another sheik about water rights. I am not with him, but he is telling me the story and I can see it. Why can I see it? Huh, we have that ability I guess, to see in each other's lives. I don't know how comfortable I am with this. (Laughter)

Q: Surprise!

Me: Here I am! I'm not even looking in a crystal ball!

He is saying to the sheik, he doesn't really want one of the daughters. So the sheik is going to teach him some of the ancient Sufi wisdom about how to open yourself to universal wisdom. It's the wisdom he used when he was on the cross. What he is saying is, he didn't want to stay on the cross forever and he didn't want to die a painful death. When people have been hanged, they suffocate when the weight of the lungs drops. And he is saying it was harder for him. He lasted a lot longer because his feet were not loose. So he worked at keeping from bleeding when he was being crucified. He practiced with the sheik. He didn't know when he was going to need this. The sheik came from an ancient Sunni/Sufi tradition. Were they Sunnis too? He's saying that eventually what he did was he just chose to stop his heart and died that way rather than waiting to suffocate. I guess he had some yogi practices, too, so he combined it with the Sufi practice, where they specialized in surviving being impaled. It involves drawing what is puncturing you into yourself, where you become one with the nail, or whatever it is. What he found when he was being crucified was that the more he did that, the more he became one with the nail, the longer he was living, so that wasn't necessarily working.

(Laughter) So he had to then use a yogi tradition where he stopped his heart.

He is saying that is one thing to tell the people who are so distressed about his crucifixion is that he had very little pain and he had a lot of personal choice in what was happening while he was being crucified. That really ties into the **Chain Gang** awe because it is about finding that joy, no matter what the circumstances are. He could connect to the ecstasy that went beyond the awe and inspiration. He was connecting with that kind of ecstasy because it was such an intense situation. He is saying it was not at all sexual.

He is saying when people have had the Stigmata, like St. Francis, where they had the bleeding from the...?

Q: Palms.

Me: Yes. He says that's what they were aiming for was the same kind of ecstasy, and so did the people who wore the hair shirts. It takes them to a different level to have to go beyond that pain, that rawness. He says that's what cutters do, that's what they are looking for. Somehow it is a connection.

Q: So the Sufis taught him how to do that?

Me: I was with him when he learned from the yogis in India, but I was not with him when he went to see the sheik. The sheik worked with him on the impaling process, but he learned to stop his heart from the yogis in India. That's good to know. I don't know that I previously knew, on any level, that he experienced very little pain.

Q: I think that is great to know, because a lot of people hang on to that with the guilt.

335

Me: That's the other part. He wants to make the statement that he was co-creating every part of his life. And that's why we were talking about Judas. Judas then had the choice of how he was going to live his life (after the crucifixion). All the apostles did. They could all manifest that joy any time they wanted to. They could all write the script. At the time it seemed like crucifixion was what was going to work best. He knew that he could have a life with me and the boys in the mountains somewhere far, far away from the public eye. But that wasn't the point. The point was to have this amazing existence that everyone talked about. The point was it would create a spectacle and a memory. If he had simply shown up as this great guy who had this wonderful light and this ability to heal, and then disappeared quietly, there wasn't the exclamation point at the end of the life. This way…

Q: It made more of an impact.

Me: Exactly. OK. I am saying to him, your body was still broken. Your body still was not in great shape after the crucifixion. It was still like brittle little pretzel pieces, even though you were in control every single minute, even though you were co-creating. So, yes, he felt blessed and yes he felt gratitude, but it was beyond that. Because it was a situation he had designed, he had co-created and he was taking responsibility for it. He was NEVER a victim is what he is saying. Interesting…

OK, and we're going to talk about Judas. They are saying Jesus was not a victim of Judas. Jesus could choose at any time how his life was going to be. Judas eventually chose to live very simply. Like a joyful beggar. There's a story that he got really fat and somehow his entrails came out.

Q: He didn't hang himself?

Me: No, he didn't hang himself. He liked to anonymously slip in and out of communities and bring joy, Judas did finally. He eventually realized that it wasn't helping anyone to be so devastated. At first he was sort of like me at the end of the bandit life, where he felt that he was the one who was left…

Q: Survivor guilt.

Me: Yes, and he was finally able to re-connect with joy. He knew how to do that. It was sort of like the Nikko life, where the pre-Jesus guy who lived in the forest could supply the environment for all the animals to coexist peaceably? He could slip into communities if they were having a plague or something like that and he sat himself down like a beggar on the street with an eye patch, and send out waves. He chanted in different languages. People thought he was crazy/schizophrenic. He anonymously brought healing to the community if there was a plague or dissension. "That is how," they are saying to me, "he lived the rest of his life."

Q: I'm glad that's cleared up because he has always had a really bad rap.

Me: That's why Jesus said, "I did it all my way. It unfolded exactly the way I designed it." Judas was into the self-flagellation and masochism, but he grew out of it. He developed another identity. You know how we were talking about that intention for material things belonged in another room?

Q: Right.

Me: He stepped out of the Judas identity and created another identity for himself in another room. He began living off the new heritage then. It is like shedding a snakeskin. The Judas identity is the snakeskin that he has shed. And he created this whole other benevolent…

Q: But purposeful, life.

Chain Gang I, 510 B.C.
Excerpted from Number 10, April 29, 2011

Q: What do you know about the cloth of Turin?

Me: Did we wrap Jesus in that?

Q: The image of his face was there, I believe that's the story? He was wrapped in that.

Me: It was something that we carried with us. Yes, we did wrap him in it. When we sealed him in the tomb, I took the cloth with me.

Q: You un-wrapped him…

Me: Because I couldn't bear…not to have it with me. It was the only physical keepsake of him I could take to France. We buried it in Spain. It wasn't far from where I was living. Outside of current day Barcelona there's a monastery very high up on a hill, Montserrat. We used to visit near where it is located. The cloth was taken from that area. The boys put it there.

Q: Your boys and Jesus'?

Me: It was sort of like a ritual where I wanted it to be pre-served. We knew from the Egyptians that when you put something into the elements it was better-protected. They had ways of preserving things. Taking it back into the hills and the caves, the boys were going to find a good space for it. It seems to me that there were some layers of rock in those areas. You could go in to find a space in the layers of rock to slip it in and keep it.

Q: To preserve it in the element of the earth.

Me: Yes.

Q: Could you ever see an image of him when you looked at the cloth?

Me: I knew it was there. I knew it smelled of rosemary. After he died, I rubbed oil into his body. We had some rosemary oil. We had some unguents and creams we used. We made a suspension with rosemary. After he died I was...so...it was just my way of giving him comfort. I had this sense that his spirit was lingering close by, just outside of his body. I knew his spirit was inside of his aura. It was my way of bringing comfort to his passing. It was so awful. It was such a terrible way to leave the body and the earth. I had a visceral sense that if I could massage his broken body with this lovely rosemary and olive oil, cream, and some rendering of sheep fat--there was a whole process around it, kind of how they make tallow for candles--and if I could imbue it with all the love that I had for him... that it would help soothe his way out of his body. Even though it happened afterwards, it's sort of like the whole idea that time is relative. I hoped that if I could capture it when his body was still warm, before the rigor mortis set in, and I delayed the rigor mortis. I massaged this into his body to give him the comfort of a loving passage. And so I knew that was on the cloth...and I knew (tearful) it was all that I had of him. I carried it with me until I was able...to let him go...later because I wanted it to be preserved. So we made a sleeve from animal skins that we tied up. It was like an envelope. We folded the cloth up in that. The boys were going to find a rock to slide it into.

Q: Could you ask the ritual that you used?

Me: With Jesus? Did I say anything?

Q: Anything during the ritual?

Me: I think I had this mantra. It was like a vigil. There were just a handful of people, and his mother came in. She laid her hand on his forehead. I think we smudged the air with sage around us, and there was some deep, low chanting. I'm seeing his cousins outside, around a fire. Holding hands, chanting, and then they came in and held hands around us... him, his mother and me. The words of the chanting were something like: The pain in my soul, I know I must let it go, and allow myself to carry your honor with me. You know, how you have the gut feeling? We all felt like we had been gutted. We all had that awful feeling like our entrails were hanging out. We had so much physical pain. We knew that to wrap ourselves in the pain would be to deny his honor. So we knew we had to chant to allow the pain not to be tied up inside of us, and to allow his honor to be carried inside of us instead. You know how when you're cold, and you want to hold yourself so tight, and you know when you're hurt, you want to hold yourself so tight? We had to allow the pain that was there to be released, not trapping it inside of us. Then we asked for the honor to come in. The honor is shimmering gold that was energy he carried with him. That's what the chanting was, an "Oh, my soul, please allow me to distance myself from this pain, so that I can allow honor that is generosity of spirit to transport us." It will carry us anywhere. It's this purity. When you hold pain and suffering too close to you it creates a rent in the protective layer around you.

Q: The rip?

Me: Yes, the tear.

Q: The tear is created from holding the pain, as if it is yours.

Me: Yes, it's the hardest thing we do, letting go of fear, and letting go of pain--because it is so horrendously annihilating. It is the generosity of spirit that needs to be held closer than the pain.

Q: That we embrace versus the pain. Is this something similar to what I've been saying about things happening and coming through you? Or is this something you actually draw around you so that it's easier to let go of the pain, versus taking it in.

Me: That's the process where you don't allow the pain to be you. You allow the pain to be separate from you. You surround yourself because you know you have to. Wrap yourself in the honor that is generosity of spirit like Jesus did. His honor was his true generosity of spirit. It was a, "I am healing. I am health. I am your healing. I am your health." He learned to be the vessel for healing. When we carried his honor next to our skin instead of the pain, it was also a way to symbolically carry him in the honor instead of the pain, so that he could make the transition easily, so that he could be who he is now. It was a way to safeguard his passage, as well as to safeguard our own passage.

Q: To relish in his honor and to hold that honor up to his enormous generosity.

Me: Exactly. After honor, integrity is superfluous. When he did a process, when he sat and meditated, you could see it around him. It was gold light and his mother could do it too. The two of them could do it.

I'm seeing the other piece of the generosity of spirit is that people aren't truly Christian until they accept all the other views. You can't be truly Christian until you have energy that is accepting of everyone. That's accepting of all people from all places. There are no exceptions.

Q: Who are they today?

Me: Who ARE they today? Who is here? Peter is here and, and Jesus is here, and all of our guides are here and they say, "Thank you for creating this wonderful space." They say they stand in a circle and hold hands around us in the process. They are saying it is an available service for anyone doing these kinds of processes. It isn't just us who deserve this. It is always here for us as we are doing this work. They are sort of like a surveillance crew. Mother Mary is here.

Q: Do they have anything more to say about the ritual?

Me: After we massaged him with rosemary oil, we wrapped him in cotton. Rosemary is the heart medicine. The olive oil and the tallow, they both have gold in them, so that represents the gold that I rubbed into his body. I didn't let anyone else help me with that part. His mother touched him, but everyone allowed me that space to have with him. That was the impression left on the cloth of Turin.

There were the words that we said with that. They were, "Oh, divine soul, allow"—and it wasn't "take this pain from me"—it was allow this pain to be gone from me. It was an allowing process. It wasn't a shifting of responsibility. Because when you say, "take this pain away from me" it is a subtle shift in responsibility. That defeats the purpose.

The Hebrew is coming through: It's like EE OO II Y T. And that was how they chanted it. And it was low.

Q: I am…

Me: I am allowing this to separate from my spirit. It feels like I am lost when I do this. And I know I must let it go. And I will allow the generosity of spirit to come out of my heart to come around me and protect me in this honor. I will keep that closer to me than this pain and this fear that I am allowing to safely leave me for the universe to safely break up for me and separate from me. Those aren't the exact words, but that's the information.

People can formulate their own words around that. There's nothing sacred about who has to deliver them. In fact it's better for people to create their own message, because it is what resonates with them.

Q: Message bottom line being "I am allowing."

Me: Yes.

Q: Not assigning someone else to do it for you.

Me: Yes. We all want to do that. They are saying to me it is an honest mistake. What they are saying is that those of us who understand ownership, get ownership, and it is a really good lesson. "I own my health, I own my spirit." When we give them away to the medical profession or the church, it can be a mistake. They may not be trustworthy for us. Fear we are allowed to release. We don't want to give it to anyone else. That's the hard part. We always want to assign it. They say to safely deliver it to the incineration in the middle of the earth. But don't assign it to any other person because that is too much to give to somebody else.

Q: Fabulous lesson in the allowing.

Me: Right. To go ahead and accept responsibility, and use the ability we have for connecting with universal wisdom.

First, we dissipate the fear.

Q: Do we have to own it first?

Me: Well, we have to disown it first. Recognize you have this fear, and then you…

Q: Identify it.

Me: Identify it. And then you disown it. "This does not belong to me." And then set it on fire and allow it to safely disseminate. And have the ability to turn. After you have gotten rid of it, you bring to yourself the "I am the generosity of spirit that is my heart." And ritual doesn't have to be so blasted serious all the time. It can be humorous.

In owning the healing, it has to resonate for us. If we tell people how the healing has to look to them, then it is…

Q: Taking away their power.

Me: Right. It takes away their ownership. It takes away their ability to create it themselves in a way that works for them through their filter. We are simply creating an opening for the healing to occur.

Q: Allow.

Me: Yes.

Q: Is it right for us as human beings at this point to say "I am" also?

Me: Absolutely. The minute we start to say "I am" is the minute we begin to become divine. I like the "allow" piece. "I am. I allow."

Q: I think that's the answer I was looking for.

When we say "I am" our personal essence and potency becomes valid in a fuller, rock solid way. There is no doubt when we say "I am" that we are taking full responsibility for the co-creation of our existence and the context of our experience, as well as cherishing the perfection inside of us.

*****

This is the story as I have received it, modified to fit the parameters the spirits gave me. It's a tremendous amount to take in. For those of you who have made it to the end with me, I appreciate your commitment and attention. It has been a highly charged journey for me in many, many ways with an ever growing cadre of committed readers and practitioners who continue to support me in this endeavor. My wish is for your journey in connecting with universal wisdom and divine love to be filled with boundless joy and awe.

Julia Turner Hultgren, July, 2012

Appendix 1

The Session Facilitators

Kat Mitchell Kurtzweil is an active member of the Association of Comprehensive Energy Psychology and is working towards her Diplomate status. She instructs interested parties in the Donna Eden Energy routines that allows the energy flow through the meridian systems in the body. These routines keep the flow consistent, affording optimal health when used on a regular basis. The routines are fun and assist in many areas of concern in the body. They can be used individually or in a daily five minute routine. Some of the highlights are reducing stress in our daily environments, calming down the central nervous systems and keeping energy at its optimal function. She is a licensed therapist and understands what damage stress can cause the mind, body and ultimately the soul's process.

Lee Mitchell is a Certified Past Life Regressionist since 2007. She works in Sarasota, Florida, Denver and Colorado Springs facilitating past life and between lives regressions. She also teaches classes on meeting your spirit guides, the earth shift, and more at many metaphysical centers in those areas. You may reach her for private readings or regressions at her website, crystalsoulpath. com, or on her phone: 719-221-4275.

Michelle Moceri is a certified Medium, a Reiki Master energy healer, is ordained in Metaphysical ministry, and has a bachelor in Metaphysical studies. Michelle felt drawn to this material and started to help Julia with the regressions in the summer of 2011. Through the channeling, it was revealed to Michelle that is she is an important part of this work. She has had many past lives with Julia and was part of the culminating life with Jesus, as a member of the White Brotherhood. She also is receiving instructions for talents to develop for the purpose of connecting to divine love and healing. Michelle is a wife and mother to three daughters and has lived in Colorado Springs since 2009.

Sue Miller has a degree in Physical Science from McPherson College. She worked as a financial advisor for ten years and is currently working as a software developer.

Claes Hultgren, Jr., along with being Julia's spouse since 1988, and father to her four children, is an MAI, MBA commercial real estate appraiser and investor, in practice for over 30 years. He is an accomplished xeriscape gardener, and is also known as the "orchid whisperer" in their social circles.

Appendix 2

Sessions in chronological order by current date

Number 1, September 28, 2010, Lee Mitchell facilitator: **Mary the Nun, 1400's A.D.***

Number 2, October 27, 2010, Lee Mitchell facilitator: **John the Baptist, 33-34 A.D.**

Number 3, January 26, 2011, Lee Mitchell facilitator: **Oil and Ash in Turkey, 23 A.D.**

Number 4, February 6, 2011, Claes Hultgren facilitator: **Spain, 48 A.D.**

Number 5, February 9, 2011, Lee Mitchell facilitator: **Mother Mary, 41 A.D.**

Number 6, February 19, 2011, Claes Hultgren facilitator: **France, 1735 A.D., Egyptian Priestess I, 200 B.C., Greek Soldiers, 1312 B.C.**

Number 7, March 7, 2011, Lee Mitchell facilitator: **Odessa, 34 A.D.***

Number 8, March 14, 2011, Claes Hultgren and Sue Miller facilitators: **Abrum, 475 B.C.**

Number 9, April 6, 2011, Lee Mitchell facilitator: **Frozen Brain, 1012 B.C.**

Number 10, April 29 I, 2011, Kat Kurtzweil facilitator: **Chain Gang I, 510 B.C.**

Number 11, April 29 II, 2011, Kat Kurtzweil facilitator: **Egyptian Priestess II, 200 B.C.**

Number 12, April 30, 2011, Kat Kurtzweil facilitator: **Caves, 20,000 B.C., Nikko, 400 B.C.**

Number 13, May 1, 2011, Kat and Lee Kurtzweil facilitator: **Bandits, 100 B.C.**

Number 14, May 2 I, 2011, Kat Kurtzweil facilitator: **Jonah, 610 B.C., Ute Brothers, 1600-1700 A.D.**

Number 15, May 2 II, 2011, Kat Kurtzweil facilitator: **Innsbruck, 730 B.C.**

Number 16, May 3 I, 2011, Kat Kurtzweil facilitator: **De'nitions, 2011 A.D.***

Number17, May 3 II, 2011, Kat Kurtzweil facilitator: **Peacock, 1400 B.C.**

Number 18, May 18, 2011, Lee Mitchell facilitator: **Brittany, 10,000 B.C.**

Number 19, June 11, 2011, Sue Miller facilitator: **Roman Twins, 50 B.C.**

Appendix 2, continued

Number 20, June 30, 2011, Michelle Moceri facilitator: **Maui, 410 B.C.***

Number 21, July 19, 2011, Michelle Moceri facilitator: **Marriage with Jesus, 16 A.D.**

Number 22, July 26, 2011, Michelle Moceri facilitator: **Jesus at Roman Party, 18 A.D.**

Number 23, August 4, 2011, Michelle Moceri facilitator: **Chain Gang II, 510 B.C.**

Number 24, September 26, 2011, Michelle Moceri facilitator: **Italian Farmer, 300 B.C.**

* These asterisked sessions were not central to the story line or held information that was made clearer in other sessions. Some transcribed sessions are available on the website www.awepath. com.